PASTRY SCHOOL

100 STEP-BY-STEP RECIPES

LE CORDON BLEU®

PASTRY SCHOOL

100 STEP-BY-STEP RECIPES

Photographs by Olivier Ploton

GRUB STREET • LONDON

FOREWORD

Throughout its more than 120 years of existence, Le Cordon Bleu has always been faithful to its philosophy of excellence. Through the world's leading network of culinary arts and hotel management institutes, present in 20 countries and close to 35 establishments, Le Cordon Bleu offers a large range of courses that range from beginner's level to degree studies in restaurant and hospitality management, and tourism.

The institute has upheld its reputation over the years. The courses offered, which incorporate the most innovative technologies, have continuously been updated in order to meet every professional requirement. Degree programmes are constantly adapted with the assistance of special partnerships set up throughout the world with governments, universities and specialist entities. Le Cordon Bleu institutes train more than 20,000 students of 100 different nationalities every year in cuisine, pastry, bread-making, wine and spirits, and hotel management. Le Cordon Bleu has opened a new, ultramodern and eco-friendly campus in Paris offering programmes for professionals and amateurs in a dedicated space overlooking the Seine.

Since its founding in 1895, the mission of the institute has been to impart the skills and knowledge inherited from the great masters of French cuisine. The institute began with the creation by Marthe Distel of a weekly culinary magazine called *La cuisinière Le Cordon Bleu*. After gaining more than 20,000 subscribers in its first year of existence, it soon occurred to the founder to invite them to free cooking lessons given by the chefs whose recipes were featured. The magazine reflected the most refined French cuisine of the time, but it was also already opening up to the cuisines of the world because it was published in a number of different languages. The first cooking classes organised by Marthe Distel were held at Le Cordon Bleu school in Paris on 15 October 1895.

Right from the start, Le Cordon Bleu demonstrated its openness to the world by receiving international students in Paris, its birthplace. Classes today are taught in French and translated into English to make them accessible to international students. The institute has expanded internationally and contributes to highlighting French culture throughout the world. While Le Cordon Bleu institutes located in the four corners of the globe still teach French culinary techniques, they also provide the means for students to showcase the culinary heritage of their countries of origin.

Le Cordon Bleu contributes to the international prestige of French culture and lifestyle by promoting excellence in gastronomy and the hospitality industry. In recent years, our activities have seen great diversification through our involvement in the distribution of gourmet food products and professional culinary equipment, the opening of restaurants, and partnerships for the production of television shows and the publication of cook books. Le Cordon Bleu regularly publishes books, many of which are acclaimed throughout the world, with some considered reference books for culinary training. More than 10 million books have been sold around the world.

Le Cordon Bleu is attentive to its professional methodology, and has worked closely with Larousse in the design of several cook books that teach French culinary techniques, the essential values of the institute, to inspire students and fine food enthusiasts. We are pleased to share with you our desire to constantly excel in the pursuit of pleasure and good food, and our passion for tradition and modernity.

Amitiés gourmandes
ANDRÉ COINTREAU
President of Le Cordon Bleu International

CONTENTS

INTRODUCTION

Le Cordon Bleu is proud to present *Pastry School,* a book that combines the culinary and educational know-how of Le Cordon Bleu institute and the quality of Éditions Larousse publications.

In this book, Le Cordon Bleu's Chefs exclusively offer their secrets to making 85 sweet creations ranging from the simplest to the most complex, in addition to 15 basic preparations that are essential in French pastry.

Each recipe in this collection of classic and modern pastry creations is presented with illustrated, step-by-step instructions for ease of understanding and to guarantee success. One whole chapter is devoted to basic pastry preparations, such as creams and doughs, which are essential to the success of your endeavours and must be mastered.

You will find recipes for gateaux, individual pastries, tarts, biscuits, confectioneries and outstanding entremets, with all levels of difficulty, worthy of a Le Cordon Bleu Chef, which you can make at home thanks to the recognised teaching methods employed by the institute.

The Chefs at Le Cordon Bleu were eager to create exclusive recipes, but also to share their tips and anecdotes, and information about recipes, techniques and ingredients.

Coming after the *Petit Larousse du Chocolat*, translated into English as *Chocolate Bible*, this new book exemplifies Le Cordon Bleu's mission: to impart skills and know-how and to showcase contemporary cuisine, both in France and around the world.

An essential pastry handbook for enthusiasts who want to make specific original creations or more traditional cakes, pastries or confections, *Pastry School* invites you to discover the world of French pastry as taught at Le Cordon Bleu and to embark on new culinary challenges like a chef.

CHEF JEAN-FRANÇOIS DEGUIGNET
Technical Director - Pastry

LE CORDON BLEU
key dates

1895 A French journalist, Marthe Distel, publishes a culinary magazine in Paris called *La Cuisinière Cordon Bleu*. In October of this year, subscribers are invited to the first Le Cordon Bleu cooking lessons.

1897 Le Cordon Bleu Paris welcomes its first Russian student.

1905 Le Cordon Bleu Paris trains its first Japanese student.

1914 Le Cordon Bleu operates four schools in Paris.

1927 The 16 November edition of *The Daily Mail* newspaper reports on a visit to Le Cordon Bleu Paris school: 'It's not unusual for as many as eight different nationalities to be represented in the classes.'

1933 Rosemary Hume and Dione Lucas, who both trained at Le Cordon Bleu Paris under Chef Henri-Paul Pellaprat, open the L'École du Petit Cordon Bleu school and Au Petit Cordon Bleu restaurant in London.

1942 Dione Lucas opens a Le Cordon Bleu school and restaurant in New York. She also writes the best-selling *The Cordon Bleu Cook Book* and becomes the first woman to host a televised cooking show in the United States.

1948 Le Cordon Bleu is accredited by the Pentagon for the professional training of young American soldiers after their tour of duty in Europe. As a former member of the Office of Strategic Services (OSS) in the United States, Julia Child qualifies and enrols at Le Cordon Bleu Paris.

1953 Le Cordon Bleu London creates the dish Coronation Chicken, which is served to foreign dignitaries attending the coronation banquet held for Queen Elizabeth II.

1954 The success of the film *Sabrina* by Billy Wilder, starring Audrey Hepburn in the title role, adds to the growing fame of Le Cordon Bleu.

1984   The Cointreau family, descendents of the founding families of Rémy Martin and Cointreau, take over the presidency of Le Cordon Bleu Paris, succeeding Elizabeth Brassart, director of the school since 1945.

1988   Le Cordon Bleu Paris moves from rue du Champ de Mars, near the Eiffel tower, to its new home in rue Léon Delhomme, in the 15th district. The school is opened by Minister Édouard Balladur.
• Le Cordon Bleu Ottawa welcomes its first students.

1991   Le Cordon Bleu Japan opens in Tokyo, and later in Kobe. The schools are known as 'Little France in Japan'.

1995   Le Cordon Bleu celebrates its centenary.
• For the first time, the authorities of the Shanghai District send chefs abroad to train at Le Cordon Bleu Paris.

1996   Le Cordon Bleu begins operations in Sydney, Australia, at the request of the government of New South Wales, and provides chef training in preparation for the 2000 Sydney Olympics. Bachelor's and master's degrees and university research are developed in Adelaide in the fields of Hospitality and Restaurant Management, Culinary Arts and Wine.

1998   Le Cordon Bleu signs and exclusive agreement with the Career Education Corporation (CEC) to bring its teaching expertise to the United States and to offer Associate Degrees with a unique curriculum in Culinary Arts and Hospitality Management.

2002   Le Cordon Bleu Korea and Le Cordon Bleu Mexico open to welcome their first students.

2003   Le Cordon Bleu Peru begins operations. It flourishes and becomes the leading culinary institute in the country.

2006   Le Cordon Bleu Thailand opens in partnership with Dusit International.

2009   All Le Cordon Bleu institutes around the world participate in the release of the film *Julie & Julia,* with Meryl Streep playing the role of Julia Child, alumna of Le Cordon Bleu Paris.

2011   Le Cordon Bleu Madrid opens in partnership with the Francisco de Vitoria University
• Le Cordon Bleu launches its first online Master of Gastronomic Tourism programme
• Japan overtakes France as the country with the most Michelin three-star restaurants.

2012 Le Cordon Bleu Malaysia opens in partnership with Sunway University College.
• Le Cordon Bleu London moves to Bloomsbury.
• Le Cordon Bleu New Zealand opens in Wellington.

2013 Official opening of Le Cordon Bleu Istanbul.
• Le Cordon Bleu Thailand receives the award for Best Culinary School in Asia.
• An agreement is signed with Ateneo de Manila University to open an institute in the Philippines.

2014 Le Cordon Bleu India opens and offers students bachelor's degrees in Hospitality and Restaurant Management.
• Le Cordon Bleu Hautes Études du Goût celebrate their 10th anniversary.

2015 The 120th anniversary of Le Cordon Bleu is celebrated all over the world.
• Le Cordon Bleu Shanghai welcomes its first students.
• Le Cordon Bleu Peru is bestowed university status.
• Le Cordon Bleu Taiwan opens in partnership with NKUHT and the Ming-Tai Institute.
• Le Cordon Bleu opens in Santiago, Chile, in partnership with Finis Terrae University.

2016 Opening of the new Le Cordon Bleu Paris facility by the Seine in the 15th district. With over 4,000 m^2 devoted to Culinary Arts and to Wine, Hospitality and Restaurant Management, Le Cordon Bleu Paris welcomes more than 1,000 students.

2017 Le Cordon Bleu becomes the first Culinary Arts institution to be awarded the prestigious Excellence Française trophy for the quality and expertise of its training programmes worldwide.
• Le Cordon Bleu Perth and Le Cordon Bleu Lebanon open their doors.

2018 Le Cordon Bleu Paris institute and the University of Paris-Dauphine sign a partnership agreement for the two Le Cordon Bleu Bachelor programmes: Business in Culinary Arts Management and Business in International Hospitality Management, providing a double diploma to the graduates.
• Le Cordon Bleu awarded the Grand Prix of Gastronomic culture by the Académie Internationale de la Gastronomie (AIG).
• Le Cordon Bleu opens institutes in São Paolo and Rio de Janeiro, Brazil.
• Le Cordon Bleu opens in Brisbane, Australia.

LE CORDON BLEU INSTITUTES
throughout the world

Le Cordon Bleu Paris
13-15 Quai André Citroën
75015 Paris, France
T: +33 (0)1 85 65 15 00
paris@cordonbleu.edu

Le Cordon Bleu London
15 Bloomsbury Square
London WC1A 2LS
United Kingdom
T: +44 (0) 207 400 3900
london@cordonbleu.edu

Le Cordon Bleu Madrid
Universidad Francisco de Vitoria
Ctra. Pozuelo-Majadahonda
Km. 1,800
Pozuelo de Alarcón, 28223
Madrid, Spain
T: +34 91 715 10 46
madrid@cordonbleu.edu

Le Cordon Bleu Istanbul
Özyeğin University
Çekmeköy Campus
Nişantepe Mevkii, Orman Sokak, No:13,
Alemdağ, Çekmeköy 34794
Istanbul, Turkey
T: +90 216 564 9000
istanbul@cordonbleu.edu

Le Cordon Bleu Lebanon
Burj on Bay Hotel
Tabarja – Kfaryassine
Lebanon
T: +961 9 85 75 57
lebanon@cordonbleu.edu

Le Cordon Bleu Japan
Le Cordon Bleu Tokyo Campus
Le Cordon Bleu Kobe Campus
Roob-1, 28-13 Sarugaku-Cho,
Daikanyama, Shibuya-Ku,
Tokyo 150-0033, Japan
T: +81 3 5489 0141
tokyo@cordonbleu.edu

Le Cordon Bleu Korea
Sookmyung Women's University
7th Fl., Social Education Bldg.,
Cheongpa-ro 47gil 100, Yongsan-Ku,
Seoul, 140-742 Korea
T: +82 2 719 6961
korea@cordonbleu.edu

Le Cordon Bleu Ottawa
453 Laurier Avenue East
Ottawa, Ontario, K1N 6R4, Canada
T: +1 613 236 CHEF (2433)
Toll free: +1 888 289 6302
Restaurant line : +1 613 236 2499
ottawa@cordonbleu.edu

Le Cordon Bleu Mexico
Universidad Anáhuac North Campus
Universidad Anáhuac South Campus
Universidad Anáhuac Querétaro Campus
Universidad Anáhuac Cancún Campus
Universidad Anáhuac Mérida Campus
Universidad Anáhuac Puebla Campus
Universidad Anáhuac Tampico Campus
Universidad Anáhuac Oaxaca Campus
Av. Universidad Anáhuac No. 46,
Col. Lomas Anáhuac Huixquilucan
Edo. De Méx C.P. 52786, México
T: +52 55 5627 0210 ext. 7132 / 7813
mexico@cordonbleu.edu

Universidad Le Cordon Bleu Peru (ULCB)
Le Cordon Bleu Peru Instituto
Le Cordon Bleu Cordontec
Av. Vasco Núñez de Balboa 530
Miraflores, Lima 18, Peru
T: +51 1 617 8300
peru@cordonbleu.edu

Le Cordon Bleu Australia
Le Cordon Bleu Adelaide Campus
Le Cordon Bleu Sydney Campus
Le Cordon Bleu Melbourne Campus
Le Cordon Bleu Perth Campus
Le Cordon Bleu Brisbane Campus
Days Road, Regency Park
South Australia 5010, Australia
Free call (Australia only):
1 800 064 802
T: +61 8 8346 3000
australia@cordonbleu.edu

Le Cordon Bleu New Zealand
52 Cuba Street
Wellington, 6011, New Zealand
T: +64 4 4729800
nz@cordonbleu.edu

Le Cordon Bleu Malaysia
Sunway University
No. 5, Jalan Universiti, Bandar Sunway,
46150 Petaling Jaya, Selangor DE,
Malaysia
T: +603 5632 1188
malaysia@cordonbleu.edu

Le Cordon Bleu Thailand
946 The Dusit Thani Building
Rama IV Road, Silom
Bangrak, Bangkok
10500 Thailand
T: +66 2 237 8877
thailand@cordonbleu.edu

Le Cordon Bleu Shanghai
2F, Building 1, No. 1458
Pu Dong Nan Road,
Shanghai China 200122
T: +86 400 118 1895
shanghai@cordonbleu.edu

Le Cordon Bleu India
G D Goenka University
Sohna Gurgaon Road
Sohna, Haryana
India
T: +91 880 099 20 22 / 23 / 24
lcb@gdgoenka.ac.in

Le Cordon Bleu Chile
Universidad Finis Terrae
Avenida Pedro de Valdivia 1509
Providencia
Santiago de Chile
T: +56 24 20 72 23

Le Cordon Bleu Rio de Janeiro
Rua da Passagem, 179, Botafogo
Rio de Janeiro, RJ, 22290-031, Brazil
T: +55 21 9940-02117

Le Cordon Bleu São Paulo
Rua Natingui, 862 Primero audar,
Vila Madalena, SP,
São Paulo 05443-001, Brazil
T: +55 11 3185-2500

Le Cordon Bleu Taiwan
NKUHT University
Ming-Tai Institute
4F, No. 200, Sec. 1, Keelung Road
Taipei 110, Taiwan
T: +886 2 7725-3600 / +886 975226418

Le Cordon Bleu, INC.
85 Broad Street – 18th floor,
New York, NY 10004 U.S.A.
T: +1 212 641 0331

www.cordonbleu.edu
e-mail: info@cordonbleu.edu

Gateaux, Cakes
& Entremets

MACARONNADE
with sugar-frosted rose petals

Serves 10

PREPARATION TIME: 1 hour 15 minutes – BAKING TIME: 30 minutes – CHILLING TIME: 50 minutes – STORAGE: 2 days in the refrigerator

DIFFICULTY: 🎩 🎩

MACARONNADE
240 g icing sugar
170 g ground almonds
4 egg whites (120 g)
Lemon juice
35 g sugar
Knife tip of red food
colouring powder

ROSE CREAM
2 gelatine leaves (4 g)
Pastry cream
300 ml milk
4 egg yolks (80 g)

50 g sugar
25 g cornflour

- - - - -

75 g room-temperature unsalted
butter
40 g white couverture chocolate
1 tbsp kirsch
8 drops rose extract
1 tbsp rose water
75 g room-temperature unsalted
butter
120 ml cream
50 g mascarpone

SUGAR-FROSTED ROSE PETALS
20 ml water
30 g sugar
Red rose petals
Sugar

FILLING
20 lychees
100 g rose petal jelly

DECORATION
Icing sugar
2 lychees

EQUIPMENT NEEDED: 2 piping bags – size 12 plain nozzle – pastry brush – cardboard cake board

Roses in pastry-making

Roses add an original flavour to desserts and can be added in different ways: essential oil, extract, syrup, and even rose petal jelly.
Highly concentrated rose essential oil is mainly used to flavour creams, mousses and ice creams. Rose petal jelly can be used to fill or garnish macarons or an entremets.

MACARONNADE with sugar-frosted rose petals

step-by-step

FOR THE MACARONNADE

1 – Preheat the oven to 180°C (gas mark 4). Draw a 22-cm circle on each of 2 sheets of baking parchment and place each one on a baking tray. Mix the icing sugar with the ground almonds in a bowl. In another bowl, whisk the egg whites with the lemon juice until firm, then incorporate the sugar to make a meringue. Add red food colouring.

2 – Use a wooden spatula to fold the dry ingredients, half at a time, into the beaten egg whites. Mix slowly, starting in the middle of the bowl and working your way up the sides.

3 – Put the mixture into one of the piping bags fitted with the nozzle and pipe 2 spirals inside the 2 circles drawn on the baking parchment sheets. Bake for 25 minutes.

FOR THE ROSE CREAM

4 – Soften the gelatine leaves in a bowl of cold water. Make a pastry cream (see page 480).

5 – Add the butter and white chocolate, and mix using a whisk. Add the kirsch, rose extract and rose water. Squeeze the gelatine to drain and incorporate into the cream. Transfer the rose cream to a bowl and refrigerate for 30 minutes.

6 – Whisk the rose cream to smooth. Whisk the butter to a creamy consistency and incorporate into the rose cream.

7 – Whip the cream with the mascarpone until firm. Incorporate into the rose cream, and then fill the other piping bag fitted with the nozzle.

FOR THE SUGAR-FROSTED ROSE PETALS

8 – Preheat the oven to 120°C (gas mark ½). Make a syrup by bringing the water and sugar to the boil in a pan. Brush the rose petals with the syrup.

9 – Sprinkle the petals with sugar and lay them on a baking tray lined with baking parchment. Bake for 5 minutes.

•••

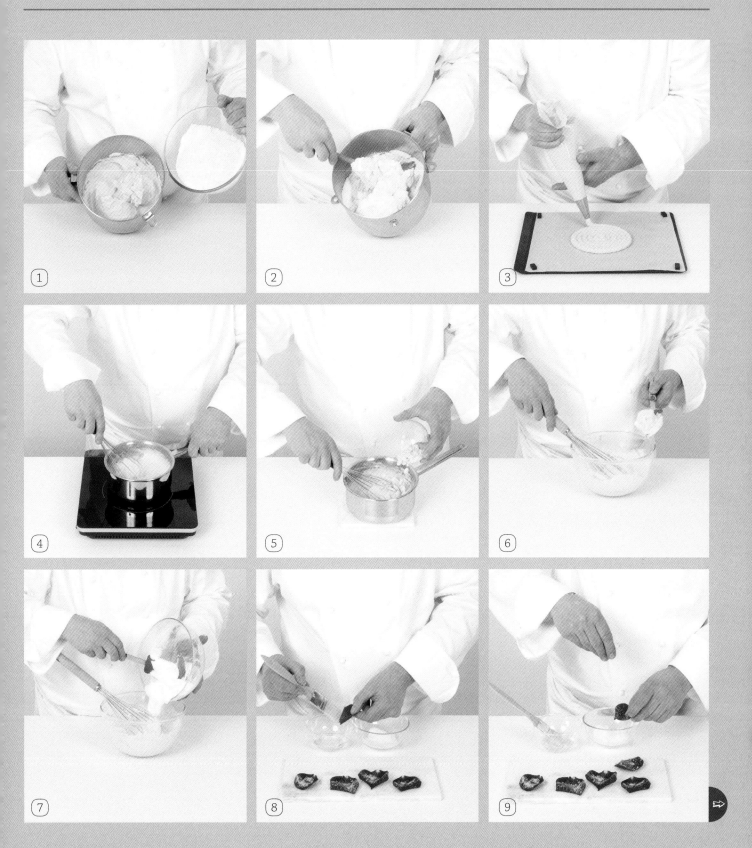

ASSEMBLY AND DECORATION

10 – Turn one of the macaronnade discs over onto the cardboard cake board and detach the baking parchment.

11 – Pipe balls of rose cream spaced evenly around the edge of the round.

12 – Peel and pit the lychees. Arrange a lychee between each ball of rose cream.

13 – Pipe a spiral of rose cream in the middle of the round, then pipe another one on top of it.

14 – Halve the remaining lychees and arrange over the cream spiral.

15 – Arrange some rose petal jelly over everything.

16 – Cover with the second macaronnade disc.

17 – Pipe three dots of rose cream on top of the macaronnade.
Dust the surface of the entremets with icing sugar.

18 – Arrange 3 sugar-frosted rose petals on top of the 3 cream dots. Decorate with 2 unpeeled lychees. Refrigerate for 20 minutes before serving.

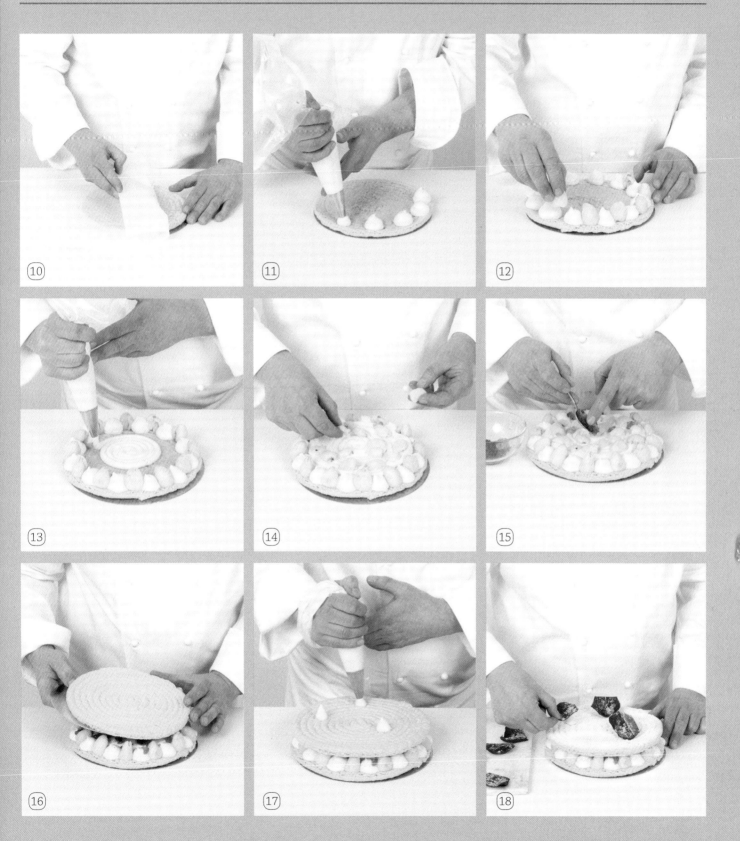

LEMON POUND CAKE

Makes 3 small cakes

PREPARATION TIME: 30 minutes – BAKING TIME: 30 minutes – STORAGE: 4 days covered in cling film

DIFFICULTY: ♙

CAKE BATTER	20 g room-temperature unsalted butter for greasing
4 eggs (200 g)	20 g plain flour for dusting
Zest of 4 lemons	
170 g sugar	100 g apricot glaze
170 g plain flour	
Pinch baking powder	LEMON GLAZE
160 g unsalted butter, melted	150 g icing sugar
	2 tbsp lemon juice

Oil, for dipping the plastic dough scraper

EQUIPMENT NEEDED: Three 14 x 6 cm loaf tins – plastic dough scraper – pastry brush

Gâteaux de voyage

Whether in the form of a loaf cake, butter cake, financier or pound cake, gâteaux de voyage - French for 'travel cakes' - are by definition cakes that travel well, without fear of spoilage. These simple and very moist cakes must be easy to pack and carry, last at least 3 days without refrigeration, and can survive the hazards of a journey. They can be given any flavour. For a lemon cake, use the juice and zest of fresh lemons for an intense flavour.

FOR THE CAKE BATTER

1 – Preheat the oven to 180°C (gas mark 4). Melt the 20 g of butter in a pan. Brush the loaf tins with the melted butter and dust with flour.

2 – Break the eggs into a large bowl. Grate the zest of the lemons into the bowl.

3 – Whisk, then add the sugar, whisking constantly until the mixture turns pale and thickens.

4 – Mix the flour with the baking powder and incorporate into the egg mixture.

5 – Add the 160 g of melted butter and whisk until smooth.

6 – Use a ladle to fill the greased tins three-quarters full.

7 – Dip the plastic dough scraper in the oil and lightly press into the centre of the batter in each tin to make a line. Bake for 30 minutes. Turn the cakes out of the tins. Leave to cool. Keep the oven temperature at 180°C.

8 – Heat the apricot glaze in a pan and brush over the surface of the cakes.

FOR THE LEMON GLAZE

9 – Heat the icing sugar and lemon juice in a pan while stirring constantly with a whisk until the mixture turns a little pasty. Brush the sides and top of the cakes with the glaze. Return to the oven for 1 minute. Allow to cool before serving.

● ● ●

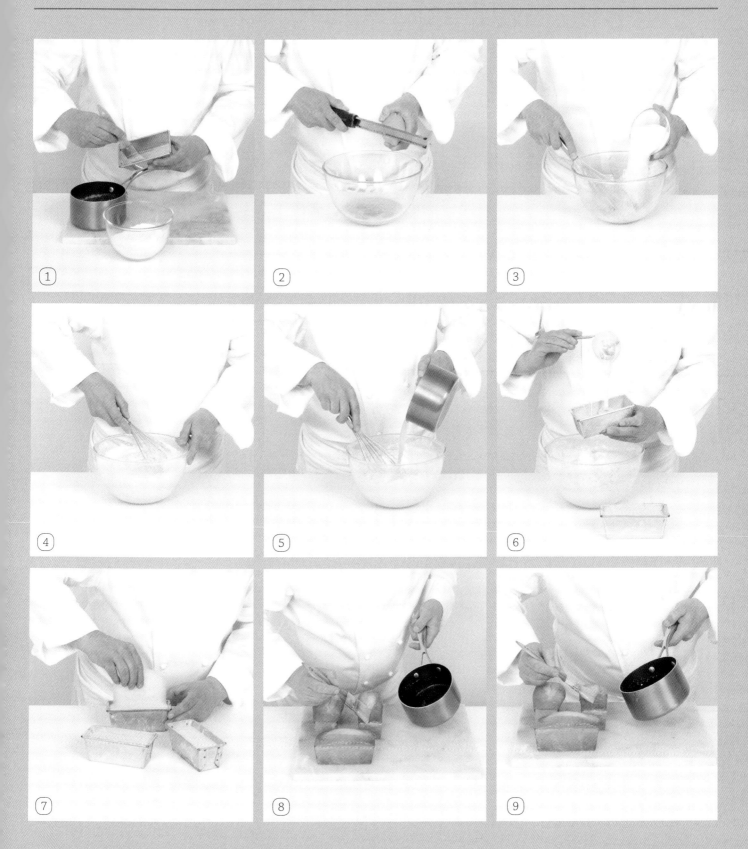

FIG, MANGO AND SPICE
dacquoise

Serves 10

PREPARATION TIME: 1 hour 15 minutes – BAKING TIME: about 25 minutes – CHILLING TIME: 1 hour – FREEZING TIME: 1 hour
STORAGE: 2 days in the refrigerator
DIFFICULTY: ♙ ♙

SPICED FIG AND RASPBERRY COMPOTE
2 gelatine leaves (4 g)
200 g figs
Pinch quatre-épices spice blend
50 g sugar
1 tsp lemon juice
60 g whole raspberries

DACQUOISE
20 g desiccated coconut
140 g icing sugar
40 g plain flour
140 g ground almonds
Pinch quatre-épices spice blend
170 g egg whites
115 g sugar

MANGO AND SPICE CREAM
3 egg yolks (60 g)
60 g sugar
25 g potato starch
250 g mango purée
35 g unsalted butter
Pinch quatre-épices spice blend
1 star anise
1 tbsp Cointreau®
75 g room-temperature unsalted butter
140 ml cream

DECORATION
1 fig
12 raspberries
Icing sugar
3 star anise

EQUIPMENT NEEDED: 18-cm tart ring – 20-cm entremets ring – piping bag – size 12 plain nozzle
size PF16 star nozzle

Quatre-épices

This is a mixture of spices comprising nutmeg, cloves, cinnamon and pepper. It should not be mistaken for allspice, also known as Jamaica pepper, a berry also known in French as 'quatre-épices' because its aroma is similar to a combination of nutmeg, cloves, cinnamon and pepper.

FOR THE SPICED FIG AND RASPBERRY COMPOTE

1 – Soften the gelatine leaves in a bowl of cold water. Cut the figs into small pieces.
2 – Combine the figs with the quatre-épices in a pan and cook for
2 minutes while stirring with a silicone spatula.
3 – Add the sugar, followed by the lemon juice and raspberries. Continue to
cook for 2–3 more minutes.
4 – Remove the pan from the heat. Squeeze the gelatine to drain and
incorporate into the mixture in the pan.
5 – Stretch cling film over the top of the 18-cm tart ring.
6 – Turn the ring over onto the work surface and fill with the compote.
Smooth with the spatula to distribute evenly inside the ring. Freeze for 1 hour.

FOR THE DACQUOISE

7 – Preheat the oven to 150°C (gas mark 2) and toast the desiccated coconut in
the oven for 4 minutes. Raise the oven temperature to 200°C (gas mark 6).
Mix together the icing sugar, flour, ground almonds and quatre-épices.
8 – Whisk the egg whites until firm enough to cling to the tip of
the whisk, then incorporate the sugar while whisking to stiff peaks.
9 – Fold in the dry ingredients, then transfer to a piping bag fitted with
size plain 12 nozzle.

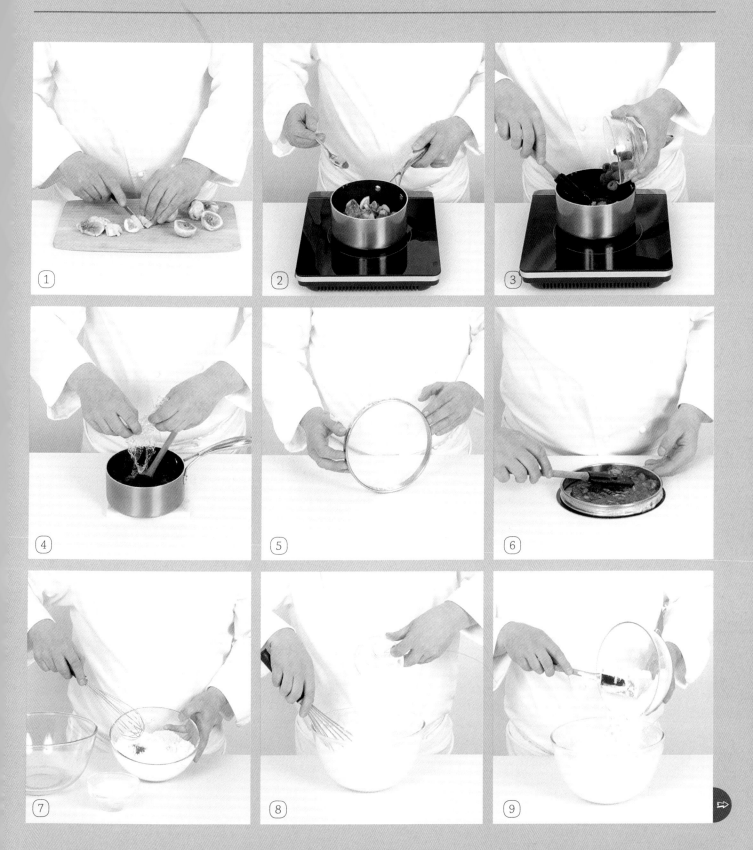

10 – Use the 20 cm entremets ring as a template to draw a circle on each of 2 sheets of baking parchment. Place each one on a baking tray. Pipe the batter in a spiral inside the 2 circles.

11 – Sprinkle the dacquoise rounds with the toasted desiccated coconut.

12 – Then dust with a little icing sugar through a sieve. Bake each disc separately for 18 minutes.

FOR THE MANGO AND SPICE CREAM

13 – Beat the egg yolks with the sugar in a bowl until the mixture turns pale and thickens, then add the potato starch.

14 – Combine the mango purée with the butter in a pan and bring to the boil.

15 – Pour into the egg mixture and mix.

16 – Transfer the mixture to the pan. Add the quatre-épices and the star anise, and bring to the boil while stirring constantly with a whisk. Take out the star anise, pour the mixture into a bowl and refrigerate for 1 hour.

17 – Whip the mango and spice cream until smooth, then add the Cointreau.® Whisk the butter to a creamy consistency. Incorporate into the mango and spice cream, whisking briskly.

18 – Whip the cream until it is firm and clings to the tip of the whisk.

• • •

CHEF'S TIP

To incorporate the cream, it should be added a little at a time to loosen the mixture into which it is being added. The consistencies will be more similar and the resulting cream will remain light.

ASSEMBLY

19 – Incorporate a third of the whipped cream into the mango and spice cream, whisking briskly, then fold in the remainder. Fill a piping bag fitted with the PF16 star nozzle.

20 – Peel off the baking parchment from the dacquoise discs.

21 – Place one round on a cardboard cake board. Remove the cling film and tart ring from the spiced fig and raspberry compote.

22 – Lay it on top of the dacquoise disc.

23 – Pipe a thick continuous swirl of spiced mango cream around the edge of the dacquoise.

24 – Pipe a spiral of spiced mango cream over the centre of the fig and raspberry compote.

25 – Cover with the second dacquoise disc.

26 – Quarter the fig. Dust the top of the dacquoise with icing sugar through a sieve.

27 – Decorate the dacquoise with the fig quarters, raspberries and star anise.

TARTE TATIN-STYLE
apple ring

Serves 10

PREPARATION TIME: 30 minutes – BAKING TIME: 1 hour 5 minutes – COOLING TIME: 4 hours – STORAGE: 2 days in the refrigerator

DIFFICULTY: 🎩

CARAMELISED APPLES	SWEET SHORTCRUST PASTRY
7 apples	125 g plain flour
150 g unsalted butter	75 g unsalted butter
150 g sugar	Pinch of salt
Pinch ground cinnamon	2 tsp icing sugar
	½ egg (30 g)
100 g unsalted butter for the mould	1 tsp water
100 g sugar for dusting and sprinkling	

EQUIPMENT NEEDED: 1 savarin mould

The tarte Tatin (upside-down tart)

The Tatin sisters are credited with this caramelised apple tart, and the original way of baking it upside down. Traditionally, the bottom of a special Tatin mould is filled with apples which are caramelised with butter and sugar together with the mould, then covered with sweet shortcrust pastry and baked in the oven. If you are unable to find a Tatin mould, caramelise the apples ahead of time in a frying pan.

TARTE TATIN-STYLE apple ring

FOR THE CARAMELISED APPLES

1 – Peel, halve and core the apples.
2 – Heat the butter and sugar in a large frying pan. Add the cinnamon and continue to cook until caramelised.
3 – Add the apple halves and cook for about 10 minutes.
4 – Preheat the oven to 220°C (gas mark 7). Butter the mould and dust with sugar.
5 – Arrange the apple halves inside the mould, packed tightly, and sprinkle with sugar. Bake for 45 minutes.

FOR THE SWEET SHORTCRUST PASTRY (see page 490)

6 – Roll out the dough and cut out a disc slightly larger than the diameter of the mould. Refrigerate.
7 – Take the mould out of the oven, allow to cool a little, then cover with the dough disc.
8 – Run the rolling pin over the top of the mould to trim off the excess dough. Lower the oven temperature to 200°C (gas mark 6) and bake the tart for 20 minutes.
9 – Let cool for at least 4 hours. Put the tart over a bain-marie before turning it out.

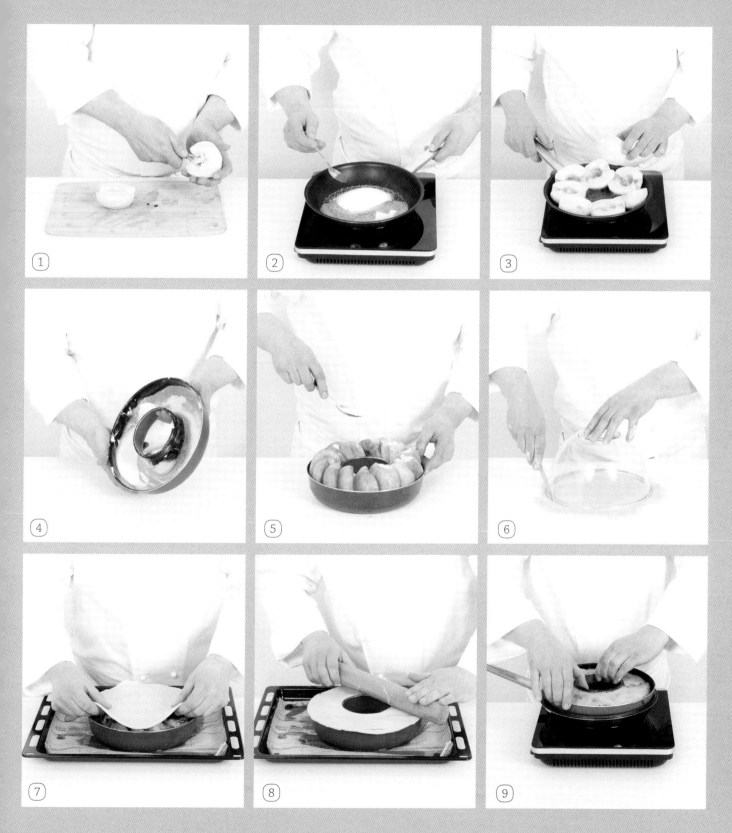

CHOCOLATE-BANANA
Brittany shortbread

Serves 8

PREPARATION TIME: 1 hour + 30 minutes for tempering the chocolate – BAKING TIME: 20–25 minutes
CHILLING TIME: 1 hour 30 minutes – STORAGE: 2 days in the refrigerator
DIFFICULTY: 🍳

CHOCOLATE-BANANA
BRITTANY SHORTBREAD
100 g lightly salted butter
50 g sugar
20 g ground hazelnuts
1 egg yolk (20 g)
100 g plain flour
½ tsp baking powder
2 tsp unsweetened cocoa powder
80 g bananas

CARAMELISED BANANAS
180 g bananas
15 g unsalted butter
30 g unrefined cane sugar
30 ml Malibu®

MILK CHOCOLATE GANACHE
180 g milk chocolate
250 ml cream

DECORATION
100 g milk couverture chocolate
Icing sugar

EQUIPMENT NEEDED: 18-cm tart ring – size 10 plain nozzle – Saint-Honoré nozzle
5-cm biscuit cutter – 2 piping bags

Piping bags and nozzles

Piping bags and nozzles are essential in pastry making. They allow creams, mousses and ganaches to be applied cleanly and uniformly when making an entremets, filling choux buns or decorating with any cream or icing. Nozzles come in both plastic and stainless steel, and piping bags can be either disposable or reusable.

FOR THE CHOCOLATE-BANANA BRITTANY SHORTBREAD

1 – Preheat the oven to 170°C (gas mark 3–4). Whisk the butter in a bowl to a creamy consistency, then add the sugar and ground hazelnuts and mix. Whisk in the egg yolk, then incorporate the flour, baking powder, cocoa powder and bananas, previously mashed with a fork. Transfer to a piping bag fitted with the size 10 plain nozzle.

2 – Butter the tart ring and lay it on a baking tray lined with baking parchment. Pipe balls of the dough close together against the sides of the ring, then pipe a spiral in the middle. Bake for 20–25 minutes.

FOR THE CARAMELISED BANANAS

3 – Slice the bananas. Heat the butter and sugar in a frying pan and allow to caramelise. Add the bananas and cook until soft. Remove the pan from the heat and add the Malibu.® Mix and leave to cool.

FOR THE MILK CHOCOLATE GANACHE

4 – Melt the chocolate in a bowl over a bain-marie. Pour in the cream and mix, then refrigerate for 30 minutes.

5 – Whisk well to emulsify. Transfer to a piping bag fitted with the Saint-Honoré nozzle.

ASSEMBLY AND DECORATION

6 – Turn out the Brittany shortbread and leave to cool. Spread the caramelised bananas over the top, leaving a 2 cm margin around the edge of the shortbread.

7 – Pipe waves of milk chocolate ganache over the top. Refrigerate for 1 hour, then dust the edges of the shortbread with icing sugar through a sieve.

8 – Temper the couverture (see pages 494–495) and spread it out over a cold work surface. When it starts to harden, while still remaining elastic, scrape with a biscuit cutter to make large shavings.

9 – Dust the shavings with icing sugar and use to decorate the shortbread.

CHEESECAKE
like an entremets

Serves 10

PREPARATION TIME: 1 hour – BAKING TIME: 20 minutes – CHILLING TIME: 3 hours 50 minutes

STORAGE: 2 days in the refrigerator

DIFFICULTY: ♙♙

SHORTBREAD BASE
240 g shortbread biscuits

90 g unsalted butter, cut into pieces

RASPBERRY FILLING
20 ml water

25 g honey

75 g sugar

180 g raspberries

2 peppercorns, crushed

2 tsp balsamic vinegar

2 gelatine leaves (4 g)

CREAM CHEESE MOUSSE
20 ml water

60 g sugar

2 egg yolks

160 g Philadelphia® cream cheese

Zest of ½ lemon

50 ml cream

3 gelatine leaves (6 g)

250 ml cream

DECORATION
100 g ladyfingers

50 g raspberries

Edible gold powder

20 g blueberries

1 tsp pistachios

Neutral glaze

Icing sugar

EQUIPMENT NEEDED: Entremets ring 20 cm across and 4.5 cm deep - cooking thermometer

Cheesecake

Cheesecake is a very popular dessert in the United States – its best-known version is from New York – and comes in many styles and flavours. The base can be made using digestive, shortbread, and even speculoos biscuits. It is filled with cream cheese, typically the iconic American brand Philadelphia®, with the addition of eggs and sugar.

FOR THE SHORTBREAD BASE

1 – In a bowl, crush the biscuits with a rolling pin, then add the butter and crush again. Finish mixing with a fork until the mixture looks like a crumble.
2 – Cover a baking tray with a sheet of baking parchment and place an entremets ring on it. Use a tablespoon to spread the shortbread base inside the ring, compacting well with the back of the spoon. Refrigerate for 30 minutes.

FOR THE RASPBERRY FILLING

3 – Combine the water, honey and sugar in a pan and heat until the temperature reads 120°C on the cooking thermometer.
4 – At 120°C, add the raspberries, peppercorns and vinegar, and cook for 2 minutes while stirring with a silicone spatula. Soften the gelatine leaves in a bowl of cold water.
5 – Squeeze the gelatine to drain, add to the pan and stir with a wooden spoon to incorporate.
6 – Use a tablespoon to spread the raspberry filling inside the ring, over the shortbread base.

FOR THE CREAM CHEESE MOUSSE

7 – Combine the sugar and water in a small saucepan and bring to the boil to make a syrup. Whisk the egg yolks in a bowl and pour over the hot syrup.
8 – Beat briskly with an electric whisk to cool the mixture and obtain a pâte à bombe.
9 – Put the cream cheese into a bowl. Grate the zest of a lemon over it. Soften the gelatine leaves in a bowl of cold water.

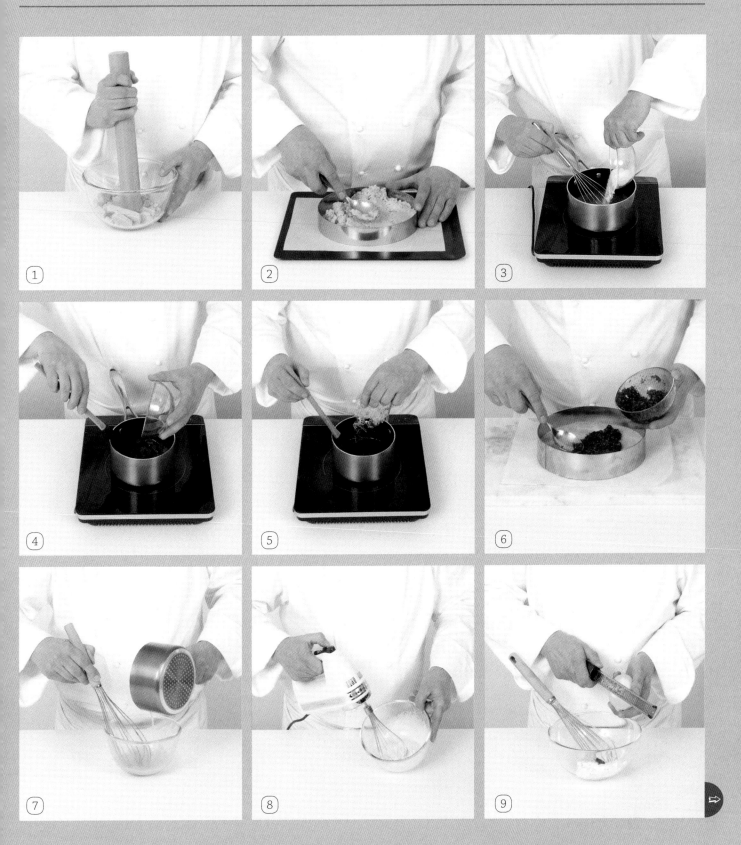

10 – Squeeze the gelatine to drain. Heat the 50 ml of cream in a pan and whisk in the gelatine to dissolve.

11 – Pour over the cream cheese and mix with a whisk.

12 – Whisk in the pâte à bombe until fully incorporated.

13 – Whisk the 250 ml of cream to soft peaks.

14 – Fold the whipped cream into the cream cheese mixture.

ASSEMBLY AND DECORATION

15 – Use a silicone spatula to spread the cream cheese mousse over the raspberry layer in the ring, starting from the edges and working your way to the middle.

16 – Smooth the surface with a palette knife to remove the excess mousse. Refrigerate the entremets for 20 minutes.

17 – Preheat the oven to 150°C (gas mark 2). Crush the ladyfingers and spread over a baking tray lined with baking parchment. Dry out in the oven for 20 minutes. Sprinkle the crumbs over the entremets and refrigerate for 3 hours.

18 – Carefully remove the ring and decorate the cheesecake with whole raspberries dipped in the gold powder, blueberries and pistachios. Heat the neutral glaze in a small saucepan, then pour into a paper cone and pipe a drop of glaze on top of each raspberry. Dust the entremets with icing sugar.

"POIRE TAPÉE", CHERRY
and dried apricot loaf cake

Serves 6

PREPARATION TIME: 30 minutes – MACERATION TIME: 10 minutes – BAKING TIME: 35–40 minutes
STORAGE: 4 days covered in cling film
DIFFICULTY: 🎩

<u>CAKE</u>

50 g "poires tapées" (dried and pressed pears)
30 g Amarena cherries
50 g soft dried apricots
2 tsp Grand Marnier®
110 g plain flour
110 g room-temperature unsalted butter
85 g icing sugar
1 large egg (60 g)
1 egg yolk (20 g)
½ tsp baking powder

<u>SYRUP</u>

30 ml water
30 ml orange juice
30 g sugar
2 tsp Grand Marnier®

20 g room-temperature unsalted butter for the mould

<u>EQUIPMENT NEEDED</u>: 18 x 6 cm loaf tin – pastry brush

"Poires tapées"

"Poires tapées" (dried and pressed pears) are a speciality of the Indre-et-Loire region of France and are still produced using traditional methods. Pears are peeled, dried in an oven, then flattened in a hammer-like press known as a *platissouerre*. They are then stored in wicker baskets. The slightly tart dried and pressed pears can be eaten plain, and they make an excellent accompaniment for both savoury and sweet dishes.

"POIRE TAPÉE", CHERRY and dried apricot loaf cake   step-by-step

FOR THE CAKE BATTER

1 – Cut the pears, cherries and dried apricots into small pieces. Macerate them in the Grand Marnier® for 10 minutes.

2 – Preheat the oven to 170°C (gas mark 3–4). Butter the tin. Mix the fruit with 2 tablespoons of the previously weighed-out flour.

3 – Cream the butter with the icing sugar.

4 – Add the whole egg and then the egg yolk, and mix well with a whisk.

5 – Use a silicone spatula to incorporate the remaining plain flour and baking powder.

6 – Add the fruit and mix gently.

7 – Distribute the batter evenly in the tin and bake for 35–40 minutes.

FOR THE SYRUP

8 – Combine the water, orange juice and sugar in a pan and bring to the boil. Remove the pan from the heat and add the Grand Marnier.® Leave to cool.

9 – When the cake comes out of the oven, brush with the syrup.

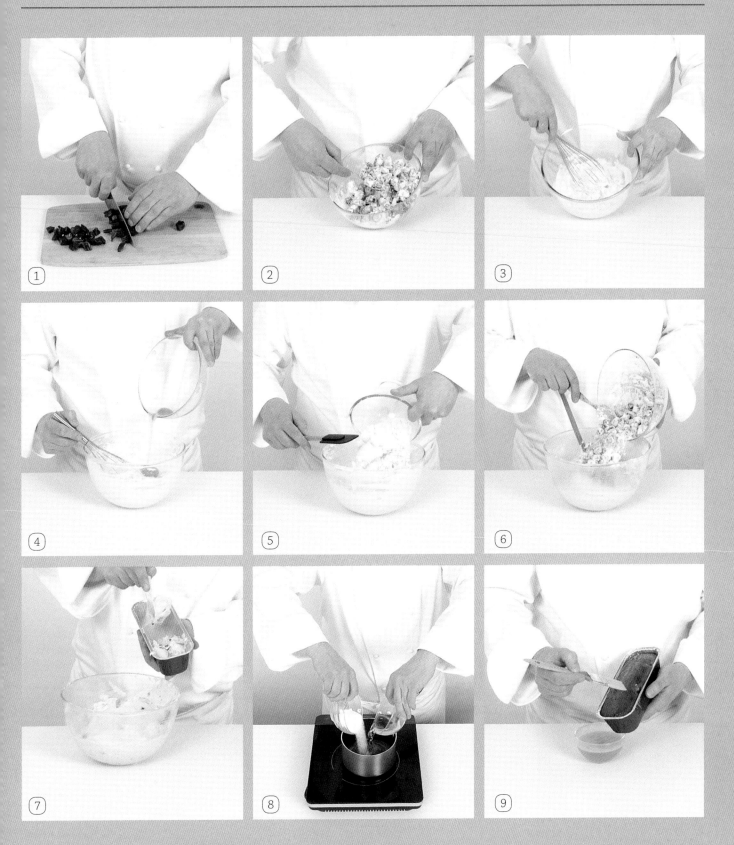

PASSION FRUIT-COCONUT
baba

Serves 10

PREPARATION TIME: 45 minutes – PROOFING TIME: 45 minutes – BAKING TIME: 40 minutes – STORAGE: 2 days in the refrigerator

DIFFICULTY: 🎩

BABA BATTER
200 g plain flour
20 g sugar
1 tsp salt
15 g fresh compressed yeast
1 tbsp warm water
2 eggs (100 g)
110 ml milk
1 tbsp Malibu®
70 g unsalted butter
20 g unsalted butter for the mould

PASSION FRUIT-COCONUT SYRUP
600 ml water
37 g sugar
120 ml coconut milk
60 g passion fruit purée
50 ml Malibu®

PASSION FRUIT GLAZE
200 g apricot glaze or apricot jam
2 passion fruits

HONEY WHIPPED CREAM
250 ml cream
40 g honey

EQUIPMENT NEEDED: 20-cm kugelhopf mould – 6-cm kugelhopf mould
2 piping bags – size E7 star nozzle – pastry brush

Fresh compressed yeast

Fresh compressed yeast is obtained from a live fungus and is used as
a leavening agent for pastries and many different varieties of bread.
The yeast 'feeds' off the glucose in flour, a reaction that causes doughs
and batters to rise. Take care never to mix it directly with salt because
the salt will kill the micro-organisms in the yeast and the dough or
batter will not rise.

FOR THE BABA BATTER

1 – Mix the flour with the sugar and salt in a bowl. Dilute the yeast in warm water, then add to the bowl.

2 – Add the eggs, followed by the milk. Whisk until smooth.

3 – Gently whisk in the Malibu®.

4 – Whisk the butter to a creamy consistency and incorporate into the batter. Continue to work the batter with an electric whisk.

5 – Work the batter until it is smooth and elastic, then transfer to a piping bag.

6 – Butter both kugelhopf moulds.

7 – Pipe batter into the larger mould, filling to two-thirds, then do the same for the smaller mould. Leave to rise for 45 minutes in a warm place. Preheat the oven to 180°C (gas mark 4). Bake the smaller baba for 20 minutes and the larger one for 40 minutes. Turn the babas out of their moulds as soon as they come out of the oven.

FOR THE PASSION FRUIT AND COCONUT SYRUP

8 – Combine the water and sugar in a pan and bring to the boil. Remove the pan from the heat and add the coconut milk, the passion fruit purée, and then the Malibu.® Pour the syrup into a large bowl.

9 – Return the larger baba to its mould, then use a ladle to gradually pour syrup over it until it is completely imbibed.

• • •

CHEF'S TIP

There is an infinite choice of flavours and aromas with which you can vary your baba, such as pineapple, grapefruit, cherry and lemon. You can also replace the traditional rum with bourbon or whisky, kirsch or Grand Marnier.®

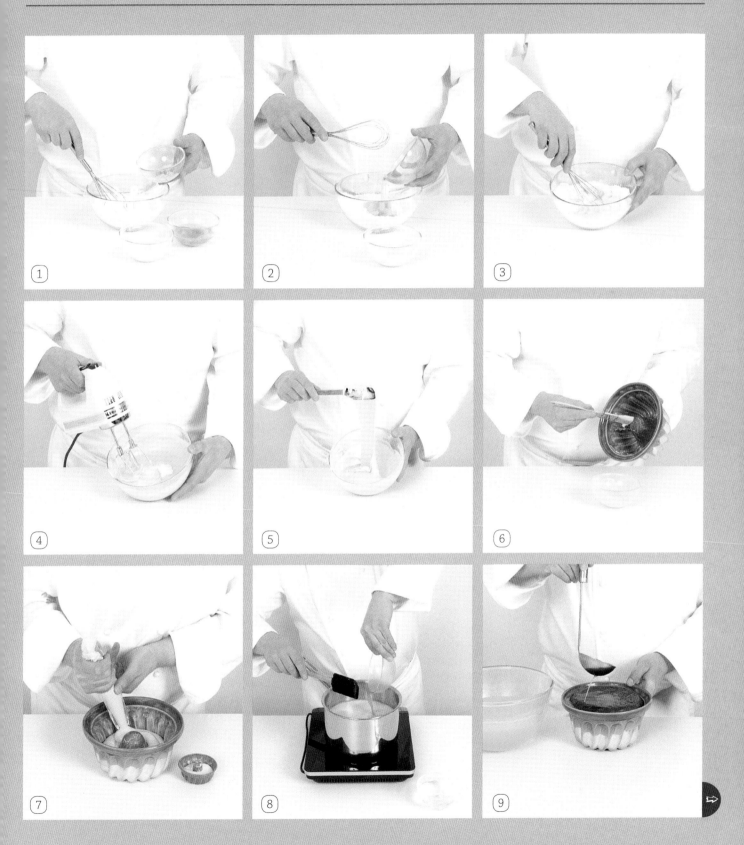

10 – Put the smaller baba directly into the bowl with the syrup. Use the ladle to imbibe it several times with syrup, then transfer to a rack over a container to drain.

11 – Put another rack over the larger mould and turn the baba out onto the rack over a large bowl.

12 – Use the ladle to pour the rest of the syrup over the baba to imbibe thoroughly, then leave to drain.

FOR THE PASSION FRUIT GLAZE

13 – Heat the apricot glaze in a pan, diluting with a little syrup. Bring to the boil while mixing with the brush until a small ball forms at the end of the brush.

14 – Halve the passion fruits, scoop out the juice and seeds, and add to the glaze.

FOR THE HONEY WHIPPED CREAM

15 – Whip the cream until it is firm and clings to the tip of the whisk, then incorporate the honey. Transfer to a piping bag fitted with the size E7 star nozzle with the cream.

ASSEMBLY AND DECORATION

16 – Stand the larger baba on a clean rack and brush with the passion fruit glaze.

17 – Fill the centre with honey whipped cream.

18 – Position the smaller baba on top of the larger one. Pipe a swirl of honey whipped cream and decorate with a few passion fruit seeds.

ST. TROPEZ "TART"

Serves 8

PREPARATION TIME: 1 hour – PROOFING TIME: 1 hour + 45 minutes – CHILLING TIME: 5 hours – BAKING TIME: 40 minutes

DIFFICULTY: ⏣ ⏣

BRIOCHE DOUGH	VANILLA-FLAVOURED CHIBOUST CREAM
5 g fresh compressed yeast	Pastry cream
20 ml milk	370 ml milk
1–2 drops vanilla extract	75 g eggs
170 g plain flour	60 g sugar
1 scant tsp salt	50 g cornflour
2 eggs (100 g)	1 vanilla pod
20 g sugar	Italian meringue
85 g unsalted butter	100 g egg whites
	40 ml water
1 egg yolk (20 g) for glazing	160 g sugar
80 g nibbed sugar	

EQUIPMENT NEEDED: Stand mixer with dough hook attachment – 22-cm tart ring – pastry brush

La tropézienne (St. Tropez "tart")

The iconic dessert of Saint-Tropez and famous throughout France, St. Tropez "tart" is a brioche split in two with a traditional filling of mousseline cream flavoured with orange flower water, and sprinkled with nibbed sugar. In this recipe, the mousseline cream is replaced by a very light and creamy Chiboust cream, a mixture of pastry cream and Italian meringue.

FOR THE BRIOCHE DOUGH

1 – Dilute the yeast in the warmed milk with vanilla.

2 – Mix the flour and salt in the mixer bowl.

3 – Pour in the milk with yeast and add the eggs. Knead for 7–8 minutes.

4 – Add the sugar and continue to knead for a few minutes.

5 – Incorporate the butter a little at a time while continuing to knead for 5 minutes, until the dough comes away from the sides of the bowl.

6 – The dough should have a smooth and elastic consistency. Transfer to a large bowl.

7 – Cover the bowl with cling film and leave the dough to proof for 1 hour in a warm place.

8 – Lightly flour your hands and fold the dough over itself several times to expel any air. Wrap in cling film and rest in the refrigerator for 4 hours.

9 – Shape the dough into a ball, then place it on the work surface and lightly flatten.

• • •

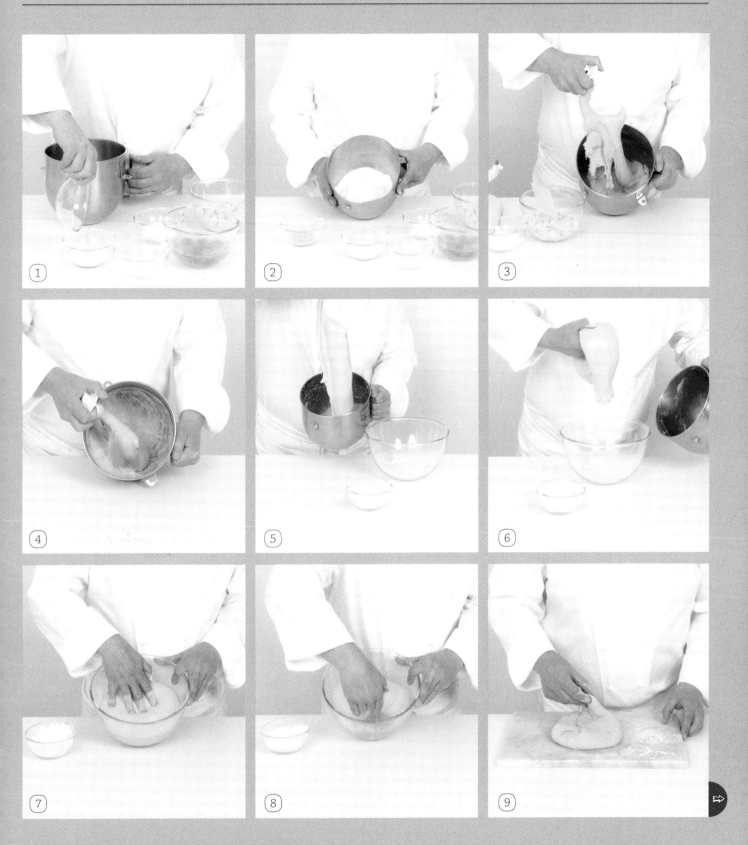

10 – Transfer the dough to a baking tray, place the tart ring around it and flatten to spread evenly inside the ring. Cover the ring with cling film or a damp cloth and leave in a warm place for about 45 minutes, until the dough doubles in size.

11 – Preheat the oven to 180°C (gas mark 4). Brush the brioche dough with the egg yolk.

12 – Sprinkle the surface with nibbed sugar. Bake for 40 minutes.

13 – Leave the brioche to cool, then split in half and remove the ring.

FOR THE VANILLA-FLAVOURED CHIBOUST CREAM

14 – Split the vanilla pod and scrape out the seeds with a knife tip. Whisk the pastry cream (see page 480) to smooth, then add the vanilla seeds. Add a little of the Italian meringue (see page 487) and whisk briskly to loosen the cream.

15 – Fold in the rest of the meringue, a third at a time.

ASSEMBLY

16 – Put the tart ring on the brioche base and spread uniformly with the Chiboust cream. Smooth with a palette knife and remove the ring.

17 – Cut the brioche top into 8 equal pieces.

18 – Arrange the pieces over the cream to give the St. Tropez "tart" its final appearance, then cut between the pieces through the base. Refrigerate for 1 hour before serving.

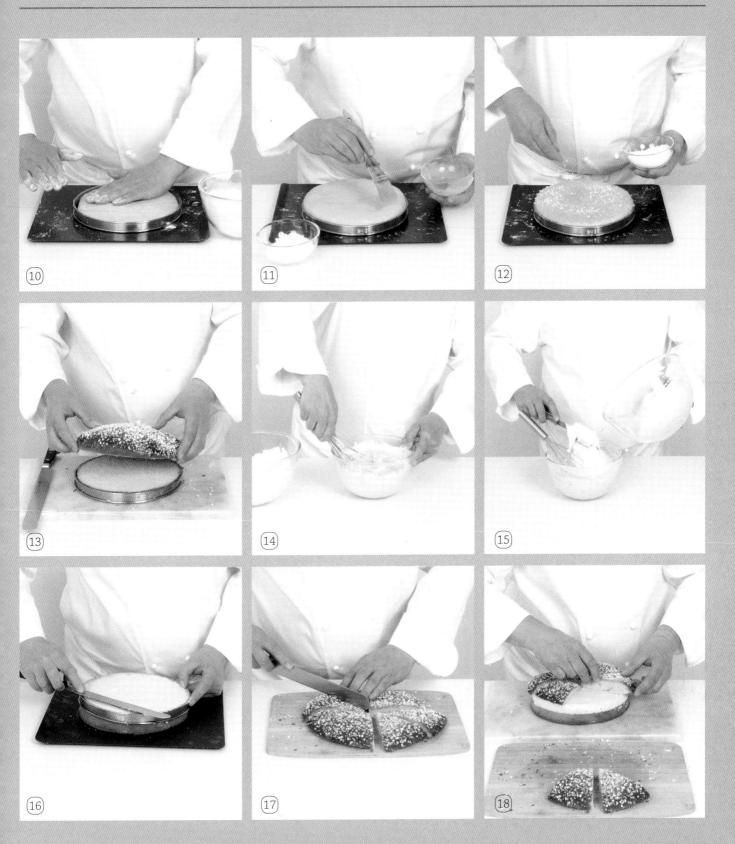

BERRY, CRISPY CEREAL AND
white chocolate entremets

Serves 10

PREPARATION TIME: 1 hour – BAKING TIME: 15 minutes – FREEZING TIME: 2 hours – STORAGE: 2 days in the refrigerator

DIFFICULTY: 🎩

SAVOY SPONGE CAKE
70 g unsalted butter
2 small eggs (80 g)
75 g sugar
65 g plain flour
Pinch of baking powder
30 g raspberries
20 g blueberries

CRISPY CEREAL BASE
130 g white chocolate
100 g cereal with red berries
30 g puffed rice
2 tsp popping sugar

WHITE CHOCOLATE AND PEAR MOUSSE
2 gelatine leaves (4 g)
100 g pear purée
1 tbsp honey
4 tbsp cream
235 g white chocolate
220 ml cream

IMBIBING LIQUEUR
2 tsp raspberry brandy

DECORATION
Icing sugar

EQUIPMENT NEEDED: 20-cm entremets ring – 18-cm entremets ring
pastry brush – 1 can red velvet spray – chef's blow torch – cardboard cake board

Adding crunch to your pastry creations

There is simple way for you to add a crunchy texture to your entremets.
Mix cereal with melted chocolate and leave to cool to create a crispy layer
that you can insert into your creation as you assemble it. Likewise, you can
also use Gavottes® crêpes (wafers), and you can also vary the flavour of this
layer as you like.

FOR THE SAVOY SPONGE CAKE

1 – Preheat the oven to 200°C (gas mark 6). Melt the butter. Whisk the eggs with the sugar. Add the flour and baking powder and mix. Incorporate the lukewarm melted butter.

2 – Pour the batter over a baking tray lined with baking parchment, without spreading.

3 – Halve the raspberries and blueberries and arrange over the batter. Bake for 15 minutes.

FOR THE CRISPY CEREAL BASE

4 – Melt the white chocolate over a bain-marie and mix in a bowl with the cereal with red berries, puffed rice and popping sugar.

5 – Place the 20 cm entremets ring on a baking tray lined with baking parchment and fill with the cereal mixture. Use a tablespoon to press on the mixture, spreading uniformly inside the ring.

6 – Make small rock-like balls with the remaining cereal mixture for the decoration and place on the same tray. Refrigerate.

FOR THE WHITE CHOCOLATE AND PEAR MOUSSE

7 – Soften the gelatine leaves in a bowl of cold water. Combine the pear purée, honey and the cream in a pan and bring to the boil. Remove the pan from the heat. Squeeze the gelatine to drain and add into the mixture in the pan. Transfer the mixture to a bowl.

8 – Chop the white chocolate and incorporate. Mix until smooth. Leave to cool. Whisk the 220 ml of cream to soft peaks and fold into the mixture.

ASSEMBLY AND DECORATION

9 – Turn the Savoy sponge cake over onto a sheet of baking parchment, and peel away the top baking parchment.

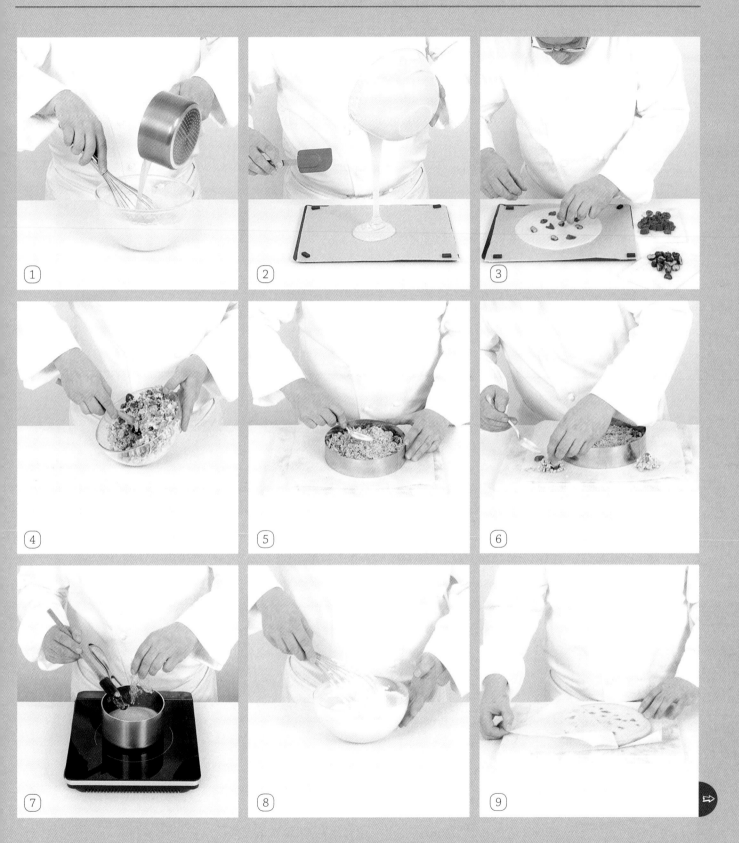

10 – Put the 18-cm entremets ring over the sponge and trim to size with
a knife.

11 – Brush the surface of the sponge with a little raspberry brandy.

12 – Pour a little white choccolate and pear mousse into the entremets ring
containing the crispy cereal base. Use a silicone spatula to spread evenly.

13 – Place the Savoy sponge cake disc on top of the mousse.

14 – Add the remaining mousse to cover and smooth with a palette knife to
remove the excess. Freeze the entremets for 2 hours.

15 – Cover the work surface with cling film and put a rack on top. Transfer the
entremets to the rack without removing the ring. Cover the surface of
the entremets uniformly with the red velvet spray.

16 – Put the entremets onto an upturned bowl and pass the blow torch around
the ring. Lower the ring to remove and transfer the entremets to the cardboard
cake board.

17 – Dust part of the surface of the entremets with icing sugar.

18 – Arrange the small cereal rocks on top.

PEAR AND TONKA BEAN
entremets

Serves 10

PREPARATION TIME: 1 hour 30 minutes + 15 minutes for the pastry cream – BAKING TIME: about 35 minutes

CHILLING TIME: 1 hour 30 minutes – STORAGE: 2 days in the refrigerator

DIFFICULTY: ◯

DRIED PEARS
4 pears
Neutral glaze

CARAMELISED PEARS
WITH TONKA BEAN
30 g unsalted butter
40 g sugar
Diced pears
⅓ tonka bean

WALNUT "BISCUIT" SPONGE
4 egg yolks (75 g)

55 g sugar
2 ½ egg whites (70 g)
20 g sugar
20 g plain flour
25 g potato starch
40 g unsalted butter, melted
30 g chopped walnuts

TONKA BEAN CREAM
Pastry cream
170 ml milk
⅓ tonka bean
4 egg yolks (80 g)

40 g sugar
1 tbsp cornflour
----
35 g dessert jelly
200 ml cream

CARAMEL GLAZE
150 g neutral glaze
1 tsp liquid caramel
Knife tip of red food colouring
powder

EQUIPMENT NEEDED: Silicone baking mat – 22-cm entremets ring – cardboard cake board

The tonka bean

Tonka beans come from the fruit of the cumaru or Brazilian teak tree, which is native to South America. Because they have an intense flavour, midway between an almond and caramel, and are toxic if used in large amounts, tonka beans are used only sparingly to flavour such preparations as creams. Grated or infused, the tonka bean combines perfectly with pear, and its original flavour is a surprise to the palate.

DRIED PEARS

1 – Preheat the oven to 180°C (gas mark 4). Before peeling the pear, cut out 2 thin slices from the centre of one of them. Then dice the remainder and set aside for the caramelised pears with tonka bean.
2 – Pan fry the 2 pear slices with stem for 5 minutes. Transfer to the silicone baking mat and dry out in the oven for 15 minutes.

FOR THE CARAMELISED PEARS WITH TONKA BEAN

3 – Heat the butter and sugar in a frying pan until they begin to caramelise, then add the diced pears and cook until soft. Grate the tonka bean over the top, mix and transfer to a bowl. Refrigerate.

FOR THE WALNUT "BISCUIT" SPONGE

4 – Keep the oven temperature at 180°C. Beat the egg yolks with the sugar in a bowl until the mixture turns pale and thickens.
5 – In a large bowl, whisk the egg whites until firm enough to cling to the tip of the whisk, then incorporate the sugar while whisking to stiff peaks.
6 – Fold in the egg yolk mixture.
7 – Then fold in the flour, potato starch and melted butter.
8 – Incorporate the chopped walnuts.
9 – Place the entremets ring on a baking tray lined with baking parchment and fill with the mixture. Bake for 22 minutes.

•••

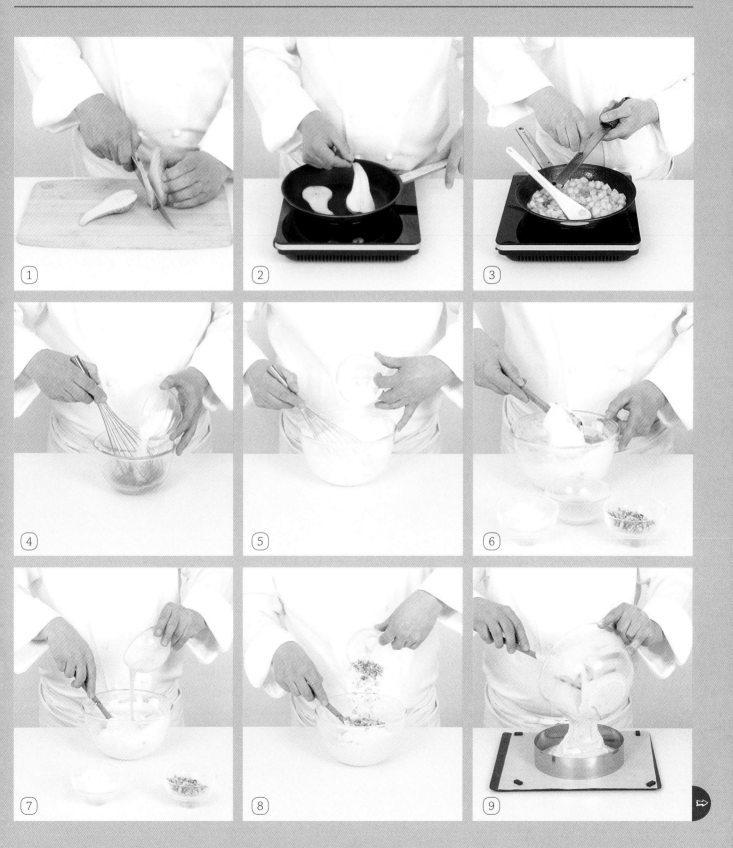

FOR THE TONKA BEAN CREAM

10 – Grate the tonka bean. Make a pastry cream (see page 480), heating the milk together with the grated tonka bean. Incorporate the dessert jelly into the hot pastry cream, then refrigerate for 30 minutes. Whip the cream until it is firm and clings to the tip of the whisk. Add a little of the whipped cream to the pastry cream while whisking to loosen. Then fold in the rest delicately.

ASSEMBLY

11 – Mix the caramelised pears with tonka bean with the tonka bean cream.
12 – Transfer the walnut "biscuit" sponge to a sheet of baking parchment, remove the ring, and cut through the middle to form a 1.5 cm thick disc.
13 – Place the entremets ring over the cardboard cake board, then put the "biscuit" sponge disc inside the ring.
14 –Fill the ring to the top with the tonka bean cream and smooth the surface with a palette knife, removing the excess. Refrigerate for 1 hour.

FOR THE CARAMEL GLAZE

15 – Mix the neutral glaze with the liquid caramel and a pinch of red food colouring.
16 – Pour the glaze over the top of the entremets.
17 – Smooth with a palette knife to remove the excess.
18 – Dip the dried pear slices in the neutral glaze and decorate the entremets.

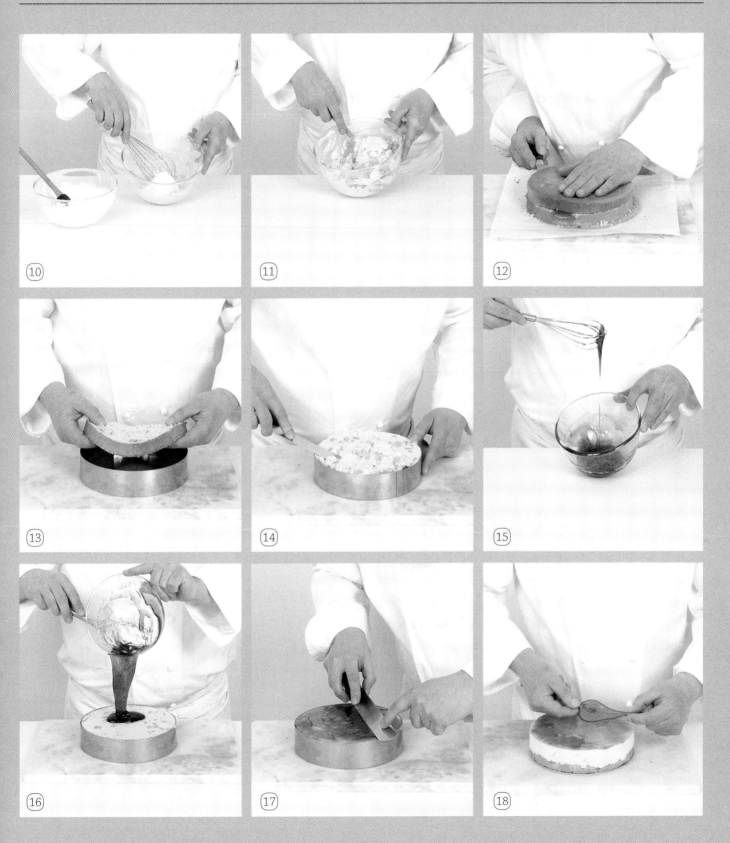

BLACK FOREST
gateau

Serves 10

PREPARATION TIME: 1 hour 15 minutes – BAKING TIME: 30 minutes – CHILLING TIME: 1 hour – STORAGE: 2 days in the refrigerator

DIFFICULTY: ○ ○

CHOCOLATE GÉNOISE SPONGE
4 eggs (200 g)
1 egg yolk (20 g)
120 g sugar
50 g plain flour
50 g potato starch
20 g unsweetened cocoa powder

CHOCOLATE SHAVINGS
200 g milk chocolate

CHANTILLY CREAM
500 ml cream
50 g icing sugar
Knife tip of vanilla powder

IMBIBING SYRUP
150 ml water
200 g sugar
30 ml kirsch

CHERRIES
350 g preserved cherries

EQUIPMENT NEEDED: Entremets ring 20 cm across and 6 cm deep – cardboard cake board

Black Forest gateau

A German speciality, the Black Forest is a gateau comprising layers of chocolate Génoise sponge imbibed with kirsch and filled with Chantilly cream and cherries. This gateau is generously covered with Chantilly cream, and the surface is decorated with cherries and chocolate shavings. The Black Forest gateau is also popular in Alsace.

FOR THE CHOCOLATE GÉNOISE SPONGE

1 – Preheat the oven to 170°C (gas mark 3–4). Beat the eggs, egg yolks and sugar in a bowl with an electric whisk. Transfer the bowl to a bain-marie and continue to whisk until the mixture turns pale and thickens.

2 – Take the bowl out of the bain-marie and continue to whisk until the mixture cools completely and acquires a ribbon consistency: it should run off the whisk without breaking, forming a ribbon.

3 – Sift the flour, potato starch and cocoa powder together, then fold into the egg mixture.

4 – Place the entremets ring on a baking tray lined with baking parchment and fill with the mixture. Bake for 30 minutes and leave to cool.

FOR THE IMBIBING SYRUP

5 – Combine the water and sugar in a pan and bring to the boil. Allow to cool, and then add the kirsch.

FOR THE CHOCOLATE SHAVINGS

6 – Melt the chocolate in a bowl over a bain-marie. Pour over a clean work surface and work with two palette knives until completely cool.

7 – Use a flexible knife to scrape the chocolate, forming shavings.

FOR THE CHANTILLY CREAM

8 – Whip the cream until it is firm and clings to the tip of the whisk. Add the icing sugar and vanilla powder and whisk lightly.

ASSEMBLY AND DECORATION

9 – Remove the ring from the Génoise sponge and cut through the middle into three uniform rounds.

•••

① ② ③
④ ⑤ ⑥
⑦ ⑧ ⑨

10 – Place a Génoise sponge disc on the cardboard cake board and brush with the imbibing syrup. Spread with a layer of Chantilly cream and smooth with a palette knife.

11 – Cover with cherries.

12 – Brush the second disc with syrup and lay over the cream.

13 – Cover with a layer of Chantilly cream. Smooth again with the palette knife and cover with more cherries.

14 – Carefully brush the third disc with syrup and lay over the cream.

15 – Use a flexible palette knife to cover the sides of the gateau with Chantilly cream.

16 – Cover the surface with cream and smooth all over with the palette knife to remove the excess.

17 – Cover the gateau with another layer of cream, tapping it with the back of a spoon to form peaks.

18 – Decorate the top and sides of the gateau with cherries and chocolate shavings. Refrigerate for 1 hour before serving.

CHEF'S TIP

A quicker way of making chocolate shavings is to scrape a chocolate bar with a vegetable peeler. However, the shavings will have a less polished appearance.

CHOCOLATE MARBLE
cakes

Makes 3 small cakes

PREPARATION TIME: 30 minutes – BAKING TIME: about 35 minutes – STORAGE: 4–5 days covered in cling film

DIFFICULTY: ○

CAKE BATTER	COCOA COLOURING
180 g room-temperature unsalted butter	20 g unsweetened cocoa powder
180 g icing sugar	100 ml milk
3 ½ eggs (180 g)	
1 vanilla pod	50 g room-temperature unsalted butter for the moulds
240 g plain flour	Flour for dusting
1 tsp baking powder	

EQUIPMENT NEEDED: Three 14 x 6 cm loaf tins

The origins of chocolate

The Maya people were the first to cultivate cacao or cocoa trees. After roasting, crushing and heating the cocoa beans, they would mix the resulting paste with water to make a bitter beverage. The Aztecs added sugar, vanilla, cinnamon and honey to make *xocolatl*. Cocoa was exported to Spain by the conquistadors in the sixteenth century, and spread throughout Europe a century later.

FOR THE CAKE BATTER

1 – Preheat the oven to 170°C (gas mark 3–4). Butter the loaf tins and dust with flour. Turn them over and tap the bottom to remove the excess. Whisk the butter in a bowl to a creamy consistency.
2 – Add the icing sugar and mix well.
3 – Whisk in the eggs.
4 – Split the vanilla pod and scrape out the seeds with a knife tip. Incorporate the seeds into the mixture.
5 – Sift the flour and baking powder together into a bowl, then incorporate a little at a time into the butter and egg mixture to make a batter.
6 – Pour a third of the batter into a separate bowl.

FOR THE COCOA BATTER

7 – In a small bowl, mix the cocoa powder with the milk to make a paste. Add the paste to the bowl containing the third of the batter and mix with a whisk.

FOR THE MARBLE CAKES

8 – Pour the plain batter into the loaf tins. Then pour the cocoa batter over the batter in the three tins.
9 – Use a fork to lightly swirl through two batters inside each tin to create a veined marble effect. Tap the bottom of each tin. Bake for about 35 minutes, or until a knife blade inserted into the cakes comes out clean.

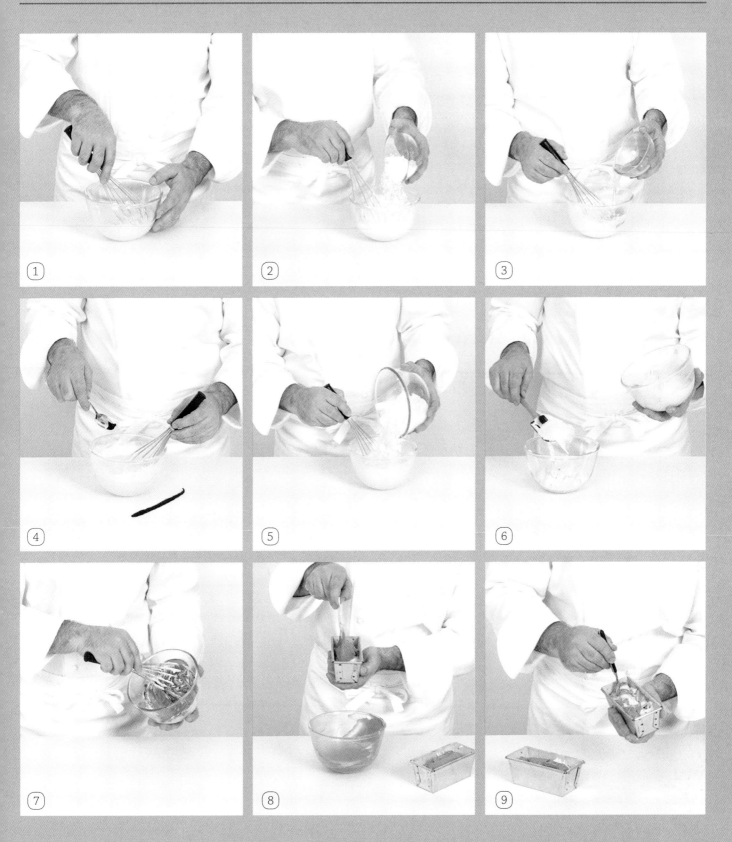

FRAISIER CAKE

Serves 8

PREPARATION TIME: 1 hour 30 minutes for the Génoise sponge + 15 minutes for the pastry cream

BAKING TIME: about 30 minutes – CHILLING TIME: 1 hour + 30 minutes for the pastry cream – STORAGE: 2 days in the refrigerator

DIFFICULTY: ♙ ♙

For the Génoise sponge
3 eggs (150 g)
110 g sugar
30 g ground almonds
115 g plain flour
20 g unsalted butter

Imbibing syrup
120 g sugar
150 ml water
20 ml kirsch

Mousseline cream
Pastry cream
370 ml milk
25 g unsalted butter
3 egg yolks (60 g)
80 g sugar
20 g plain flour
25 g cornflour
----
200 g unsalted butter

Filling + Decoration
400 g strawberries
1 bunch redcurrants
3 raspberries

EQUIPMENT NEEDED: 16-cm entremets ring – 14-cm entremets ring – piping bag
size 10 plain nozzle – cardboard cake board

A classic of French pastry

The fraisier is an entremets-style cake comprising syrup-imbibed Génoise sponge layers, buttercream, and strawberries. Today the buttercream is often replaced by mousseline cream – a pastry cream with added butter – because it is lighter and smoother.

FOR THE GÉNOISE SPONGE:

1 – Preheat the oven to 170°C (gas mark 3–4). Place the 16-cm entremets ring on a baking tray lined with baking parchment and fill with the Génoise sponge mixture (see page 484). Bake for 30–35 minutes and leave to cool.
Cut through the middle of the sponge to make two uniform discs.
2 – Use the smaller entremets ring to trim the discs to a diameter of 14 cm, and set aside the offcuts for the decoration.

FOR THE IMBIBING SYRUP

3 – Heat the water and sugar in a pan. Remove the pan from the heat and leave to cool, then add the kirsch.

FOR THE MOUSSELINE CREAM

4 – Pour the pastry cream (see page 480) into a bowl. Whisk to smooth.
5 – Whisk the butter in a bowl to a creamy consistency. Add to the pastry cream and whisk again. Transfer to a piping bag fitted with the size 10 plain nozzle.

ASSEMBLY AND DECORATION

6 – Place the 16-cm entremets ring on the cardboard cake board and pipe a ring of mousseline cream around the inside of the ring, over the cardboard.
7 – Brush the first Génoise sponge disc with syrup and lay it on the cake board inside the entremets ring, over the mousseline cream ring.
8 – Then pipe another ring of cream over the sides of the sponge, then in a spiral over the centre.
9 – Halve the strawberries and arrange them with their cut sides against the entremets ring.

• • •

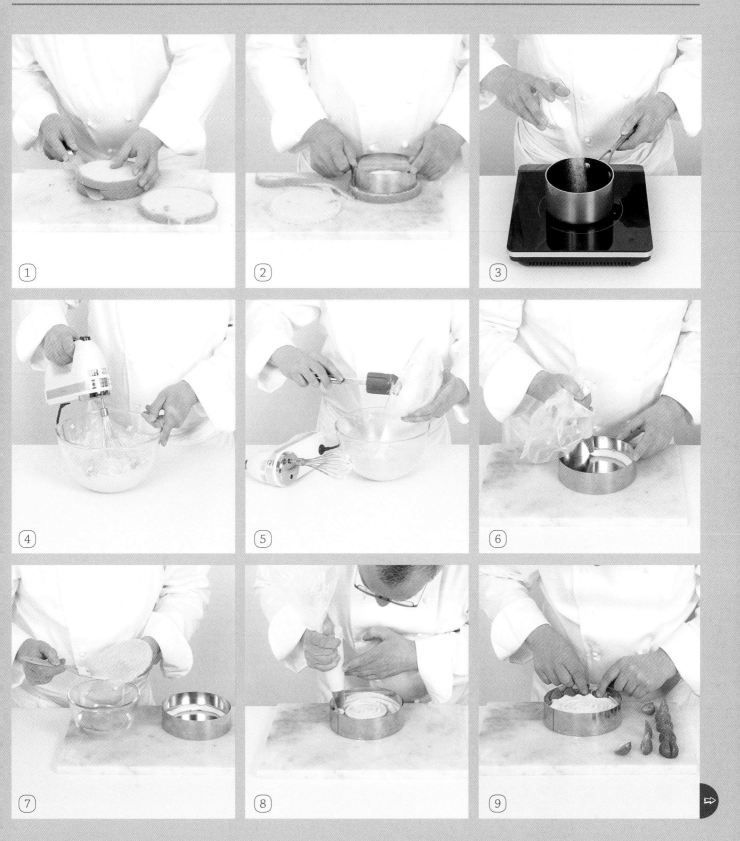

10 – Pipe cream over the strawberries to cover.

11 – Then press a spatula over the cream to completely cover.

12 – Arrange strawberries over the inside of the sponge disc, to the edge of the covered strawberries.

13 – Pipe a layer of mousseline cream over the strawberries to cover well, and smooth with a palette knife.

14 – Cover with the second sponge disc and brush with syrup.

15 – Pipe a spiral of cream over the sponge to form another layer. Smooth with the palette knife.

16 – Crumble the sponge offcuts and sprinkle the crumbs over the cream. Refrigerate for 1 hour.

17 – Dust the fraisier with icing sugar, then carefully remove the ring.

18 – Decorate with raspberries, strawberries and redcurrants as desired.

CHEF'S TIP

For a more traditional style, you can substitute the cake crumb and icing sugar decoration with pink almond paste and embellish with a few red berries. You can also finish your fraisier cake with Italian meringue (see page 487), to give it a very professional look.

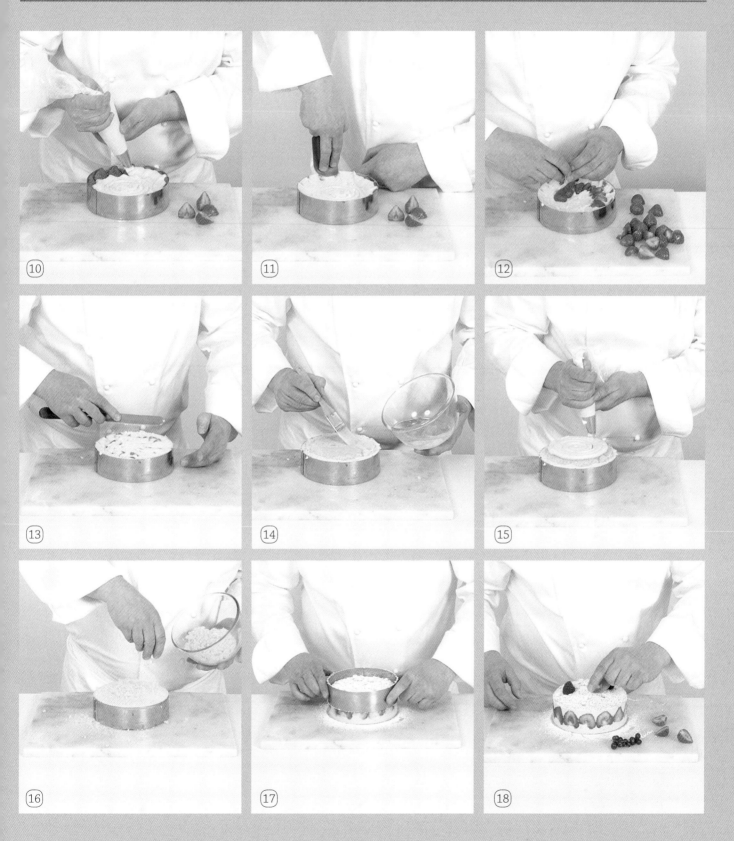

SWISS ALMOND-FILLED CAKE

Serves 8

PREPARATION TIME: 45 minutes + 15 minutes for the pastry — BAKING TIME: 40 minutes

CHILLING TIME: 10 minutes + 30 minutes for the pastry — STORAGE: 3 days in an airtight container.

DIFFICULTY: ♙

DICED APPLE
1 apple
30 g sugar
30 ml water

SWEET PASTRY DOUGH
105 g plain flour
50 g unsalted butter
50 g icing sugar
15 g ground almonds
½ egg (25 g)

Unsalted butter and plain flour for the mould

ALMOND FILLING
140 g room-temperature unsalted butter
120 g sugar
30 g ground almonds
1½ eggs (75 g)
1 egg yolk (20 g)
Pinch of vanilla powder
30 g plain flour
1 egg white (30 g)
20 g sugar

DECORATION
Icing sugar

EQUIPMENT NEEDED: Entremets ring 16 cm across and 4.5 cm deep

Softened butter

In culinary terminology, softened butter is butter that has been worked or whisked to give it a creamy consistency.

It is used in this form to incorporate into a preparation because it is much easier to mix. It allows a mixture to be emulsified well and to become smooth. Softened butter should never become runny, so it should never be overworked.

FOR THE DICED APPLE

1 – Peel and core the apple, then cut into 1 cm dice. Put into a pan with the sugar and water, and cook until soft.

FOR THE TART CASE

2 – Dust the work surface with flour and roll out the sweet pastry dough (see page 488) to a thickness of 2 mm. Use the entremets ring to cut the dough into a disc and transfer to a baking tray lined with baking parchment. Butter and flour the ring and position it around the dough.

3 – Roll the surplus pastry into a sausage shape. Flatten it with the rolling pin and roll out into a rectangle 2 mm thick.

4 – Use a knife to cleanly cut out a strip 16 cm long and 4.5 cm wide, using the height of the entremets ring as your guide.

5 – Lightly dust the strip of dough with flour and roll it around the rolling pin. Unroll the dough along the inside of the ring, pressing lightly to line it well with dough. Use a knife to trim off any dough rising above the rim of the ring. Refrigerate for 10 minutes.

FOR THE ALMOND FILLING

6 – Soften the butter by whisking and cream well with the 120 g of sugar. Incorporate the ground almonds. Mix the eggs and egg yolk, then add to the creamed butter half at a time, whisking well with each addition. Whisk in the vanilla, followed by the flour.

7 – Whisk the egg white until it is firm and clings to the tip of the whisk, then incorporate the 20 g of sugar while whisking to stiff peaks. Fold into the filling mixture.

ASSEMBLY AND DECORATION

8 – Preheat the oven to 170°C (gas mark 3–4). Cover the bottom of the pastry case with the diced apple.

9 – Pour the almond filling over the apple and smooth well with a palette knife. Bake for 40 minutes. Leave to cool, then remove the ring. Lightly dust the tart with icing sugar.

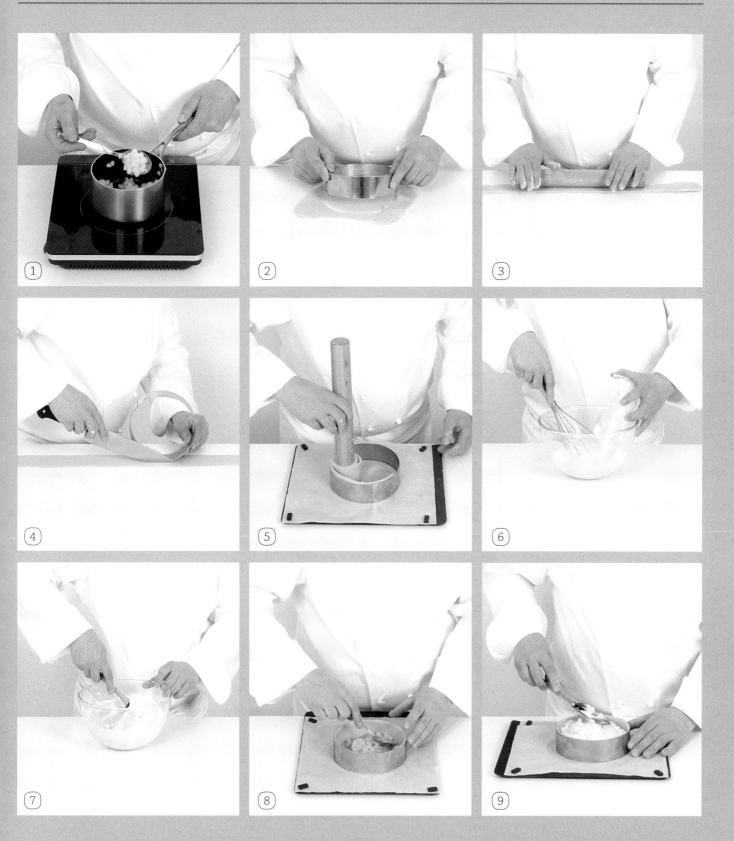

Individual pastries & Plated desserts

CHOCOLATE AND RASPBERRY
éclairs

Makes 15 éclairs

PREPARATION TIME: 1 hour + 15 minutes for the choux pastry – BAKING TIME: 35 minutes – STORAGE: 2 days in the refrigerator

DIFFICULTY: ♙

CHOUX PASTRY
170 ml milk
70 g unsalted butter
1½ tsp sugar
½ tsp fine salt
100 g plain flour
3 eggs (140 g)

DECORATION
200 g red fondant icing
150 g neutral glaze
Knife tip of red food colouring powder
Knife tip of edible gold powder
125 g raspberries

CHOCOLATE AND RASPBERRY MOUSSE
90 g milk chocolate
100 g raspberry purée
1 tsp dessert jelly
1 tsp sugar
200 ml cream

EQUIPMENT NEEDED: 2 piping bags – size PF16 star nozzle – size 10 plain nozzle – size 6 plain nozzle

The origins of the éclair

The éclair appeared in Lyon in the late nineteenth century. The master pastry chef Antonin Carême modernised what was known at the time as *pain à la duchesse*, a short log made from choux pastry and almonds, by filling it with pastry cream. Nowadays, the éclair comes in many different flavours besides the traditional chocolate, vanilla and coffee.

CHOCOLATE AND RASPBERRY éclairs

step-by-step

FOR THE CHOUX PASTRY AND ÉCLAIRS

1 – Preheat the oven to 180°C (gas mark 4). Fill a piping bag fitted with the size PF16 star nozzle with the choux pastry (see page 483).

2 – Line a baking tray with baking parchment and pipe thick fingers of choux pastry 10 cm long in staggered rows to keep separate. Bake for 35 minutes, slightly opening the oven door every 2 minutes to vent the steam.

FOR THE CHOCOLATE AND RASPBERRY MOUSSE

3 – Chop the chocolate and put into a bowl. In a pan, heat the raspberry purée, then add the dessert jelly and sugar. Mix, then remove the pan from the heat.

4 – Immediately pour the mixture over the chocolate, mix and leave to cool.

5 – Whisk the cream to soft peaks, then fold into the chocolate and raspberry mixture. Transfer to a piping bag fitted with the size 10 plain nozzle.

ASSEMBLY AND DECORATION

6 – Make three holes on the underside of each éclair by piercing with the size 6 plain nozzle, turning it a little. Fill the éclairs with the mousse by piping it through the holes. Use a teaspoon to remove the excess mousse.

7 – Finely roll out the fondant icing and cut out 10 x 2 cm rectangles. Lightly brush the surface of the éclairs with neutral glaze and position a fondant icing rectangle over each one.

8 – Mix the neutral glaze with the food colouring and gold powder, then dip the surface of the éclairs in the glaze and smooth around with your finger.

9 – Dip raspberries in the gold powder and arrange one on top of each éclair.

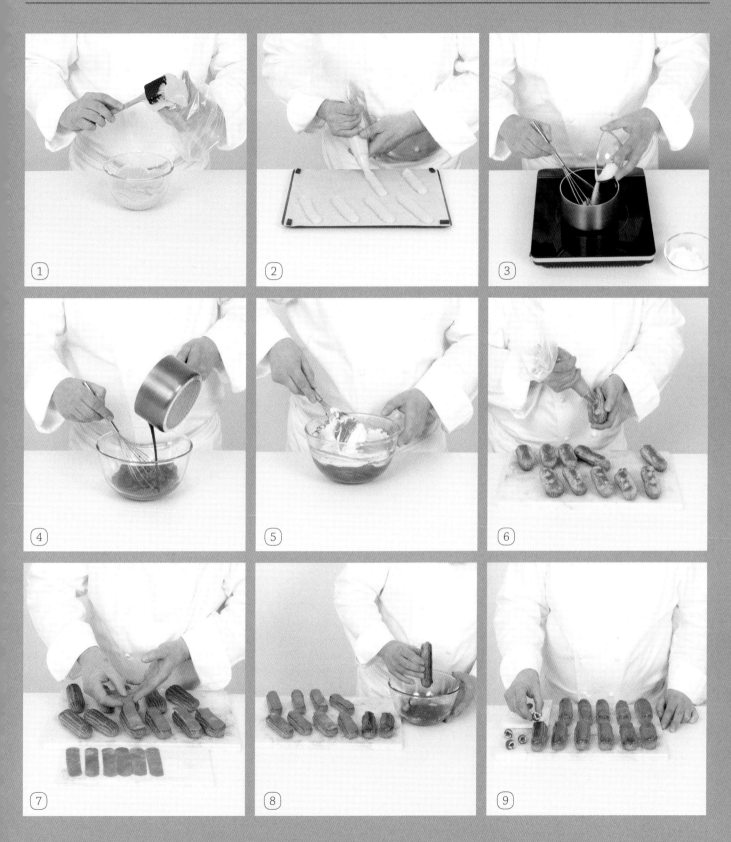

CHOUX BUNS WITH CRAQUELIN
and chocolate

Makes 15 buns

PREPARATION TIME: 1 hour 30 minutes – BAKING TIME: 35 minutes – CHILLING TIME: 1 hour 15 minutes
STORAGE: 2 days in the refrigerator

DIFFICULTY: 🎩

CHOCOLATE CRAQUELIN
75 g room-temperature unsalted butter
75 g plain flour
80 g unrefined cane sugar
12 g unsweetened cocoa powder

CHOUX PASTRY
170 ml milk
70 g unsalted butter
1½ tsp sugar
½ tsp fine salt
100 g plain flour
3 eggs (140 g)

CHOCOLATE CREAM
Pastry cream
370 ml milk
25 g unsalted butter
3 egg yolks (70 g)
80 g sugar
20 g plain flour
25 g cornflour

----

100 g dark chocolate (72% cocoa)
70 ml cream

CHOCOLATE GLAZE
160 g dark chocolate (72% cocoa)
2 tsp unsweetened cocoa powder
30 ml water
130 ml cream
80 g glucose
20 g neutral glaze

EQUIPMENT NEEDED: 2 piping bags – size 10 plain nozzle – size 6 plain nozzle
5-cm round biscuit cutter – 1 can edible gold spray (optional)

The key stage for making choux pastry

Collapsing choux pastry is every gourmet's nightmare. To overcome this difficulty, there is a crucial stage in its making – drying out. Because choux pastry contains a lot of water, in order to prevent a disaster, it has to be dried out in a pan before baking. This will allow the choux buns to rise properly as they are baked and to acquire their characteristic dry appearance.

FOR THE CHOCOLATE CRAQUELIN

1 – Combine the butter, flour, sugar and cocoa powder in a bowl. Mix with your fingers to form a dough, then smear (fraser) to a smooth consistency. Refrigerate for 15 minutes.

2 – Transfer the craquelin dough to a floured sheet of baking parchment and roll it out very finely with a rolling pin.

FOR THE CHOUX PASTRY AND CHOUX BUNS

3 – Fill a piping bag fitted with the size 10 plain nozzle with the choux pastry (see page 483). Preheat the oven to 180°C (gas mark 4). Line a baking tray with baking parchment and pipe balls about 5 cm across in staggered rows over the tray.

4 – Use the biscuit cutter to cut out rounds of craquelin. Place one round on top of each choux ball. Bake for 35 minutes, slightly opening the oven door every 2 minutes to vent the steam.

FOR THE CHOCOLATE CREAM

5 – Make a pastry cream (see page 480). Chop the chocolate and put into a bowl. Pour in the hot pastry cream and mix. Refrigerate for 1 hour.

6 – Whip the cream until it is firm and clings to the tip of the whisk. Whisk the pastry cream and whisk in a little of the whipped cream. Then gently incorporate the rest. Transfer to a piping bag fitted with the size 10 plain nozzle.

FOR THE CHOCOLATE GLAZE

7 – Chop the chocolate and put into a bowl with the cocoa powder. Combine the water, cream and glucose in a pan and heat. Pour the hot mixture over the chocolate, then incorporate the glaze. Pass through a conical sieve into a bowl. Cover with cling film and leave to cool.

ASSEMBLY AND DECORATION

8 – Pierce a hole in the underside of each choux bun with the size 6 plain nozzle, then fill the buns by piping the cream through the hole. Use a teaspoon to remove the excess cream.

9 – Dip the top of the choux buns in the warm glaze, then smooth with your finger.

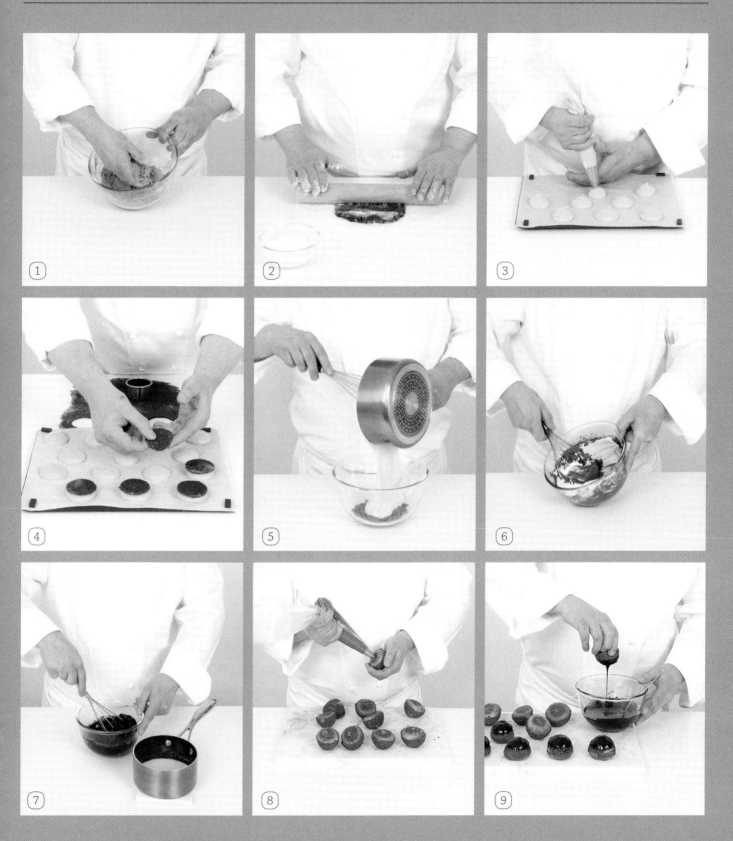

BRITTANY SHORTBREAD
with meringue and Menton lemon

Makes 10 shortbreads

PREPARATION TIME: 1 hour 15 minutes + 10 minutes for the meringue – BAKING TIME: 1 hour 30 minutes – CHILLING TIME: 2 hours

STORAGE: 2 days in the refrigerator

DIFFICULTY: 🎩 🎩

MERINGUES	MENTON LEMON CREAM
2 egg whites (50 g)	2½ gelatine leaves (5 g)
100 g sugar	3–4 eggs (180 g)
60 g icing sugar	210 g sugar
Zest of 1 lemon	10 g cornflour
1 tsp chopped pistachio nuts	140 ml Menton lemon juice
	Zest of 2 Menton lemons
	265 g unsalted butter, cut into pieces
BRITTANY SHORTBREAD WITH LEMON	
25 g ground almonds	CANDIED MENTON LEMON ZEST
150 g room-temperature lightly salted butter	Zest of 1 Menton lemon
60 g sugar	100 ml water
Zest of 1 lemon	100 g sugar
1 egg yolk (25 g)	
130 g plain flour	
½ tsp baking powder	Unsalted butter for the moulds

EQUIPMENT NEEDED: Ten 8-cm pastry rings – 3 piping bags – size 8 plain nozzle

Menton lemon

Prized for its unique flavour and delicate scent, the Menton lemon is grown in the mountainous region around Menton, France.

The lemons are traditionally hand-picked and left untreated. The town of Menton holds a festival to honour this fruit every year.

FOR THE MERINGUES

1 – Preheat the oven to 120°C (gas mark ½). Make a French meringue (see page 486) and transfer to a piping bag fitted with the plain nozzle. Line a baking tray with baking parchment and pipe half the meringue out as small drops in staggered rows.

2 – Then spread the rest of the meringue over the same tray and sprinkle with the chopped pistachios. Bake for 1 hour and leave to cool. Break the meringue sheet with pistachios into pieces.

FOR THE BRITTANY SHORTBREAD WITH LEMON

3 – Raise the oven temperature to 180°C (gas mark 4). Whisk the ground almonds with the butter, sugar and lemon zest in a bowl.

4 – Whisk in the egg yolk, then fold in the flour and baking powder with a silicon spatula.

5 – Use a silicone spatula to transfer the pastry to a piping bag with the plain nozzle.

6 – Butter the ten tart rings and set them on a baking tray lined with baking parchment.

7 – Pipe spirals of shortbread dough inside the rings. Bake for about 20 minutes, until golden. When the shortbreads come out of the oven, run the blade of a small knife around the inside of the rings and remove. Leave to cool.

FOR THE MENTON LEMON CREAM

8 – Soften the gelatine leaves in a bowl of cold water. In another bowl, beat the eggs with the sugar until the mixture turns pale and thickens.

9 – Add the cornflour.

• • •

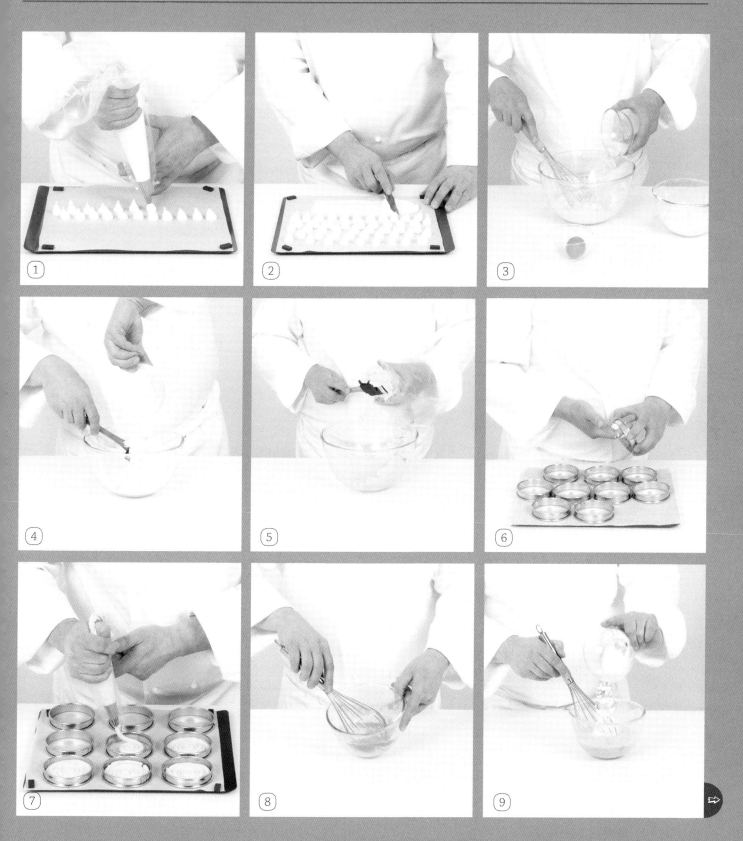

10 – Combine the lemon juice with the zest in a pan and bring to the boil. Pour the mixture into the egg and sugar mixture while whisking briskly.

11 – Return the mixture to the pan and cook over a low heat, stirring constantly with the whisk until it comes to a gentle boil. Immediately remove the pan from the heat.

12 – Pour the cream into a large bowl. Squeeze the gelatine to drain and incorporate into the cream. Allow to cool for a few minutes, then add the butter.

13 – Use a hand-held blender to blend until very smooth. Refrigerate for 2 hours.

FOR THE CANDIED MENTON LEMON ZEST

14 – Cut the lemon zest into very thin strips.

15 – Bring water to the boil in a pan and blanch the zest.
Change the water and repeat the process. Next, combine the water and sugar in a pan and bring to the boil. Add the zest and cook for 10 minutes. Take the zest out of the pan and drain on kitchen paper.

ASSEMBLY

16 – Lightly whisk the Menton lemon cream to smooth. Transfer to a piping bag fitted with the plain nozzle, then pipe small dots on each shortbread.

17 – Top each pastry with three meringue drops and 2 pieces of meringue with pistachio.

18 – Decorate with the candied lemon zest.

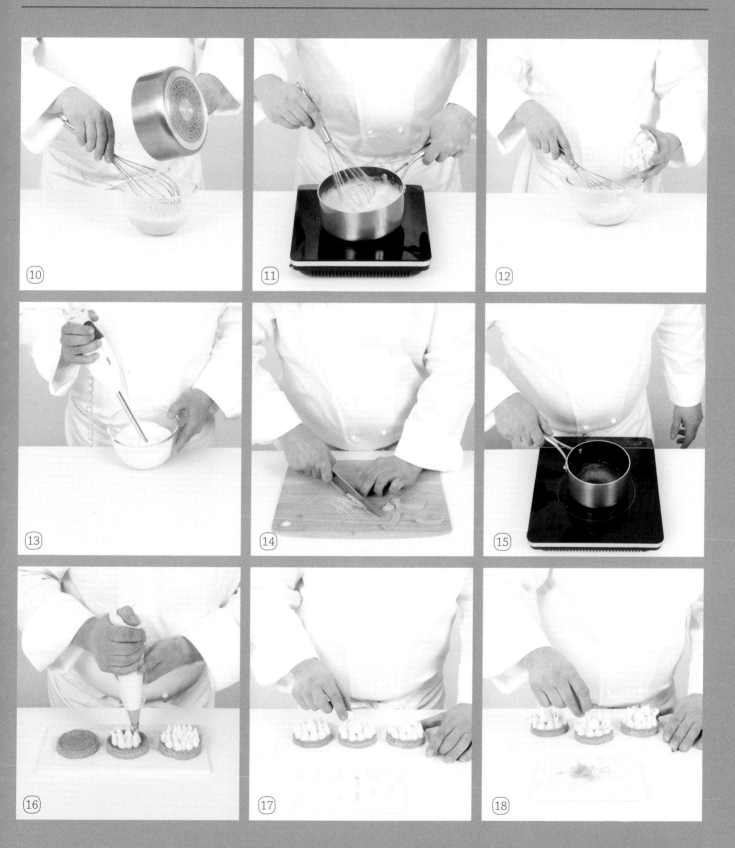

COCONUT AND GINGER
religieuses

Makes 12 religieuses

PREPARATION TIME: 45 minutes + 15 minutes for the choux pastry + 15 minutes for the pastry cream – BAKING TIME: 35 minutes
CHILLING TIME: 30 minutes – STORAGE: 2 days in the refrigerator
DIFFICULTY: ♙

CHOUX PASTRY	COCONUT AND GINGER CREAM
170 ml milk	Pastry cream
70 g unsalted butter	200 ml milk
1½ tsp sugar	200 ml coconut milk
⅓ tsp fine salt	3 egg yolks (70 g)
100 g plain flour	80 g sugar
3 eggs (140 g)	20 g plain flour
	25 g cornflour
1 beaten egg for glazing	-------
	5 g fresh ginger
	140 ml cream
	DECORATION
	100 g neutral glaze
	100 g desiccated coconut

EQUIPMENT NEEDED: 2 piping bags – size 10 plain nozzle – pastry brush – size D7 star nozzle – size 6 plain nozzle

Ginger

Ginger is the aromatic rhizome or rootstock of a plant native to India and Malaysia that is cultivated in many Asian countries.

It is valued in all its forms, whether ground, fresh or crystallised, and features in different sweet and savoury culinary preparations. Do not hesitate to try it together with coconut, with which it forms a perfect and timeless combination.

FOR THE CHOUX PASTRY AND CHOUX BUNS

1 – Preheat the oven to 170°C (gas mark 3–4). Fill a piping bag fitted with the size 10 plain nozzle with the choux pastry (see page 483). Pipe twelve 5 cm balls and twelve 2.5 cm balls of choux pastry on a baking tray.

2 – Brush with the beaten egg glaze and lightly flatten with a fork. Bake for 35 minutes, slightly opening the oven door every 2 minutes to vent the steam.

FOR THE COCONUT AND GINGER CREAM

3 – Make a pastry cream (see page 480), mixing the milk with the coconut milk. Peel the ginger and grate over the hot coconut pastry cream. Immediately transfer the mixture to a bowl. Cover with cling film and refrigerate for 30 minutes.

4 – Whisk the coconut and ginger cream to smooth.

5 – Whip the cream until it is firm and clings to the tip of the whisk. Incorporate a third of the whipped cream into the pastry cream and mix well to loosen. Then gently whisk in the remaining cream. Transfer to a piping bag fitted with the size D7 star nozzle.

ASSEMBLY AND DECORATION

6 – Make a hole on the underside of each choux bun by piercing with the size 6 plain nozzle, turning it a little.

7 – Fill each choux bun with the coconut and ginger cream. Use a teaspoon to remove the excess cream.

8 – Put the neutral glaze into one bowl and the desiccated coconut into another. Dip the surface of each choux bun into the glaze, wipe off the excess with your finger, then dip in the coconut.

9 – Pipe a swirl of coconut and ginger cream on top of the larger choux buns, then top each one with a smaller bun.

CHEF'S TIP

To enhance the ginger flavour of the coconut and ginger cream, grate the ginger into the pan with the milk and coconut milk before heating.

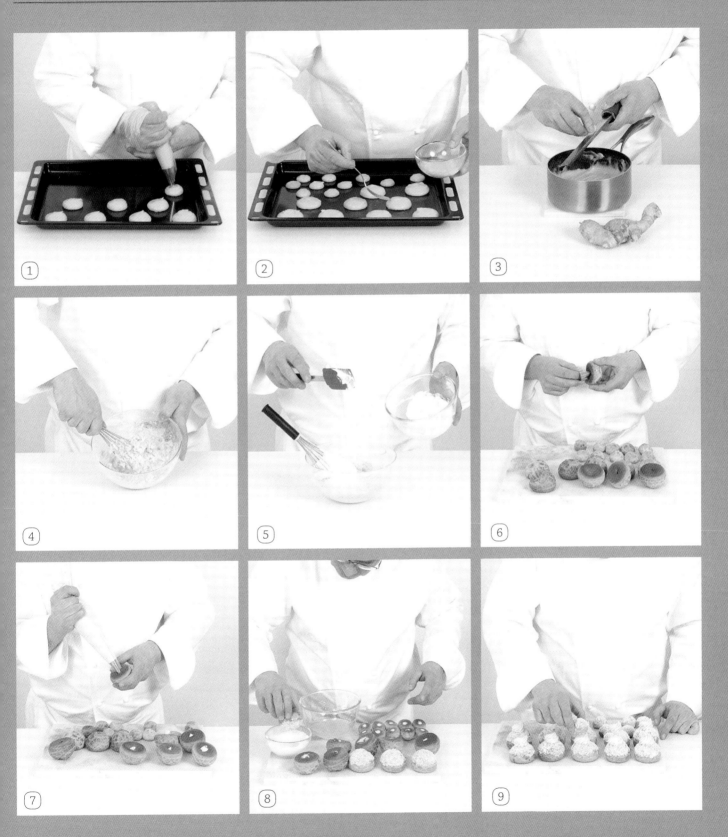

VIOLET ÉCLAIRS

Makes 15 éclairs

PREPARATION TIME: 1 hour + 15 minutes for the choux pastry + 15 minutes for the pastry cream – BAKING TIME: 35 minutes

CHILLING TIME: 1 hour 15 minutes – STORAGE: 2 days in the refrigerator

DIFFICULTY: 🎩

CRAQUELIN
65 g room-temperature unsalted butter
85 g plain flour
80 g unrefined cane sugar

CHOUX PASTRY
170 ml milk
70 g unsalted butter
1½ tsp sugar
½ tsp fine salt
100 g plain flour
3 eggs (140 g)

VIOLET
PASTRY CREAM
550 ml milk
40 g unsalted butter
5 egg yolks (105 g)
120 g sugar
30 g plain flour
35 g cornflour
----
7 drops violet essence

DECORATION
200 g violet fondant icing
75 g raspberry jam
300 g neutral glaze
Knife tip of violet food colouring powder
Knife tip of edible metallic silver glitter
Silver sugar pearls

EQUIPMENT NEEDED: 2 piping bags – size PF16 star nozzle – size 10 plain nozzle – size 6 plain nozzle

Violet pastries

The fragrant and delicate violet is one of the oldest edible flowers in use. It is associated with the city of Toulouse, where it is found mainly as crystallised flowers and used in pastries, but also in the form of essence used to flavour all sorts of indulgences. Try combining the flavour of violet with its colour by tinting your creams, macarons and glazes with violet food colouring.

FOR THE CRAQUELIN

1 – Combine the butter, flour and sugar in a bowl. Mix with your fingers to form a dough, then smear (fraser) to a smooth consistency. Refrigerate for 15 minutes.

2 – Transfer the craquelin dough to a floured sheet of baking parchment and roll it out very finely with a rolling pin.

FOR THE CHOUX PASTRY AND ÉCLAIRS

3 – Fill a piping bag fitted with the size PF16 star nozzle with the choux pastry (see page 483). Line a baking tray with baking parchment and pipe thick fingers of choux pastry 10 cm long in staggered rows to keep separate.

4 – Preheat the oven to 180°C (gas mark 4). Cut the craquelin into 10 x 2 cm strips and lay one strip on each choux pastry finger. Bake for 35 minutes, slightly opening the oven door every 2 minutes to vent the steam.

FOR THE VIOLET PASTRY CREAM

5 – Put the hot pastry cream (see page 480) into a bowl and incorporate the violet essence. Refrigerate for 1 hour, then whisk the cream to smooth. Transfer to a piping bag fitted with the size 10 plain nozzle.

ASSEMBLY AND DECORATION

6 – Make three holes on the underside of each éclair by piercing with the size 6 plain nozzle, turning it a little. Fill the éclairs with the violet pastry cream by piping it through the holes. Use a teaspoon to remove the excess cream.

7 – Finely roll out the fondant icing and cut out 10 x 2 cm rectangles.

8 – Use a teaspoon to spread a little jam on each éclair, and top with a fondant icing strip.

9 – Mix the neutral glaze with the food colouring and silver glitter, then dip the surface of the éclairs in the glaze and smooth with your finger. Decorate with silver sugar pearls.

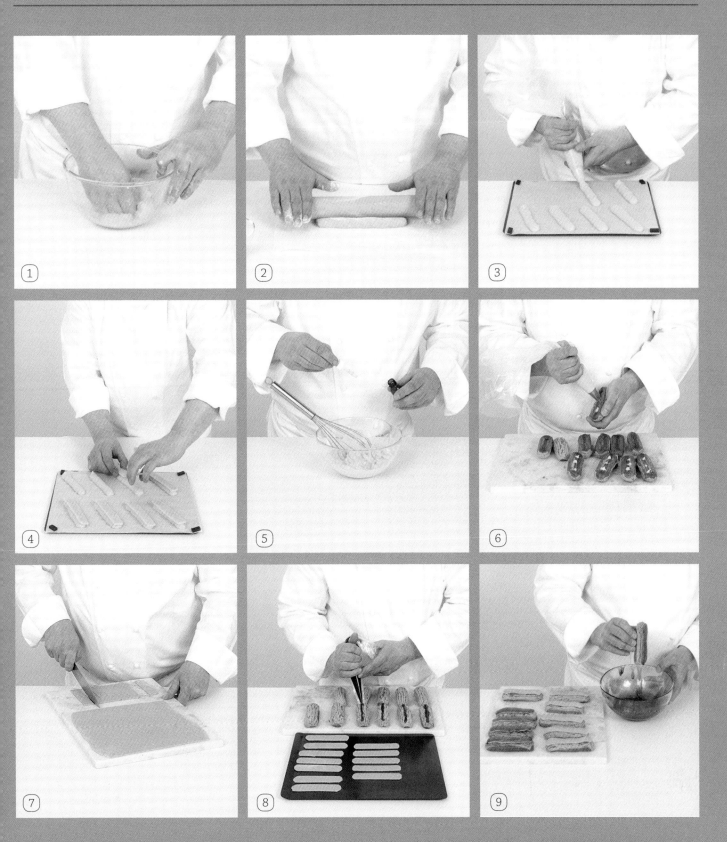

MONT BLANC
with kumquat

Makes 10 Mont Blanc

PREPARATION TIME: 50 minutes + 10 minutes for the meringue + 30 minutes for tempering – BAKING TIME: About 1 hour 30 minutes
CHILLING TIME: 40 minutes – STORAGE: 2 days in the refrigerator

DIFFICULTY: ♙ ♙

MERINGUE AND CHOCOLATE SHELLS
3 egg whites
100 g sugar
100 g icing sugar
50 g milk couverture chocolate

Unsalted butter and plain flour for the tray

CANDIED KUMQUATS
150 g kumquats
150 ml water
150 g sugar

CHANTILLY CREAM
100 ml cream
1 tbsp icing sugar

CHESTNUT CREAM
400 g chestnut paste
40 ml rum
200 g room-temperature unsalted butter

DECORATION
100 g candied chestnuts, cut into pieces
Icing sugar

EQUIPMENT NEEDED: 2 piping bags – 6-cm round biscuit cutter – size 20 plain nozzle
pastry brush – size 10 plain nozzle

Kumquat

The kumquat is the smallest of the citrus fruits. This round or oval fruit grows no larger than 5 cm. It has a soft, sweet peel and its flesh is tart. It is native to China. Kumquats can be eaten fresh, with the peel, or candied. They can also be used in certain cakes and to make jams.

FOR THE MERINGUE AND CHOCOLATE SHELLS

1 – Preheat the oven to 100°C (gas mark ¼). Fill a piping bag fitted with the size 20 nozzle with a French meringue (see page 486).

2 – Butter and flour a baking tray, and use the biscuit cutter to mark the outline of 10 circles over the tray. Pipe 10 small dome-shaped mounds of meringue, each about the diameter of the marked 6-cm circle. Bake for 25 minutes.

3 – Take the meringue domes out of the oven and use a paring knife to hollow out the inside of each one to make shells. Return them to the oven for 40 minutes.

4 – Leave the shells to cool, then use a grater to make a flat base on the rounded side.

5 – Temper the couverture chocolate (see pages 494–495).

6 – Brush the inside of the meringue shells with the tempered chocolate. Refrigerate for 10 minutes.

FOR THE CANDIED KUMQUATS

7 – Put the whole, unpeeled kumquats into a pan filled with cold water and blanch briefly. Change the water and repeat the process. Drain the kumquats.

8 – Combine the water and sugar in another pan and heat to make a syrup. Add the kumquats. Cook over a low heat for about 30 minutes.

9 – Drain, setting aside the syrup. Cut the kumquats into small pieces.

• • •

CHEF'S TIP

You can replace the candied kumquats with candied orange peel.

FOR THE CHANTILLY CREAM

10 – Whip the cream until it is firm and clings to the tip of the whisk, then incorporate the icing sugar.

11 – Use a tablespoon to fill the meringue and chocolate shells with Chantilly cream.

FOR THE CHESTNUT CREAM

12 – In a bowl, work the chestnut paste with a spatula. Gradually incorporate the rum to loosen.

13 – Gently incorporate the butter, and whisk the mixture to continue to loosen. Transfer to a piping bag fitted with the size 10 plain nozzle.

ASSEMBLY AND DECORATION

14 – Pipe a tall, narrow cone of chestnut cream in the middle of the shells.

15 – Carefully arrange pieces of candied chestnuts and kumquats over the cream.

16 – Pipe chestnut cream in a spiral around the central cone.

17 – Use a sieve to dust with icing sugar.

18 – Decorate the cream spiral with pieces of candied chestnuts and kumquats, then refrigerate for at least 30 minutes. Take the Mont Blancs out of the refrigerator 15–20 minutes before serving.

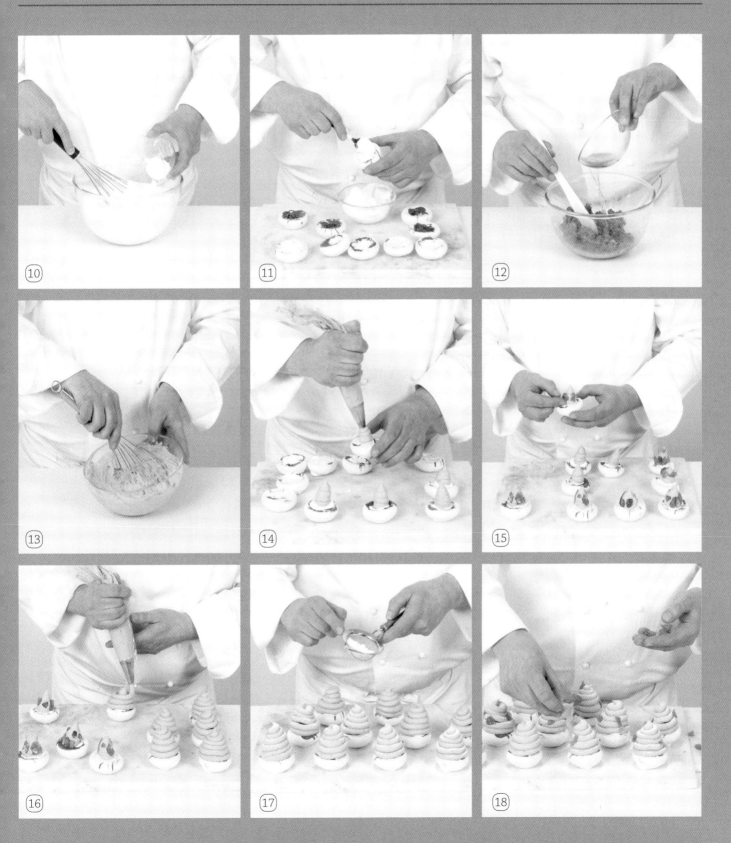

YUZU AND BLOND CHOCOLATE
choux buns

Makes 15 buns

PREPARATION TIME: 1 hour + 15 minutes for the choux pastry + 15 minutes for the pastry cream – BAKING TIME: 35 minutes CHILLING TIME: 1 hour 25 minutes – STORAGE: 2 days in the refrigerator

DIFFICULTY: ♙

CRAQUELIN
65 g room-temperature unsalted butter
85 g plain flour
80 g unrefined cane sugar

CHOUX PASTRY
170 ml milk
70 g unsalted butter
1½ tsp sugar
½ tsp fine salt
100 g plain flour
3 eggs (140 g)

YUZU PASTRY CREAM
370 ml milk
25 g unsalted butter
3 egg yolks (70 g)
80 g sugar
20 g plain flour
25 g cornflour

Zest of 1 yuzu
40 ml yuzu juice

CHOCOLATE AND CARAMEL MOUSSE
200 ml cream
35 g white chocolate
65 g milk chocolate
1 tsp liquid caramel
2 tsp icing sugar

DECORATION
Icing sugar

EQUIPMENT NEEDED: 3 piping bags – size 10 plain nozzle – size PF16 star nozzle – 5-cm round biscuit cutter

Yuzu

Yuzu, a citrus fruit native to Asia, is highly prized in pastry making.
It is the colour of a lemon and the size of an orange, but it has a unique flavour, halfway between a grapefruit and a mandarin. Its juice and zest are used to flavour creams and frozen desserts, and its peel is typically candied. You can find products made from yuzu in shops.

FOR THE CRAQUELIN

1 – Combine the butter, flour and sugar in a bowl.

2 – Mix with your fingers to form a dough, then smear (fraser) to a smooth consistency. Refrigerate for 15 minutes.

3 – Transfer the craquelin dough to a floured sheet of baking parchment and roll it out very finely with a rolling pin.

FOR THE CHOUX PASTRY AND CHOUX BUNS

4 – Fill a piping bag fitted with the size 10 plain nozzle with the choux pastry (see page 483).

5 – Line a baking tray with baking parchment and pipe balls of choux pastry about 5 cm across in staggered rows to keep separate while baking.

6 – Preheat the oven to 180°C (gas mark 4). Use the biscuit cutter to cut out rounds in the craquelin and place one round on top of each choux ball. Bake for 35 minutes, slightly opening the oven door every 2 minutes to vent the steam.

FOR THE YUZU PASTRY CREAM

7 – Put the hot pastry cream (see page 480) into a bowl and grate the zest of the yuzu into it. Mix.

8 – Incorporate the yuzu juice and refrigerate for 1 hour.

FOR THE CHOCOLATE AND CARAMEL MOUSSE

9 – Whisk the cream to soft peaks, then divide into two portions.

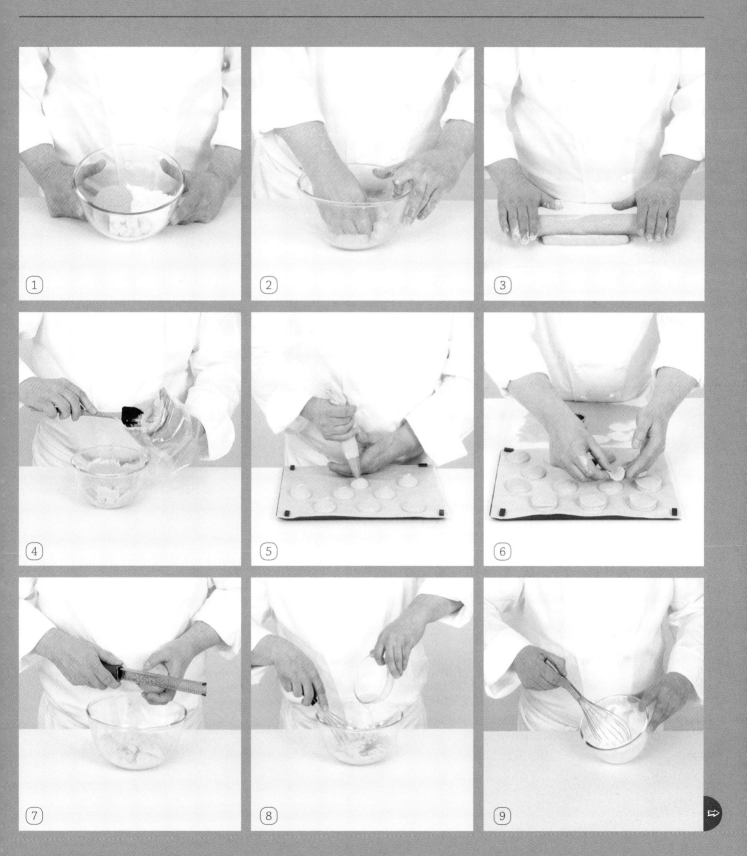

10 – Melt the white chocolate and milk chocolate over a bain-marie. Add the caramel and mix.
11 – Fold the chocolate mixture into the first portion of the whipped cream.
12 – Add the icing sugar to the second portion of whipped cream.
13 – Add the portion of cream with the icing sugar to the portion with the chocolate and mix only lightly to create a marbled effect. Transfer to a piping bag fitted with the PF16 star nozzle. Refrigerate for 10 minutes.

ASSEMBLY AND DECORATION

14 – Cut off the top of the choux buns to make lids.
15 – Use a sieve to dust the lids with icing sugar.
16 – Whisk the yuzu pastry cream to smooth, then fill a piping bag fitted with the size 10 plain nozzle and fill the choux buns to the brim.
17 – Pipe a swirl of chocolate and caramel mousse over the yuzu pastry cream.
18 – Cover each choux bun with its lid.

> ### CHEF'S TIP
>
> If the craquelin sticks to the baking parchment, dust the top of the craquelin with flour and lay a second sheet of baking parchment over it. Turn the craquelin over and remove the parchment from what was initially the bottom.
> The yuzu is added to the pastry cream after it is cooked so as not to alter its flavour during the cooking process.

VANILLA CHANTILLY
and fresh fruit mille-feuilles

Makes 4 mille-feuilles

PREPARATION TIME: 45 minutes + 1 hour 30 minutes for the puff pastry – BAKING TIME: 30 minutes
STORAGE: 2 days in the refrigerator

DIFFICULTY: ♙ ♙

<u>PUFF PASTRY</u>
55 ml water
½ tsp salt
25 g unsalted butter
100 g plain flour
85 g dry butter

Icing sugar

<u>VANILLA CHANTILLY CREAM</u>
300 ml cream
1 vanilla pod
25 g icing sugar

60 g raspberry seed jam

<u>FRESH FRUIT</u>
1 fig
4 raspberries
1 clementine
2 strawberries
1 bunch redcurrants

<u>DECORATION</u>
Fondant icing
Raspberry seed jam

<u>EQUIPMENT NEEDED:</u> 2 piping bags – size 8 plain nozzle – flower fondant plunger cutter

Vanilla

The first vanilla pods were picked from wild orchids in Mexico, and they were introduced into Europe by Christopher Columbus in the sixteenth century. It was impossible for this plant to be cultivated outside of its natural habitat until it was realised that a specific Mexican bee was responsible for its pollination. Pollination of the orchid by hand started on the island of Réunion and later Madagascar, which along with Indonesia are the leading producers of vanilla.

FOR THE PUFF PASTRY RECTANGLES

1 – Preheat the oven to 200°C (gas mark 6). Roll out the puff pastry (see page 491) to a thickness of 2 mm.

2 – Cut a 30 x 24 cm rectangle and dock lightly all over with a fork.

3 – Put the dough rectangle onto a baking tray lined with baking parchment and bake for 10 minutes. When the pastry begins to rise, lay a sheet of baking parchment on top and cover with a rack.

4 – Lower the oven temperature to 180°C (gas mark 4) and continue to bake for 20 more minutes. Take the puff pastry out of the oven and raise the temperature to 200°C (gas mark 6). Dust the puff pastry with icing sugar and return to the oven until the sugar caramelises.

5 – Cut the rectangle lengthways into four 4 cm wide strips.

6 – The cut across every 10 cm, making twelve 10 x 4 cm rectangles.

FOR THE CHANTILLY CREAM

7 – Whip the cream to soft peaks. Scrape the seeds out of the vanilla pod and incorporate the seeds into the cream. Set aside the split pod for the decoration.

8 – Add the icing sugar and continue to whisk until the cream becomes firm. Transfer to a piping bag fitted with the size 8 plain nozzle.

ASSEMBLY AND DECORATION

9 – Pipe small balls of Chantilly cream, without spacing, over eight pastry rectangles.

10 – Fill a piping bag with the raspberry seed jam and carefully pipe a line between the Chantilly cream balls on four of the pastry rectangles (the lines should be shorter than the length of the cream).

11 – Roll out the fondant icing to a thickness of 2 mm. Cut out small flowers from the fondant with the cutter, and put a drop of raspberry seed jam in the centre of each flower.

12 – Peel and segment the clementine, then slice the segments in half. Halve the strawberries and finely slice the fig.

13 – Pipe three balls of Chantilly cream over each of the four remaining pastry rectangles.

14 – Arrange 2 clementine slices, 1 fig slice, 1 raspberry, 1 redcurrant and 1 strawberry half on each one.

15 – Cut the vanilla pod into thin strips.

16 – Decorate the puff pastry rectangles with the vanilla pod strips and sugar flowers.

17 – Lay a puff pastry rectangle containing only Chantilly cream over each of the four rectangles with cream and raspberry seed jam.

18 – Cover each mille-feuilles with a pastry rectangle topped with fruit.

CHEF'S TIP

While the home-made puff pastry is the featured component of this dessert, you can also use a ready-made puff pastry if you have little time to make it.

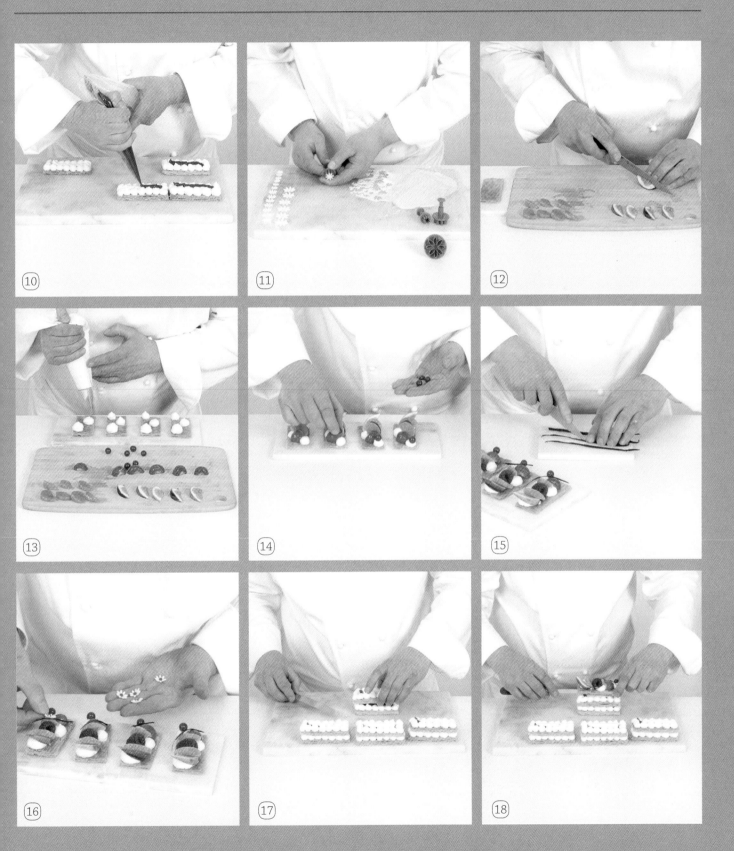

VICTORIA PINEAPPLE
éclairs

Makes 15 éclairs

PREPARATION TIME: 1 hour + 15 minutes for the choux pastry + 15 minutes for the pastry cream
BAKING TIME: 35 minutes – CHILLING TIME: 1 hour – STORAGE: 2 days in the refrigerator
DIFFICULTY: 🍥

<u>CHOUX PASTRY</u>
170 ml milk
70 g unsalted butter
1½ tsp sugar
½ tsp fine salt
100 g plain flour
3 eggs (140 g)

<u>CARAMELISED PINEAPPLE</u>
1 Victoria pineapple (about 200 g in size)
20 g unsalted butter
35 g unrefined cane sugar
2 tsp Malibu®

<u>VANILLA CREAM</u>
<u>Pastry cream</u>
370 ml milk
25 g unsalted butter
3 egg yolks (70 g)
80 g sugar
20 g plain flour
25 g cornflour

----

1 vanilla pod
140 ml cream

<u>GLAZE</u>
500 g fondant
Knife tip of yellow food colouring
Knife tip of vanilla powder
50 g glucose

<u>DECORATION</u>
50 g slivered almonds
Knife tip of edible gold powder

<u>EQUIPMENT NEEDED:</u> 2 piping bags – size PF16 star nozzle – size 12 plain nozzle – size 6 plain nozzle

Victoria pineapple

Considered by many to be the world's best variety of pineapple, the Victoria pineapple, which is smaller than the others, owes its name to Queen Victoria, who was very partial to them. Native to the island of Mauritius or of Réunion, the Victoria pineapple is distinguished by its bright yellow flesh, which is particularly soft and sweet, and its subtle tropical fragrance.

INDIVIDUAL PASTRIES & PLATED DESSERTS

VICTORIA PINEAPPLE *éclairs*

step-by-step

FOR THE CHOUX PASTRY AND ÉCLAIRS

1 – Fill a piping bag fitted with the size PF16 star nozzle with choux pastry (see page 483). Preheat the oven to 180°C (gas mark 4). Line a baking tray with baking parchment and pipe thick fingers of choux pastry 10 cm long in staggered rows to keep separate. Bake for 35 minutes, slightly opening the oven door every 2 minutes to vent the steam.

FOR THE CARAMELISED PINEAPPLE

2 – Peel and thinly slice the pineapple, then cut into small dice.
3 – In a frying pan, caramelise the butter with the sugar, then add the diced pineapple and cook for 3 minutes. Add the Malibu® and continue to cook for 1 more minute. Drain the pineapple.

FOR THE VANILLA CREAM

4 – Split the vanilla pod and scrape out the seeds. Put the hot pastry cream (see page 480) into a bowl and incorporate the vanilla seeds. Refrigerate for at least 1 hour.
5 – Whip the cream until it is firm and clings to the tip of the whisk. Whisk the pastry cream to smooth. Add a little of the whipped cream to the pastry cream while whisking to loosen. Then fold in the rest.

ASSEMBLY

6 – Mix the diced pineapple with the vanilla cream and fill a piping bag fitted with the size 12 plain nozzle.
7 – Split the éclairs lengthwise and fill with the cream.

GLAZING AND DECORATION

8 – Combine the fondant with the vanilla powder, vanilla and food colouring in a pan and heat until the temperature reads 30°C on the cooking thermometer. Add the glucose and a little water if the glaze is too thick. Remove the pan from the heat and leave to cool. Dip the top surface of each éclair in the glaze and smooth with your finger.
9 – Mix the slivered almonds with the gold powder and decorate the éclairs.

PARIS-BREST REVISITED
with a tropical centre

Makes 15 pastries

PREPARATION TIME: 1 hour + 15 minutes for the choux pastry + 15 minutes for the pastry cream
BAKING TIME: 35 minutes – CHILLING TIME: 1 hour 45 minutes – STORAGE: 2 days in the refrigerator
DIFFICULTY: 🎩 🎩

CRAQUELIN
65 g room-temperature unsalted butter
85 g plain flour
80 g unrefined cane sugar

CHOUX PASTRY
170 ml milk
70 g unsalted butter
1½ tsp sugar
½ tsp fine salt
100 g plain flour
3 eggs (140 g)

TROPICAL FRUIT COULIS
125 g mango purée
50 g passion fruit purée
Zest of ¼ lime
40 g sugar
½ tsp pectin
25 g glucose

CRUNCHY
HAZELNUTS
70 g roasted hazelnuts
20 ml water
30 g sugar

PRALINE CREAM
Pastry cream
370 ml milk
25 g unsalted butter
3 egg yolks (70 g)
80 g sugar
20 g plain flour
25 g cornflour

200 g praline paste
310 g unsalted butter
140 ml cream

DECORATION
Icing sugar

EQUIPMENT NEEDED: Size 10 nozzle – 3-cm biscuit cutter – 3 piping bags – size PF16 star nozzle

The origins of the Paris-Brest

The Paris-Brest is made from choux pastry and traditionally comes in the shape of a crown, filled with praline mousseline cream and sprinkled with flaked almonds. Louis Durand, a famous nineteenth-century pastry chef, was inspired by the cycling race between Paris and Brest to invent this dessert, hence the name. Nowadays, the Paris-Brest is very popular and has inspired new variations.

FOR THE CRAQUELIN

1 – Combine the butter, flour and sugar in a bowl. Mix with your fingers to form a dough, then smear (fraser) to a smooth consistency. Refrigerate for 15 minutes.

2 – Transfer the craquelin dough to a floured sheet of baking parchment. Roll it out very finely with a rolling pin.

FOR THE CHOUX PASTRY AND CHOUX BUNS

3 – Fill a piping bag fitted with the size 10 plain nozzle with the choux pastry (see page 483).

4 – Line a baking tray with baking parchment and pipe 3-cm balls of choux pastry, joined together in groups of three.

5 – Preheat the oven to 180°C (gas mark 4). Cut the craquelin into 3-cm rounds and lay one on each choux pastry ball. Bake for 35 minutes, slightly opening the oven door every 2 minutes to vent the steam.

FOR THE TROPICAL FRUIT COULIS

6 – Combine the mango and passion fruit purées in a pan and heat. Grate the lime zest into the pan.

7 – Mix the sugar with the pectin and sprinkle into the pan. Add the glucose and bring the mixture to the boil, whisking continuously. Transfer to a bowl and refrigerate for 30 minutes.

FOR THE CRUNCHY HAZELNUTS

8 – Use a pan to crush the hazelnuts into small pieces.

9 – Combine the water and sugar in a pan and bring to the boil for 2 minutes while stirring with a wooden spoon, then add the hazelnuts. Cook while stirring constantly until lightly caramelised. Immediately pour the mixture onto a baking tray lined with baking parchment and leave to cool.

•••

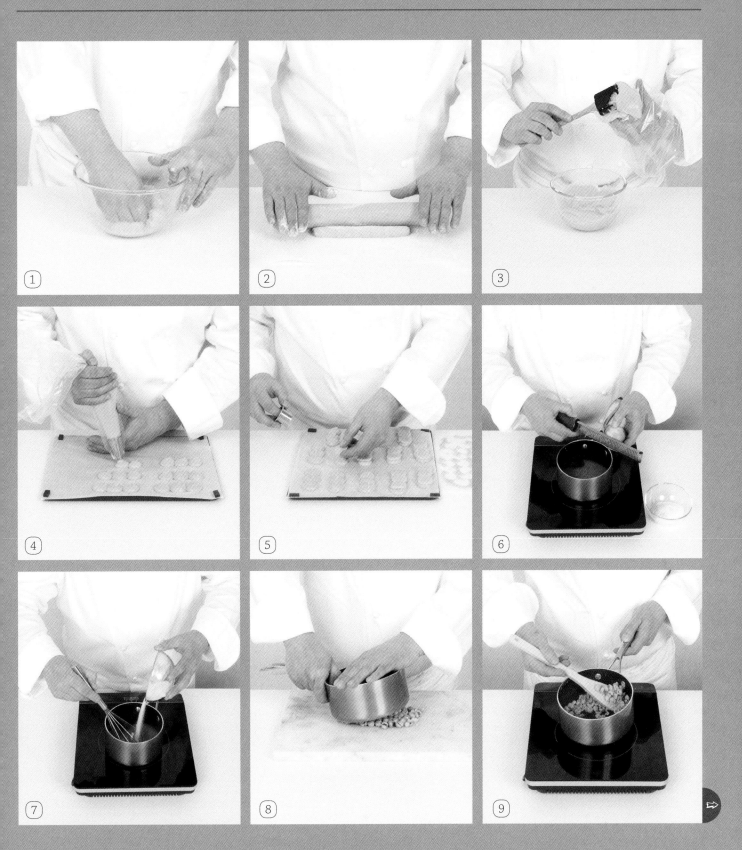

FOR THE PRALINE CREAM

10 – Make a pastry cream (see page 480) and incorporate the praline paste while still hot. Refrigerate for 1 hour.

11 – Whisk the praline pastry cream to smooth. Whisk the butter to a creamy consistency and incorporate into the pastry cream. Whisk well to emulsify and until the cream turns a lighter colour.

12 – Whip the cream until it is firm and clings to the tip of the whisk, then gently incorporate into the praline cream. Transfer to a piping bag fitted with the PF16 star nozzle.

ASSEMBLY AND DECORATION

13 – Cut off the tops of the choux buns to make lids, and fill the buns to two-thirds with the praline cream.

14 – Whisk the tropical fruit coulis to smooth, then fill a piping bag and cut off the end. Pipe a little coulis into the centre of the praline cream.

15 – Pipe a swirl of praline cream to cover.

16 – Add a few pieces of crunchy hazelnut.

17 – Trim the choux bun lids with the biscuit cutter to form 3 cm rounds.

18 – Sprinkle with icing sugar and put a lid on each of the choux buns.

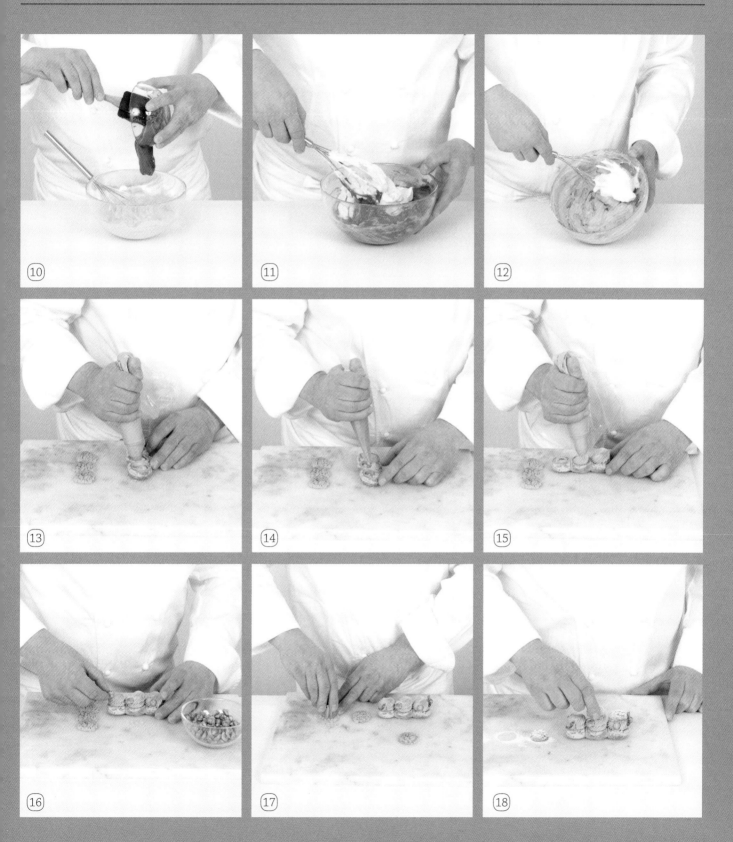

MINI BLUEBERRY
cheesecakes

Makes 6 mini cheesecakes

Preparation time: 45 minutes – Baking time: 1 hour – Chilling time: 12 hours – Storage: 2 days in the refrigerator

DIFFICULTY: ♙

BASE
Shortbread pastry
100 g plain flour
60 g unsalted butter
10 g ground almonds
30 g icing sugar
Pinch of salt
½ small egg (20 g)

----

25 g unsalted butter, melted

Oil for the moulds

FILLING
1 vanilla pod
490 g Philadelphia® cream cheese, at room-temperature
140 g sugar
3 eggs (150 g)
140 ml cream

BLUEBERRY COMPOTE
250 g blueberries
30 g sugar
2 tsp water
¼ tsp cornflour

DECORATION
125 g blueberries

EQUIPMENT NEEDED: Six entremets rings 6 cm across and 6 cm deep – silicone baking mat

Adding a finishing touch to a cheesecake

When you make a plain or lightly vanilla-flavoured cheesecake, think about decorating it with fresh fruit. And to give it an even more indulgent presentation, you can make a quick and easy fruit compote for added texture to tantalise the palate. A set of mini cheesecakes will make a more original dessert.

FOR THE SHORTBREAD PASTRY

1 – Preheat the oven to 170°C (gas mark 3–4). Combine the flour, butter, icing sugar, salt and ground almonds in a bowl. Work the pastry by rubbing between your hands and mixing with your fingertips. Incorporate the half egg and mix with a wooden spatula.

2 – Transfer the pastry to a work surface and smear (fraser) until smooth.

3 – Lightly dust the work surface with flour and roll out the dough to a thickness of 4 mm. Transfer to a baking tray lined with the silicone baking mat. Bake for 12–15 minutes, until golden. Leave to cool.

FOR THE SHORTBREAD BASE

4 – Oil the entremets rings and arrange on a baking tray lined with parchment paper. Crush the shortbread in a bowl.

5 – Add the melted butter and mix.

6 – Divide the pastry crumbs into the rings and pack down well. Refrigerate.

FOR THE FILLING

7 – Split the vanilla pod and scrape out the seeds with a knife tip.

8 – Preheat the oven to 90°C (gas mark ¼). Mix the cream cheese with the sugar. Add the eggs one at a time, mixing only lightly.

9 – Add the vanilla seeds.

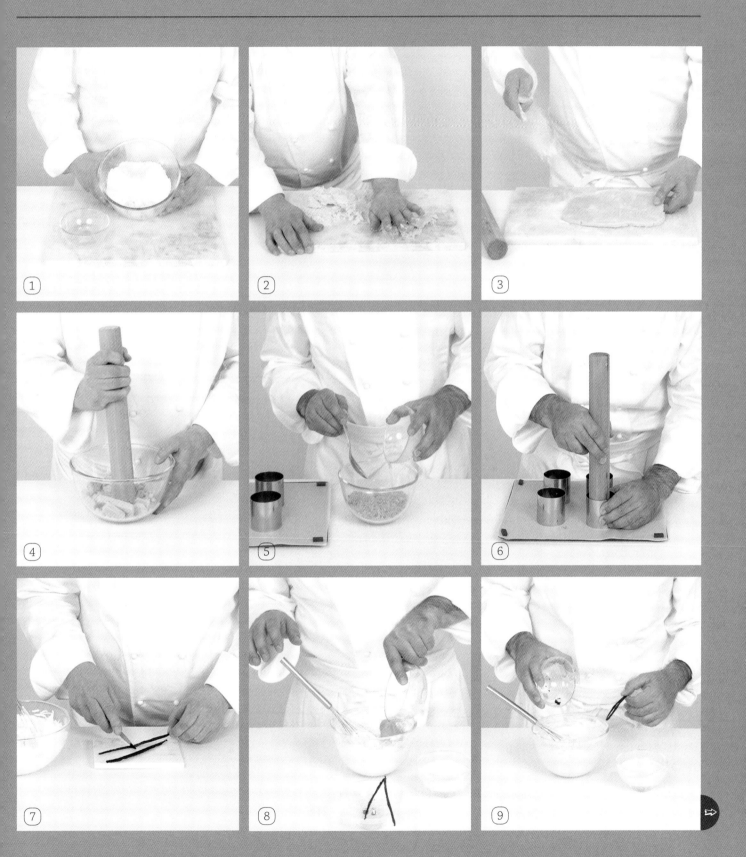

10 – Finally, incorporate the cream, taking care not to over-mix.

11 – Pour the mixture into the rings, filling to 1 cm below the rim. Bake in the oven for about 1 hour, or until a knife blade inserted into the cheesecakes comes out clean. Leave to cool, then refrigerate for 12 hours.

FOR THE BLUEBERRY COMPOTE

12 – Combine the blueberries with the sugar and water in a pan and cook until the blueberries are reduced to the consistency of a compote.

13 – Dilute the cornflour in a bowl with a tablespoon of cold water.

14 – Stir into the compote. Bring to a gentle boil for 3 minutes, then remove the pan from the heat. Refrigerate for 12 hours.

DECORATING

15 – Use a teaspoon to add blueberry compote to the entremets rings, filling to the brim. Smooth the surface with a flexible palette knife.

16 – Lightly warm the entremets rings between your hands.

17 – Carefully remove the rings.

18 – Decorate each mini cheesecake with fresh blueberries and serve immediately while still very cold.

CHEF'S TIP

In order to allow the blueberry compote to hold its shape better, you can add a gelatine leaf, previously softened in cold water and squeezed out, to lightly set it.

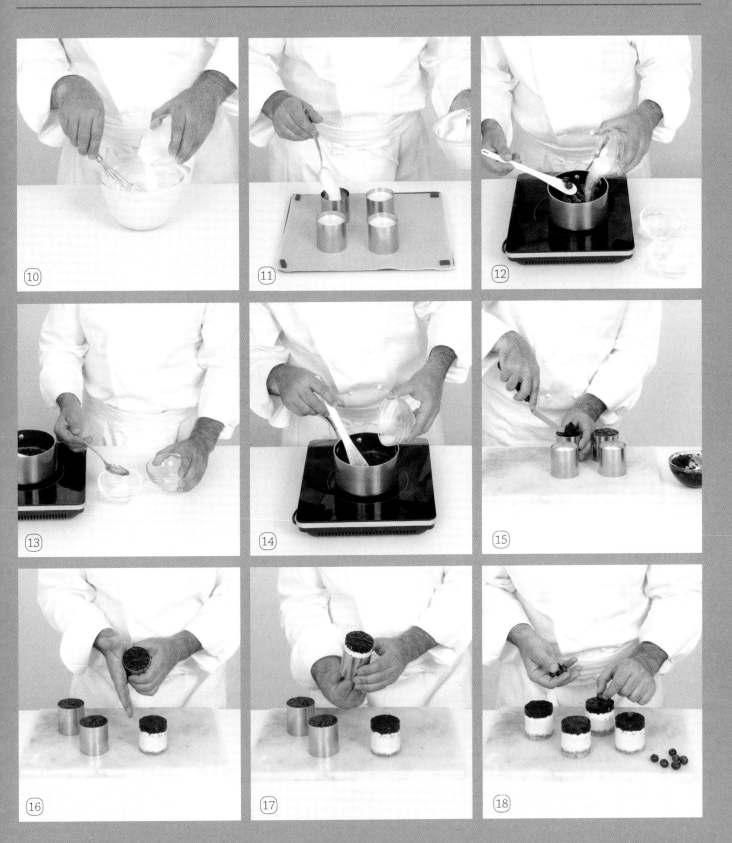

HOT VANILLA SOUFFLÉS

Makes 6 soufflés

PREPARATION TIME: 15 minutes + 15 minutes for the pastry cream
CHILLING TIME: 30 minutes for the pastry cream – BAKING TIME: 15 minutes
DIFFICULTY: ♙

VANILLA CREAM
Pastry cream
180 ml milk
1 egg (45 g)
45 g sugar
2 tsp custard powder
2 tsp cornflour
----
2 vanilla pods
5 egg whites (230 g)
110 g sugar

DECORATION
Icing sugar

Room-temperature unsalted butter and sugar
for the moulds

EQUIPMENT NEEDED: Six soufflé moulds 10 cm across and 5 cm deep – piping bag

Proper preparation of soufflé moulds

Whether you are making a large or individual soufflé, a successful outcome
can be a challenge. A soufflé has to rise well and it must have a very light
texture. It has to be served as soon as it comes out of the oven. The key stage
is preparing the moulds, which have to be perfectly clean and dry from the
start. Another tip for success is to butter them generously and coat with
sugar so that the mixture can rise easily up the sides. Take care not to leave
fingerprints inside the mould.

HOT VANILLA SOUFFLÉS

step-by-step

SOUFFLÉ MOULD PREPARATION

1 – Whisk the butter to a creamy consistency, then butter the soufflé moulds well.
2 – Pour sugar into the moulds, then turn them over to allow the excess sugar to run out, leaving the bottom and sides of each mould coated in sugar.

FOR THE VANILLA CREAM

3 – Preheat the oven to 180°C (gas mark 4). Whisk the pastry cream (see page 480) to smooth. Split the vanilla pod and scrape out the seeds with a knife tip. Add the seeds to the cream (you can also add them to the milk before making the pastry cream).
4 – Whisk the egg whites to soft peaks. Incorporate the sugar and continue to whisk until the mixture becomes smooth and glossy, about 30 seconds.
5 – Add a quarter of the beaten egg whites to the pastry cream and whisk briskly.
6 – Gently incorporate another two quarters of the egg whites with a whisk, then fold in the remaining quarter.
7 – Fill a piping bag with the vanilla cream and cut off the end to make an opening of about 2 cm. Pipe the vanilla cream into the moulds, filling to the top.
8 – Use a palette knife to smooth the surface.
9 – Run your thumb around the top of the inside of the moulds to leave a 5 mm wide groove between the soufflé mixture and the rim. This will allow the soufflés to rise more easily. Bake for 15 minutes. Do not open the oven door in this time. As soon as the soufflés come out of the oven, sprinkle with icing sugar and serve immediately.

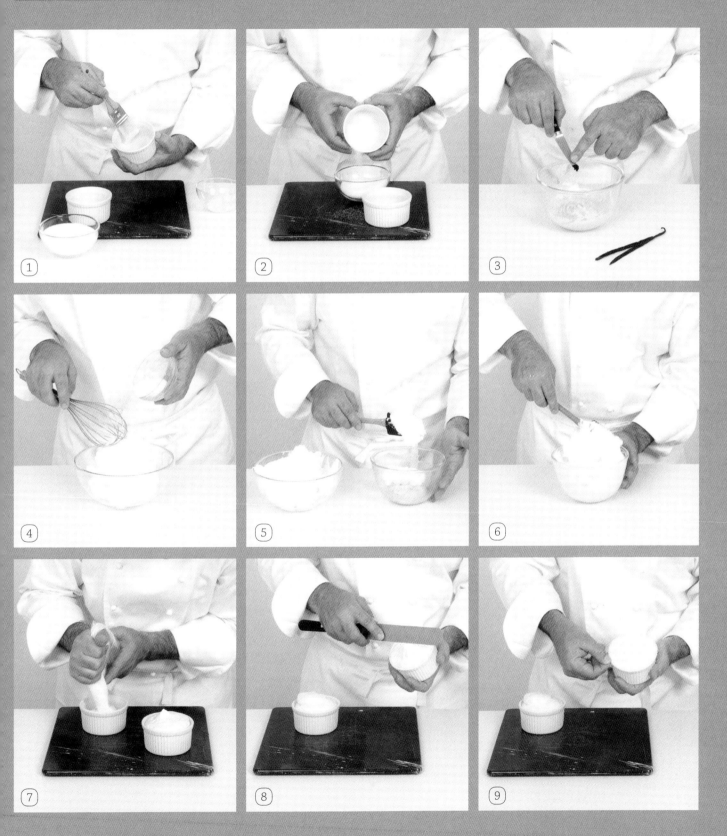

CRUNCHY ÉCLAIRS
with salted butter caramel

Makes 15 éclairs

_____

PREPARATION TIME: 1 hour + 15 minutes for the choux pastry + 15 minutes for the pastry cream – BAKING TIME: 1 hour
CHILLING TIME: 1 hour 30 minutes – STORAGE: 2 days in the refrigerator

DIFFICULTY: ♕ ♕

CHOUX PASTRY
170 ml milk
70 g unsalted butter
7 g sugar
2 g fine salt
100 g plain flour
3 eggs (140 g)

CRUNCHY CUBES
2 tsp unrefined cane sugar
2 tsp nibbed sugar
20 g unskinned ground hazelnuts
20 g plain flour
Knife tip of fine salt

20 g unsalted butter
Edible gold powder

SALTED BUTTER CARAMEL
50 g glucose
50 g fondant
40 g lightly salted butter
60 ml cream
50 g sugar
Knife tip of vanilla powder

CARAMEL PASTRY CREAM
Pastry cream
370 ml milk

25 g unsalted butter
3 egg yolks (70 g)
80 g sugar
20 g plain flour
25 g cornflour
100 g salted butter caramel

CARAMEL FONDANT
500 g fondant
150 g salted butter caramel
50 g glucose

DECORATION
"Fleur de sel" fine sea salt

EQUIPMENT NEEDED: 2 piping bags – size PF16 star nozzle – size 6 plain nozzle – size 10 plain nozzle

Salted butter caramel

The story of salted butter caramel, with its delicious combination of sugar and salt, is a curious one. It originated in Brittany, the only region that continued to produce salted butter owing to its exemption from the tax on salt imposed on the rest of France in the fourteenth century. Salted butter would endure in Brittany, and it was later combined with caramel to create the delicious mixture that is so highly prized today.

FOR THE CHOUX PASTRY AND ÉCLAIRS

1 – Fill a piping bag fitted with the size PF16 star nozzle with choux pastry (see page 483).

2 – Preheat the oven to 180°C (gas mark 4). Line a baking tray with baking parchment and pipe thick, 10 cm-long fingers of choux pastry in staggered rows to keep separate. Bake for 35 minutes, slightly opening the oven door every 2 minutes to vent the steam.

FOR THE CRUNCHY CUBES

3 – Line a baking tray with baking parchment and preheat the oven to 170°C (gas mark 3–4). Combine all the ingredients in a bowl.

4 – Rub the butter into the other ingredients with your fingers until the mixture has a 'sandy' texture, then smear the dough (fraser) until smooth.

5 – Transfer the dough to a work surface covered with a sheet of baking parchment, and flatten with your palm to a thickness of about 1 cm.

6 – Use a knife to cut into strips.

7 – Cut the strips into cubes and bake in the oven for 25 minutes.

FOR THE SALTED BUTTER CARAMEL

8 – Combine the glucose with the fondant in a pan and bring to a gentle boil, then add the lightly salted butter.

9 – Combine the cream, sugar and vanilla powder in a bowl and add to the pan. Heat over a low heat. Transfer to a bowl and refrigerate for 30 minutes.

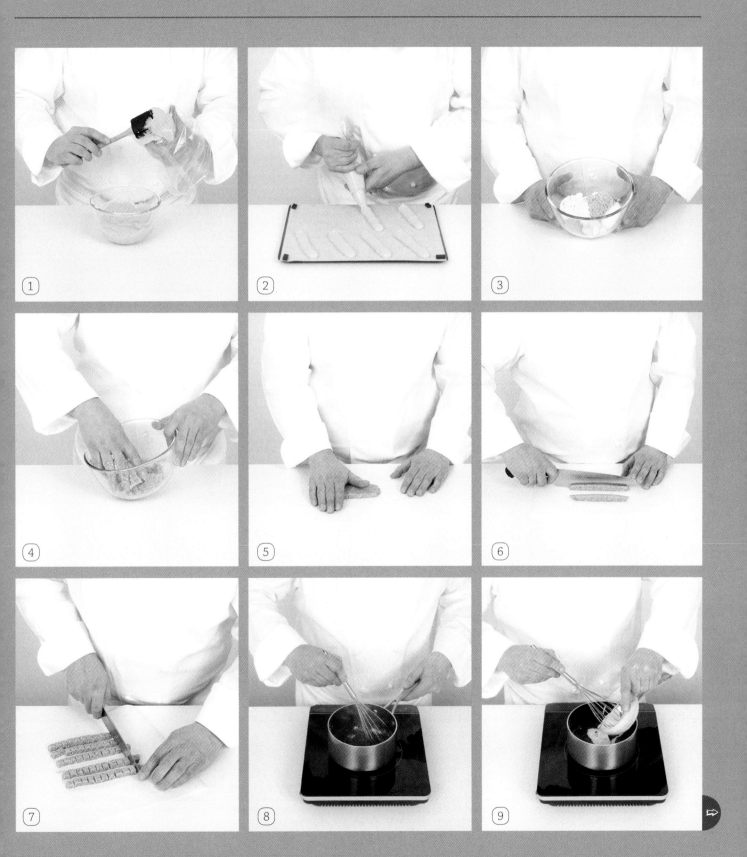

FOR THE CARAMEL PASTRY CREAM

10 – Put the hot pastry cream (see page 480) into a bowl and incorporate the cold salted butter caramel. Refrigerate for 1 hour.

ASSEMBLY

11 – Make three holes on the underside of each choux bun by piercing with the size 6 plain nozzle, turning it a little.

12 – Whisk the caramel pastry cream till smooth, then transfer to a piping bag fitted with the size 10 plain nozzle. Fill the éclairs by piping the cream through the holes. Use a teaspoon to remove the excess cream.

FOR THE CARAMEL FONDANT

13 – In a pan, heat the fondant with the salted butter caramel, mixing well with a wooden spatula.

14 – Add the glucose and heat, stirring well.

DECORATING

15 – Dip the surface of each éclair in the fondant.

16 – Smooth around the fondant with your finger.

17 – Combine the crunchy cubes in a bowl with gold powder and mix to coat well.

18 – Arrange three crunchy cubes on each éclair and decorate with a little "fleur de sel" fine sea salt.

SOFT CENTRED
chocolate "fondants"

Makes 10 "fondants"

PREPARATION TIME: 20 minutes – BAKING TIME: 6–7 minutes – STORAGE: 2 weeks in the refrigerator

DIFFICULTY: ⌂

SOFT CENTRED CHOCOLATE "FONDANT" MIXTURE
8 eggs (400 g)
270 g sugar
300 g dark chocolate
270 g room-temperature unsalted butter
80 g plain flour
45 g potato starch

FILLING
20 squares dark chocolate

Unsalted butter and plain flour for the muffin cases

EQUIPMENT NEEDED: Ten muffin cases 7.5 cm across and 4 cm deep

100 per cent chocolate

This quick and easy-to-make dessert is perfect for ending a meal with a chocolate note, or as an afternoon snack. Because it has a molten centre, it must be served hot, as soon as it comes out of the oven, and it can be accompanied by a scoop of vanilla ice cream or a crème anglaise.

FOR THE SOFT CENTRED CHOCOLATE "FONDANT" MIXTURE

1 – Butter the muffin cases and dust with flour. Turn over to remove the excess flour.

2 – Combine the eggs and sugar in a bowl over a bain-marie and beat with an electric whisk until the mixture is warm to the touch.

3 – Remove from the bain-marie and continue to beat with the whisk at high speed until the mixture cools and thickens to a ribbon consistency: it should run off the whisk without breaking, forming a ribbon.

4 – Chop the chocolate and melt in a bowl over a bain-marie. Add the butter and mix well until smooth.

5 – Fold the flour and potato starch into the egg-sugar mixture.

6 – Use a wooden spoon to fold in the chocolate mixture.

ASSEMBLY

7 – Preheat the oven to 190°C (gas mark 5). Fill the muffin cases halfway with the mixture.

8 – Put 2 squares of chocolate into the centre of each case.

9 – Finish filling the cases with the mixture. Bake for 6–7 minutes. Wait for 5 minutes before taking the soft centred chocolate "fondants" out of their cases, then serve immediately.

CHEF'S TIP

You can easily create variations on this recipe. Substitute the dark chocolate with a fruit purée, such as raspberry or mango, or a hazelnut or caramel spread for a gooey centre with different flavours and colours.

Tarts & Tartlets

BRITTANY SHORTBREAD-STYLE TART
with fresh fruit and caramelised pineapple

Serves 8

Preparation time: 45 minutes + 30 minutes for the pastry cream – Baking time: 25 minutes – Storage: 2 days in the refrigerator

DIFFICULTY: 🎩 🎩

BRITTANY SHORTBREAD PASTRY
150 g room-temperature unsalted butter
120 g icing sugar
Knife tip of vanilla powder
Pinch of salt
1 egg (50 g)
50 ml cream
155 g plain flour
1 tsp baking powder (4 g)

20 g unsalted butter for the tart ring

PASTRY CREAM
200 ml milk
15 g unsalted butter
2 egg yolks (40 g)
45 g sugar
10 g plain flour
10 g cornflour
75 ml cream

CARAMELISED PINEAPPLE
1 Victoria pineapple
30 g unsalted butter
30 g unrefined cane sugar

FRESH FRUIT
2 oranges
1 grapefruit
1 mango
200 g strawberries
125 g raspberries
100 g blueberries
2 bunches redcurrants

DECORATION
Icing sugar
Neutral glaze

EQUIPMENT NEEDED: 22-cm tart ring – 2 piping bags – size 12 plain nozzle – melon baller

Brittany shortbread

Brittany shortbread is a crumbly biscuit made using flour, butter and sometimes egg yolks, mixed to a 'sandy' consistency. Brittany shortbread today has expanded its use to sweet creations, particularly for making tart bases and individual pastries. It can be flavoured with chocolate, lemon, etc.

FOR THE BRITTANY SHORTBREAD PASTRY

1 – Whisk the butter with the icing sugar, vanilla powder and salt to a creamy consistency.
2 – Add the egg, followed by the cream, and mix well.
3 – Incorporate the flour, followed by the baking powder, and transfer to a piping bag fitted with the plain nozzle.
4 – Preheat the oven to 170°C (gas mark 3–4). Butter the tart ring and lay it on a baking tray lined with baking parchment. Stick a strip of baking parchment slightly taller than the height of the ring over the buttered inside of the ring.
5 – Pipe a spiral of shortbread pastry dough inside the ring.
6 – Pipe a ring of shortbread pastry dough over the base, along the inside of the tart ring to add thickness. Bake for 25 minutes.

FOR THE CARAMELISED PINEAPPLE

7 – Dice the pineapple.
8 – Cook the diced pineapple with the butter and sugar in a frying pan over a low heat for about 5 minutes.

FOR THE FRESH FRUIT

9 – Segment the oranges and grapefruit. To do this, first cut a fine slice from the top and bottom of each fruit. Then stand the fruit on the work surface and use a small knife to pare off the peel, following the curve of the fruit, removing all the skin and pith and leaving only the flesh.

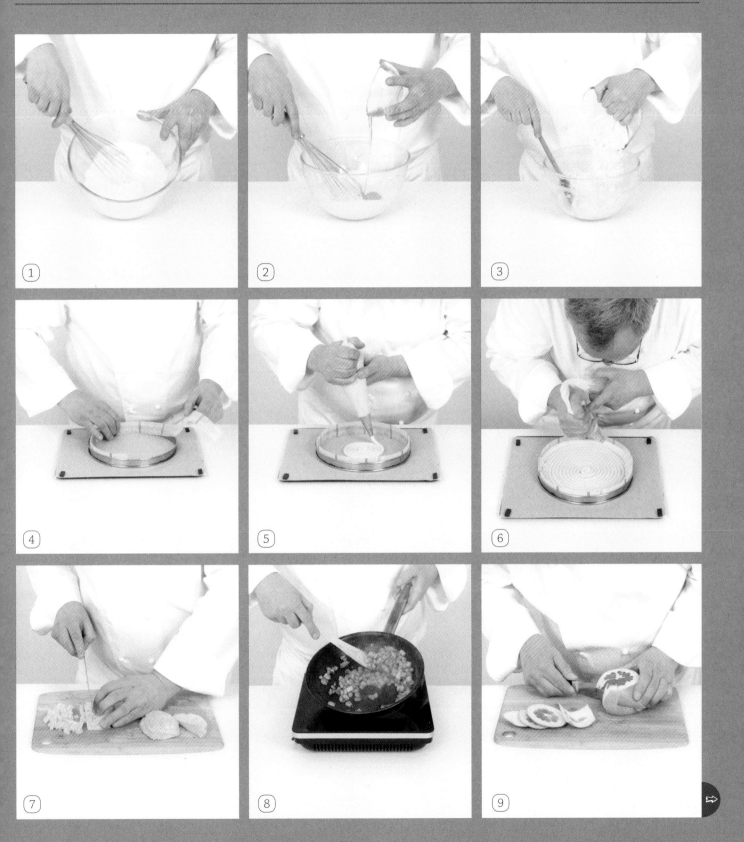

1

2

3

4

5

6

7

8

9

10 – To release orange and grapefruit segments, cut between the membranes. Remove any seeds.

11 – Peel the mango and use the melon baller to scoop out little balls of flesh.

ASSEMBLY

12 – Pour the pastry cream (see page 480) into a bowl and whisk to smooth. Mix in the caramelised pineapple dice.

13 – Spread the pastry cream with diced pineapple over the shortbread tart base.

14 – Dust along the edge of the tart with icing sugar.

15 – Halve the strawberries and arrange over the tart.

16 – Then arrange the citrus segments and mango balls.

17 – Brush with neutral glaze.

18 – Dust a few raspberries with icing sugar and arrange on the tart. Add the blueberries and redcurrants.

PASSION FRUIT AND CARAMEL TART

Serves 8

PREPARATION TIME: 45 minutes + 15 minutes for the pastry – CHILLING TIME: 30 minutes for the pastry – BAKING TIME: 30 minutes
DIFFICULTY: ♙

<u>SWEET PASTRY DOUGH</u>
50 g room-temperature unsalted butter
50 g icing sugar
½ egg (20 g)
100 g plain flour
20 g ground almonds

Unsalted butter for the ring

<u>ALMOND AND PASSION FRUIT FILLING</u>
50 g room-temperature unsalted butter
80 g passion fruit purée
100 g ground almonds
Pinch of salt
50 g sugar
2 eggs (100 g)

1½ egg whites (50 g)
20 g sugar

<u>FOR THE PASSION FRUIT CARAMEL</u>
30 g passion fruit purée
30 g sweetened condensed milk
50 ml cream
30 g glucose
60 g sugar
75 g lightly salted butter

<u>DECORATION</u>
20 g neutral glaze
50 g slivered almonds
Pinch of edible gold powder
1 passion fruit

<u>EQUIPMENT NEEDED:</u> 16-cm and 4.5 cm deep entremets ring – piping bag – size 8 plain nozzle

Cooking caramel

Caramel is the result of sugar cooked at a temperature above 150°C, as shown on a cooking thermometer, and its colour varies depending on how long it is cooked. Sugar loses some of its sweetness when it is cooked into caramel. Each type of caramel has its use. However, you must pay attention because the consistency and smell of overcooked caramel makes it unusable.

PASSION FRUIT AND CARAMEL TART

step-by-step

FOR THE TART BASE

1 – Cover a baking tray with a sheet of baking parchment. Lightly flour the work surface and roll out the sweet pastry dough (see pages 488 and 489) to a thickness of about 3 mm. Use the entremets ring to mark out a pastry disc. Remove the excess pastry, and put the disc onto a baking tray lined with baking parchment.

FOR THE ALMOND AND PASSION FRUIT FILLING

2 – Preheat the oven to 170°C (gas mark 3–4). Put the butter into a bowl. Reduce the passion fruit purée by half in a pan and immediately pour over the butter. Whisk until smooth. Mix the ground almonds with the salt and sugar in a bowl. Add to the butter mixture, then incorporate the eggs.
3 – Whisk the egg whites until firm, then incorporate the sugar while whisking to stiff peaks. Add a little of the beaten egg white to the mixture, whisk briskly, then fold in the rest.
4 – Butter the entremets ring and line with a strip of baking parchment a little higher than the ring's height. Place the ring on a baking tray and put the tart base inside. Pour in the almond and passion fruit filling and smooth with a silicone spatula. Bake for 30 minutes.

FOR THE PASSION FRUIT CARAMEL

5 – Reduce the passion fruit purée by half in a pan. Combine with the condensed milk and cream and mix with a wooden spatula. In another pan, heat the glucose and gradually add the sugar. Mix and cook to a golden brown caramel.
6 – Add the passion fruit mixture and bring to the boil. Incorporate the butter. Leave to cool, then transfer the caramel to a piping bag fitted with the plain nozzle.

DECORATING

7 – Put the tart on cardboard cake board and remove the ring. Pipe a spiral of passion fruit caramel on top of the tart.
8 – Brush the sides of the tart with neutral glaze.
9 – Preheat the oven to 160°C (gas mark 3). Toast the slivered almonds in a pan, then mix with the gold powder. Cover the side of the tart with the almonds. Scoop the seeds out of the passion fruit and decorate the surface of the tart with them.

CHOCOLATE-PRALINE TART with caramelised nuts

Serves 8

PREPARATION TIME: 1 hour + 15 minutes for the pastry – BAKING TIME: 20 minutes – CHILLING TIME: 15 minutes + 30 minutes for the pastry + 10 minutes after lining the tart ring – STORAGE: 2 days in the refrigerator

DIFFICULTY: ♔

Sweet pastry dough

- 200 g plain flour
- 120 g unsalted butter
- 1 small egg (40 g)
- 65 g icing sugar
- 25 g ground almonds

Unsalted butter for greasing

Chocolate and praline cream

- 200 ml cream
- Pinch of vanilla powder
- 200 g dark chocolate (54% cocoa)
- 35 g praline paste
- 55 g unsalted butter

Caramelised nuts

- 50 ml water
- 100 g sugar
- 50 g blanched almonds
- 60 g skinned hazelnuts

Chocolate glaze

- 130 g dark couverture chocolate
- 60 ml water
- 60 g glucose

EQUIPMENT NEEDED: 22-cm tart ring

Caramelised nuts

Caramelising nuts such as almonds, hazelnuts and pistachios gives them a sweet flavour, crispy texture and golden appearance that make them ideal for decorating tarts and other pastries. Simple and easy-to-make caramelised nuts can also be enjoyed as a light snack. All you need is to make a syrup with sugar and water, and to roll the nuts in it until they caramelise.

CHOCOLATE-PRALINE TART with caramelised nuts

FOR THE TART CASE

1 Lightly flour the work surface and roll out the sweet pastry dough (see page 488) to a thickness of about 3 mm. Using the tart ring as a guide, cut out a disc with a diameter 5 cm larger than that of the ring, about 27 cm.

2 – Preheat the oven to 170°C (gas mark 3–4). Butter the tart ring and line (see page 493) with the pastry. Put the lined ring onto a baking tray lined with baking parchment and refrigerate for 10 minutes. Blind bake the tart case (see page 494) in the oven for 10 minutes. Take out the baking beans, then bake for 10 more minutes until golden. Leave to cool, then remove the ring.

FOR THE CHOCOLATE AND PRALINE CREAM

3 – Bring the cream to room temperature. Add the vanilla powder to the cream. Melt the chocolate in a bowl over a bain-marie, then incorporate the vanilla-flavoured cream. Mix in the praline paste, followed by the butter. Leave to cool.

4 – Pour the chocolate and praline cream into the tart case and refrigerate for 15 minutes.

FOR THE CARAMELISED NUTS

5 – Combine the water and sugar in a pan and bring to the boil for 4 minutes. Add the almonds and hazelnuts and heat while stirring until caramelised.

6 – Transfer the caramelised nuts to a tray lined with parchment paper, separate them with a knife and leave to cool.

FOR THE CHOCOLATE GLAZE

7 – Chop the chocolate and place in a bowl. Combine the water with the glucose in a pan and bring to the boil. Pour over the chocolate. Mix.

8 – Pour the glaze over the chocolate and praline cream, then pick up the tart with your hands and tilt slightly to spread the glaze evenly.

9 – Decorate with the caramelised nuts.

CHOCOLATE-MARSHMALLOW
tartlets

Makes 10

PREPARATION TIME: 1 hour + 15 minutes for the pastry – BAKING TIME: about 20 minutes – CHILLING TIME: 30 minutes + 30 minutes for the pastry + 10 minutes after lining the tartlet rings – STORAGE: 2 days in the refrigerator

DIFFICULTY: ♟ ♟

<u>MARSHMALLOW</u>
2¾ gelatine leaves (5.5 g)
20 ml water
45 g sugar
20 g glucose
25 g Trimoline® (inverted sugar)
25 g Trimoline® (inverted sugar)
Knife tip of violet food colouring powder
3 drops violet flavouring
----
35 g potato starch
35 g icing sugar

Oil for the tray
Unsalted butter for the tartlet rings

<u>SWEET PASTRY DOUGH</u>
200 g plain flour
90 g unsalted butter
90 g icing sugar
30 g ground almonds
1 egg (50 g)

<u>CHOCOLATE FILLING</u>
30 g unsalted butter
50 g dark chocolate (70 % cocoa)
2 egg whites (45 g)
40 g sugar
1 tbsp plain flour
30 g ground almonds

<u>CHOCOLATE GANACHE GLAZE</u>
100 g dark couverture chocolate (70% cocoa)
40 g unsalted butter
40 ml water
60 ml cream
45 g sugar

<u>DECORATION</u>
Icing sugar

<u>EQUIPMENT NEEDED:</u> 2 piping bags – size 8 plain nozzle – ten 8-cm tartlet rings

Pastry rings

For a long time the domain of professionals, pastry rings are now easy to find in shops. They come in different shapes and sizes, and are replacing tins and moulds because they allow tarts and tartlets to be baked more evenly, they are easy to remove, and they also make it possible for amateurs to give their pastries a professional look.

FOR THE MARSHMALLOW

1 – Soften the gelatine leaves by soaking in a bowl of cold water. Combine the water, sugar, glucose and first 25 g of Trimoline® in a small saucepan and bring to the boil. Squeeze out as much water as possible from the gelatine and combine in a bowl with the remaining 25 g of Trimoline®. Pour in the hot syrup.
2 – Add the violet food colouring.
3 – Add the violet flavouring and whisk until the mixture turns smooth, then cool. Transfer to a piping bag fitted with the plain nozzle.
4 – Oil a baking tray. Pipe strings of marshmallow over the tray, spaced a little apart.
5 – Mix the potato starch with the icing sugar in a bowl. Using a small sieve, dust the marshmallow strings with the mixture to prevent from sticking. Leave the marshmallow to dry out for 2 hours, then turn over and dust again with the starch and sugar mixture.
6 – Tie knots in the marshmallow strings and cut off the ends.

FOR THE TARTLET CASES

7 – Butter the tartlet rings.
8 – Lightly flour the work surface and roll out the sweet pastry dough (see pages 488 and 489) to a thickness of about 3 mm.
9 – Using a tartlet ring as a guide, cut out discs with a diameter 5 cm larger than that of the ring, about 13 cm.

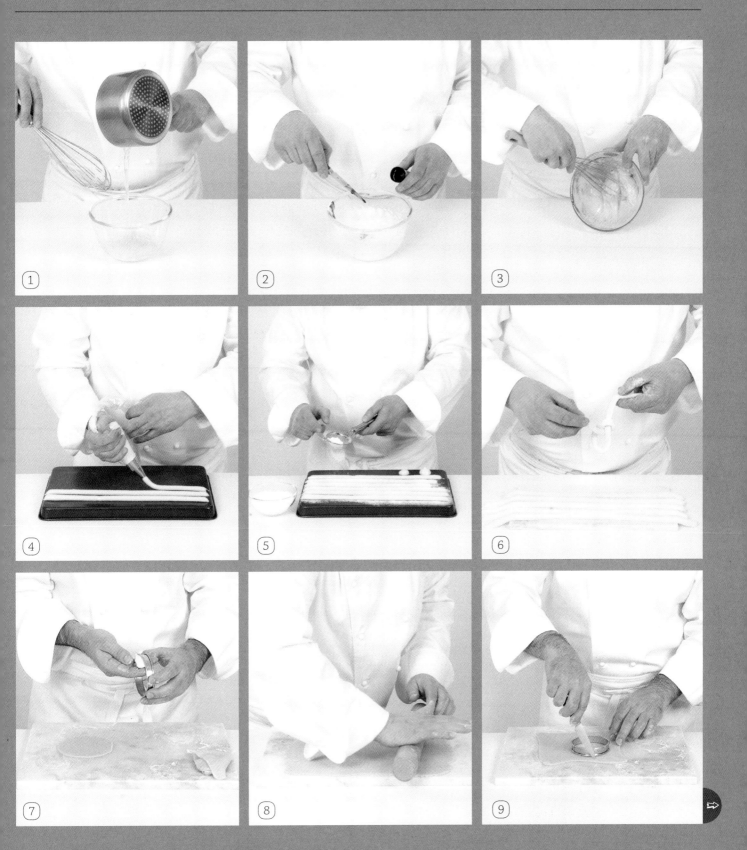

10 – Line the tartlet rings with the dough (see page 493) and refrigerate for 10 minutes. Preheat the oven to 170°C (gas mark 3–4), then blind bake the tartlet cases (see page 494) for 15 minutes.

FOR THE CHOCOLATE FILLING

11 – Preheat the oven to 200°C (gas mark 6). Put the butter into a bowl. Melt the chocolate in a bowl over a bain-marie and immediately pour over the butter. Mix well.
12 – Whisk the egg whites until firm, then incorporate the sugar whilst whisking to stiff peaks.
13 – Carefully add the beaten egg whites to the chocolate and butter mixture.
14 – Fold in using a silicone spatula. Then fold in the flour and ground almonds.
15 – Transfer to a piping bag fitted with the plain nozzle with the mixture and pipe in a spiral to cover the base of the tartlet cases. Bake for 4 minutes.

FOR THE CHOCOLATE GANACHE GLAZE

16 – Chop the chocolate and put into a bowl with the butter. Combine the water, cream and sugar in a pan and bring to the boil. Pour the hot cream mixture over the chocolate and butter mixture and stir gently with a whisk.

ASSEMBLY AND DECORATION

17 – Use a tablespoon to spread the ganache glaze over the chocolate filling inside the tartlet cases and refrigerate for 20 minutes.
18 – Dust the edges of the tartlets with icing sugar. Arrange the marshmallow knots on top.

APRICOT, HAZELNUT
and cinnamon tart

Serves 8–10

PREPARATION TIME: 45 minutes + 15 minutes for the pastry – CHILLING TIME: 30 minutes for the pastry
BAKING TIME: 1 hour – STORAGE: 2 days in the refrigerator

DIFFICULTY: ♙ ♙

SWEET SHORTCRUST PASTRY
160 g plain flour
90 g unsalted butter
½ tsp salt
1 tbsp icing sugar
1 tsp water
1 egg (50 g)
Pinch of vanilla powder

20 g unsalted butter for the tart tin

HAZELNUT CREAM
60 g unsalted butter
60 g sugar
60 g ground hazelnuts
1 large egg (60 g)
1 tsp plain flour
20 g ground hazelnuts

APRICOTS
800 g tinned apricot halves

CINNAMON MIXTURE
25 g unsalted butter
1 egg (50 g)
50 g sugar
Pinch of ground cinnamon

DECORATION
Icing sugar

EQUIPMENT NEEDED: 24-cm fluted tart tin

Apricots in pastry-making

The small orange-yellow apricot, a symbol of summer, has velvety skin and sweet and juicy flesh. While it is quite delicate when fresh, it is largely used in pastry-making as a preserve, in syrup and cut in halves.

FOR THE TART CASE

1 – Butter the tart tin. Lightly flour the work surface and roll out the sweet shortcrust pastry (see page 490) to a thickness of about 3 mm. Using the tart tin as a guide, cut out a disc with a diameter 5 cm larger than that of the tin, about 30 cm.

2 – Line the tart tin with the dough (see page 493) and dock all over with a fork.

FOR THE HAZELNUT CREAM

3 – Whisk the butter in a bowl to a creamy consistency, then incorporate the sugar and 60 g of ground hazelnuts.

4 – Add the egg, whisk briskly, then incorporate the flour.

ASSEMBLY

5 – Pour the hazelnut cream into the tart case and smooth using the back of a tablespoon.

6 – Sprinkle with the 20 g of ground hazelnuts.

7 – Drain the apricot halves of syrup and arrange over the hazelnut cream.

FOR THE CINNAMON MIXTURE

8 – Preheat the oven to 220°C (gas mark 7). Cook the butter in a pan to a nut brown butter. Whisk the egg, sugar and ground cinnamon in a bowl, then pour into the nut brown butter and whisk briskly.

9 – Use a tablespoon to spread the cinnamon mixture over the apricot halves. Bake for 15 minutes, until the tart begins to turn golden, then reduce the oven temperature to 190°C (gas mark 5) and continue to bake for 45 more minutes. Leave the tart to cool a little, then carefully remove from the tin and dust with icing sugar through a sieve.

CHEF'S TIP

You can substitute the ground hazelnuts for sprinkling over the hazelnut cream with Génoise or "biscuit" sponge crumbs. This step is essential in order to soak up the liquid from the apricots. You can also use fresh apricots in season.

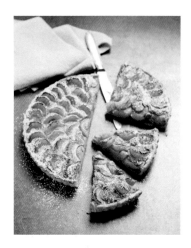

BLUEBERRY TART

Serves 8–10

PREPARATION TIME: 1 hour + 15 minutes for the pastry – BAKING TIME: about 35 minutes

CHILLING TIME: 30 minutes for the pastry + 10 minutes after lining the tart ring – STORAGE: 2 days in the refrigerator

DIFFICULTY: ♙

S<small>WEET PASTRY DOUGH</small>	A<small>LMOND CREAM</small>
200 g plain flour	60 g unsalted butter
120 g unsalted butter	60 g sugar
70 g icing sugar	60 g ground almonds
½ tsp salt	1 vanilla pod
30 g ground almonds	1 egg (50 g)
1 small egg (40 g)	

50 g room-temperature unsalted butter for the tart tin
Plain flour for the tin

D<small>ECORATION</small>
50 g apricot glaze
250 g blueberries
20 g icing sugar

E<small>QUIPMENT NEEDED</small>: 24-cm fluted tart tin – pastry brush

Choosing blueberries

The purplish-blue blueberry is a relative of the cranberry and can be picked in the forests of Alsace, Lorraine and Franche-Comté regions from June to mid-October. Make sure to carefully wash wild blueberries before eating them, to guard against the risk of contracting hydatid disease.
Choose well-rounded and uniform berries with the characteristic star-shaped hole. Avoid any wrinkled berries.

FOR THE TART CASE

1 – Preheat the oven to 170°C (gas mark 3–4). Butter the tart tin. Roll out the sweet pastry dough (see pages 488 and 489) to a thickness of about 3 mm. Using the tart tin as a guide, cut out a disc with a diameter 5 cm larger than that of the tin, about 30 cm. Line the tart tin with the dough (see page 493).

FOR THE ALMOND CREAM

2 – Whisk the butter in a bowl to a creamy consistency, then add the sugar and mix.
3 – Incorporate the ground almonds.
4 – Split the vanilla pod, scrape out the seeds with a knife tip and add to the bowl. Mix.
5 – Incorporate the egg.

ASSEMBLY AND DECORATION

6 – Pour the almond cream into the tart case and spread uniformly with a silicone spatula. Bake for about 35 minutes. Leave to cool.
7 – Remove the tart from the tin. Brush the almond cream with the apricot glaze.
8 – Arrange blueberries over the tart.
9 – Use a sieve to dust with icing sugar.

CHEF'S TIP

Always pour and spread the almond cream to halfway up the tart case, regardless of the diameter of the tart tin or ring.
This is the reasoning behind the quantity given in this recipe.

TROPICAL FRUIT TART
with raspberries

Serves 6–8

PREPARATION TIME: 1 hour 30 minutes – BAKING TIME: 35 minutes – FREEZING TIME: 2 hours 10 minutes

DIFFICULTY: ♙ ♙ ♙

BRITTANY SHORTBREAD
20 g ground almonds

125 g room-temperature lightly salted butter

50 g sugar

1 egg yolk (20 g)

100 g plain flour

½ tsp baking powder

TROPICAL FRUIT CRÉMEUX
65 g mango purée

85 g passion fruit purée

25 g glucose

50 g sugar

½ tsp pectin

COCONUT MOUSSE
70 ml coconut milk

20 g sugar

20 g desiccated coconut

1½ gelatine leaves (3 g)

160 ml cream

DECORATION
150 g neutral glaze

250 g raspberries

Icing sugar

EQUIPMENT NEEDED: 2 piping bags – 20-cm tart ring
16-cm entremets ring – cardboard cake board – size 10 plain nozzle

Finishing with neutral glaze

Neutral glaze is easy to use and allows you to embellish any dessert. Used by leading chefs for a perfect final touch, it adds a professional finish to your work. Its neutral sweet flavour suits any creation, and it adds a lovely sheen to tarts and cakes.

FOR THE BRITTANY SHORTBREAD

1 – Preheat the oven to 160°C (gas mark 3). Whisk the ground almonds with the butter and sugar in a bowl.

2 – Whisk in the egg yolk.

3 – Sift the flour and baking powder together into a bowl, then fold into the dough.

4 – Transfer to a piping bag fitted with the plain nozzle. Cut out a 20-cm-long strip of baking parchment a little higher than the height of the tart ring and line the inside of the ring. Place the tart ring on a baking tray lined with baking parchment. Pipe the shortbread dough in a spiral inside the tart ring. Bake for 35 minutes.

FOR THE TROPICAL FRUIT CRÉMEUX

5 – Combine both purées with the glucose in a pan and heat. Mix the sugar with the pectin and sprinkle over the purées, then bring to the boil.

6 – Leave to cool, work with a whisk, then fill a paper cone with a little of the crémeux. Set aside the rest in the refrigerator.

FOR THE COCONUT MOUSSE

7 – Soften the gelatine leaves in a bowl of cold water.
Combine the coconut milk with the sugar and desiccated coconut in a pan, bring to the boil and transfer to a bowl.

8 – Squeeze the gelatine to drain and whisk into the hot liquid. Leave to cool.

9 – Whip the cream to soft peaks.

• • •

10 – Incorporate a third of the cream into the coconut mixture and whisk briskly.

11 – Add the rest of the cream, whisking lightly, then finish mixing with a silicone spatula.

ASSEMBLY AND DECORATION

12 – Stretch cling film over the top of the 16-cm entremets ring. Turn the ring over onto the cardboard cake board, then using the paper cone, pipe a few different-sized spots of tropical fruit crémeux on the cling film. Freeze for 10 minutes.

13 – Pour the mousse into the ring over the tropical fruit crémeux spots, then smooth with a silicone spatula. Freeze for 2 hours.

14 – Remove the tart ring from the shortbread base, pour over the tropical fruit crémeux and spread well with the back of a tablespoon.

15 – Take the frozen coconut mousse out of the freezer, turn it over and remove the cling film. Pour the neutral glaze over the mousse and smooth with a palette knife.

16 – Remove the entremets ring from the mousse and put the mousse on top of the shortbread and tropical fruit crémeux.

17 – Use a sieve to dust the raspberries with icing sugar.

18 – Decorate the sides of the tart with the raspberries.

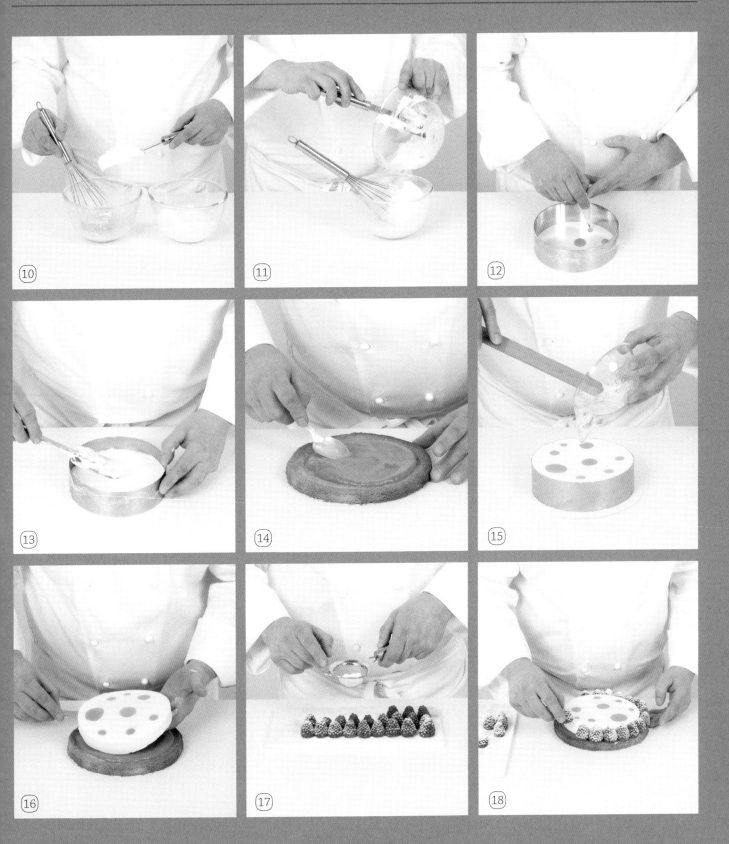

GRAPEFRUIT MERINGUE TART

Serves 8

PREPARATION TIME: 45 minutes + 15 minutes for the pastry + 15 minutes for the Italian meringue – BAKING TIME: 1 hour + 15 minutes

CHILLING TIME: 30 minutes for the pastry + 10 minutes after lining the tart ring – STORAGE: 1 day

DIFFICULTY: ♧ ♧

SWEET PASTRY DOUGH
200 g plain flour
120 g unsalted butter
65 g icing sugar
20 g ground almonds
1 small egg (40 g)

Unsalted butter for the tart ring

GRAPEFRUIT FILLING
2½ eggs (130 g)
160 g sugar
30 g ground almonds
25 g potato starch
130 g grapefruit juice
30 g unsalted butter, melted

CANDIED GRAPEFRUIT ZEST
Zest of ¼ grapefruit
100 ml water
100 g sugar
2 tsp grenadine

GRAPEFRUIT SEGMENTS
3 grapefruits
Neutral glaze

ITALIAN MERINGUE
2 egg whites (60 g)
120 g sugar
60 ml water

EQUIPMENT NEEDED: 22-cm tart ring

Paring and segmenting citrus fruit

Paring a citrus fruit means completely removing its peel and pith. This is normally done in order to remove the segments (or supremes) of the fruit – separating the segments from their membranes with a knife – or to cut the fruit into slices. The peel can be candied.

FOR THE TART CASE

1 – Preheat the oven to 170°C (gas mark 3–4). Lightly flour the work surface and roll out the sweet pastry dough (see pages 488 and 489) to a thickness of about 3 mm. Using the tart ring as a guide, cut out a disc with a diameter 5 cm larger than that of the ring, or about 27 cm.
2 – Butter the tart ring, line with the dough (see page 493) and place on a baking tray lined with baking parchment. Blind bake the tart case (see page 494) for 20 minutes. Keep the oven temperature at 170°C.

FOR THE GRAPEFRUIT FILLING

3 – Whisk the eggs with the sugar in a bowl.
4 – Add the ground almonds and potato starch, and whisk well.
5 – Incorporate the grapefruit juice, followed by the melted butter.
6 – Pour the filling into the tart case and bake for 40 minutes. Leave to cool to room temperature.

FOR THE CANDIED GRAPEFRUIT ZEST

7 – Peel the zest from the grapefruit.
8 – Cut into julienne strips.
9 – Blanch the strips in a pan of boiling water with a pinch of salt. Change the water and repeat the process.

10 – Make a syrup by combining the water and sugar in a pan and bringing to the boil, then add the grenadine. Add the grapefruit zest and cook over a low heat for about 15 minutes.

11 – Take the zest out of the pan and drain the excess syrup on kitchen paper.

FOR THE GRAPEFRUIT SEGMENTS

12 – Segment the grapefruit. To do this, first cut a fine slice from the top and bottom of the fruit. Then stand the fruit on the work surface and use a small knife to pare off the peel, following the curve of the fruit, removing all the skin and pith and leaving only the flesh.

13 – To release grapefruit segments, cut between the membranes. Remove any seeds.

FOR THE ITALIAN MERINGUE

14 – Make an Italian meringue (see page 487).

ASSEMBLY AND DECORATION

15 – Tip the meringue over the grapefruit filling in the tart case, leaving a 2-cm margin around the edge for the grapefruit segments.

16 – Gently tap the meringue with a silicone spatula to make peaks. Colour the meringue under the oven grill for a few minutes.

17 – Arrange the grapefruit segments around the meringue.

18 – Brush grapefruit segments with neutral glaze and decorate the tart with strips of candied grapefruit zest.

PASSION FRUIT-CHOCOLATE TART

Serves 8

PREPARATION TIME: 1 hour + 15 minutes for the pastry – BAKING TIME: 33 minutes – CHILLING TIME: 30 minutes +
30 minutes for the pastry + 10 minutes after lining the tart ring – STORAGE: 2 days in the refrigerator

DIFFICULTY: ♟ ♟

SWEET PASTRY DOUGH
200 g plain flour
120 g unsalted butter
65 g icing sugar
20 g ground almonds
1 small egg (40 g)

Unsalted butter for the tart ring

CHOCOLATE "MI-CUIT" CREAM
50 g milk chocolate
30 g dark chocolate (70% cocoa)
1½ eggs (75 g)
65 g sugar
2 tsp Malibu®
60 g room-temperature unsalted butter

PASSION FRUIT CRÉMEUX
1½ gelatine leaves (3 g)
2 eggs (100 g)
85 g sugar
80 g passion fruit purée
140 g unsalted butter

PASSION FRUIT GLAZE
100 g neutral glaze
1 passion fruit

CHOCOLATE SHAVINGS
1 bar milk chocolate

EQUIPMENT NEEDED: 22-cm tart ring

Passion fruit

This tangy and very fragrant fruit, native to Brazil, owes its name to the flower
from which it is derived, the passiflora, a word created from the Latin terms
passio (passion) and *flor* (flower). 'Passion' is a reference to the appearance of
the flower, which missionary explorers thought resembles the different items
associated with the Passion of Christ, such as the Crown of Thorns, a hammer
and nails.

FOR THE TART CASE

1 – Preheat the oven to 170°C (gas mark 3). Lightly flour the work surface and roll out the sweet pastry dough (see pages 488 and 489) to a thickness of about 3 mm. Using the tart ring as a guide, cut out a disc with a diameter 5 cm larger than that of the ring, about 27 cm.

2 – Butter the tart ring, line with the dough (see page 493) and place on a baking tray lined with baking parchment.

3 – Blind bake the tart case (see page 494) for 10 minutes, then take out the baking beans and bake for 15 more minutes.

FOR THE CHOCOLATE "MI-CUIT" CREAM

4 – Melt both chocolates together in a bowl over a bain-marie. Raise the oven temperature to 180°C (gas mark 4).

5 – Whisk the eggs with the sugar and Malibu® in a bowl.

6 – Whisk the butter to a creamy consistency and incorporate into the melted chocolate. Add to the eggs, sugar and Malibu® mixture and whisk to combine.

7 – Pour the filling into the tart case and bake for 8 minutes. Leave to cool.

FOR THE PASSION FRUIT CRÉMEUX

8 – Soften the gelatine leaves in a bowl of cold water. Whisk the eggs and sugar in a bowl until the mixture turns pale and thickens.

9 – Heat the passion fruit purée and immediately whisk into the egg-sugar mixture.

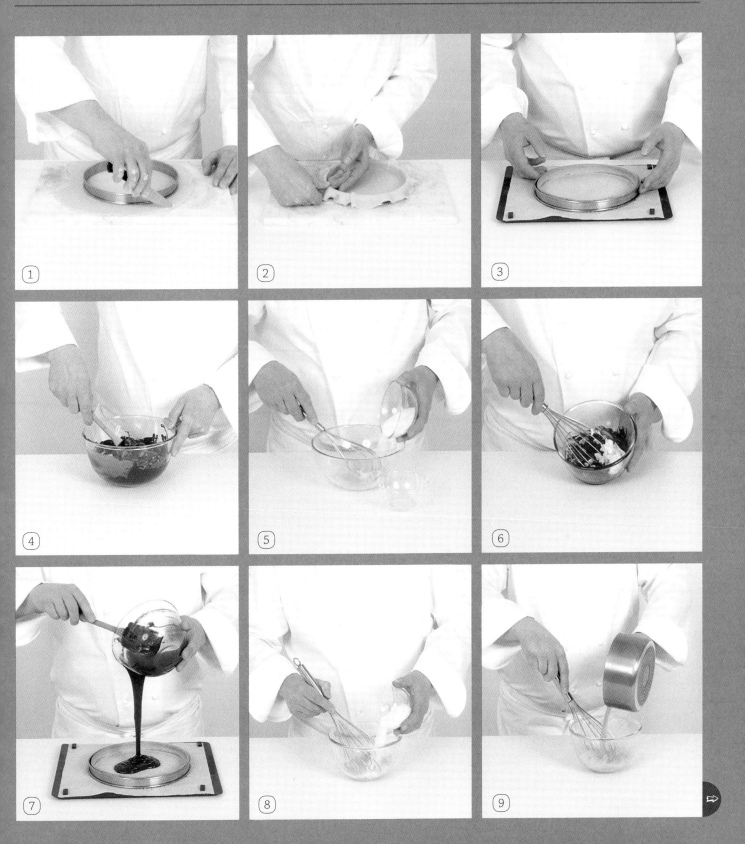

10 – Return the mixture to the pan and bring to a gentle boil while stirring constantly.

11 – Remove the pan from the heat. Squeeze the gelatine to drain and incorporate into the mixture in the pan.

12 – Transfer the mixture to a bowl and leave to cool for 5 minutes. Incorporate the butter a little at a time.

ASSEMBLY

13 – Remove the tart ring. Pour the passion fruit crémeux over the chocolate filling.

14 – Gently shake the tart from right to left to spread evenly. Refrigerate for 30 minutes.

15 – Pour the glaze over the tart and smooth the surface with a palette knife.

16 – Scoop out the juice and seeds from the passion fruit into a small bowl and mix gently with a whisk to remove any fruit fibres. Use a fork to carefully spread the seeds over the surface of the tart.

DECORATING

17 – Scrape the chocolate bar with a vegetable peeler to make shavings.

18 – Use to decorate the tart.

CHEF'S TIP

You can substitute the chocolate shavings with raspberries as decoration to give the tart more colour.

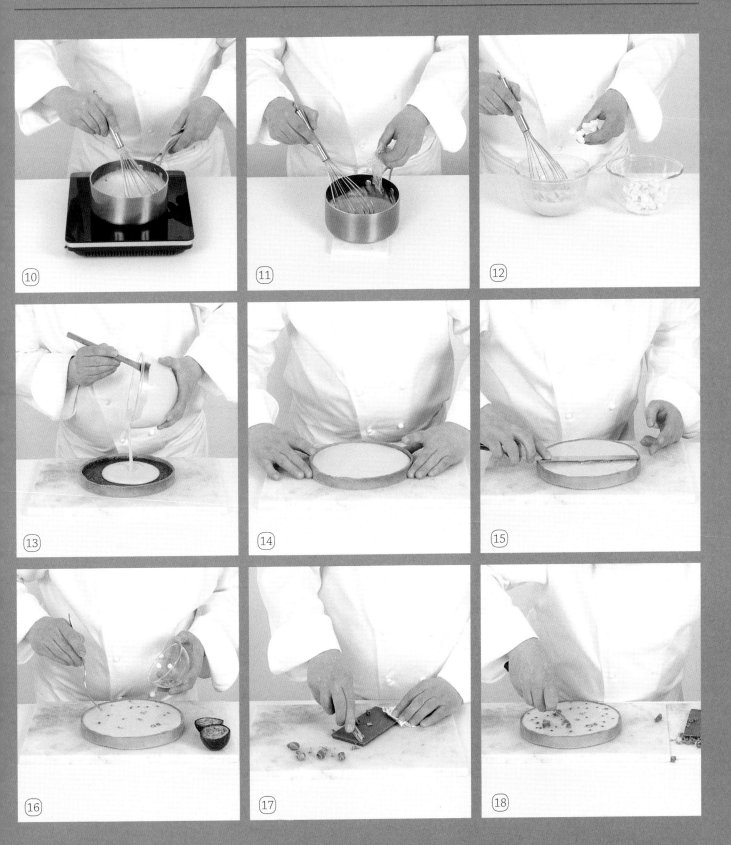

APPLE-HAZELNUT
tart with praline cream

Serves 8

PREPARATION TIME: 1 hour + 15 minutes for the pastry – BAKING TIME: 50 minutes
CHILLING TIME: 1 hour 30 minutes for the pastry + 10 minutes after lining the tart ring – STORAGE: 2 days in the refrigerator
DIFFICULTY: ♙

SWEET PASTRY DOUGH
200 g plain flour
120 g unsalted butter
65 g icing sugar
20 g ground almonds
1 small egg (40 g)

Unsalted butter for the tart ring

HAZELNUT FILLING
1 large egg (60 g)
50 g sugar
25 g unsalted butter, melted
30 g hazelnut paste

CARAMELISED APPLES
5 apples
40 g unsalted butter
40 g sugar

CANDIED HAZELNUTS
20 ml water
50 g sugar
50 g skinned hazelnuts

MASCARPONE AND HAZELNUT CREAM
120 ml cream
70 g mascarpone
20 g hazelnut paste

DECORATION
100 g neutral glaze
Icing sugar

EQUIPMENT NEEDED: 22-cm tart ring – cooking thermometer – pastry brush – cardboard cake board

Apples for tarts

It is often difficult to choose the right type of apple from among the more than one hundred available varieties, depending on how it is to be used: raw, in a tart, or in a compote. For tarts, such as this recipe, Golden Delicious, Rubinette, King of the Pippins or Belle de Boskoop apples are recommended because they are suitable for cooking in a frying pan or in the oven.

FOR THE TART CASE

1 – Preheat the oven to 180°C (gas mark 4). Lightly flour the work surface and roll out the sweet pastry dough (see pages 488 and 489) to a thickness of about 3 mm. Line the tart ring with the dough (see page 493).

2 – Blind bake the tart case (see page 494) for 10 minutes.

FOR THE HAZELNUT FILLING

3 – Mix the egg, sugar and melted butter in a bowl with a whisk, then incorporate the hazelnut paste. Pour into the tart case. Refrigerate.

FOR THE CARAMELISED APPLES

4 – Peel, core and quarter the apples. Cook the butter and sugar in a frying pan to a caramel, then add the apples. Cook for 5 minutes, then leave to cool.

FOR THE CANDIED HAZELNUTS

5 – Make a thick syrup by heating the water and sugar in a pan to 110°C, as shown on the cooking thermometer. Add the hazelnuts and cook until they turn white, about 2 minutes, while stirring constantly. Transfer to a tray and cool.

FOR THE MASCARPONE AND HAZELNUT CREAM

6 – Whip the cream in a bowl until firm and clings to the tip of the whisk. Whisk the mascarpone and incorporate the whipped cream. Gradually incorporate the hazelnut paste. Refrigerate for 1 hour.

ASSEMBLY AND DECORATION

7 – Increase the oven temperature to 200°C (gas mark 6). Arrange the apples on the tart in a rosette pattern. Bake for 40 minutes. Leave to cool.

8 – Brush the apples with the neutral glaze. Then use a small sieve to dust around the edge of the tart with icing sugar.

9 – Sprinkle the tart with candied hazelnuts and serve with the mascarpone and hazelnut cream quenelles.

CHEF'S TIP

Use two tablespoons dipped in hot water to make quenelles. To do this, take a little of the hazelnut and mascarpone cream and pass from one spoon to the other. Repeat the process until a smooth, oval quenelle is formed.

①

②

③

④

⑤

⑥

⑦

⑧

⑨

LEMON-MINT TARTLETS
with berries and kumquat

Makes 10 tartlets

PREPARATION TIME: 1 hour + 15 minutes for the pastry – BAKING TIME: 20 minutes
CHILLING TIME: 30 minutes + 30 minutes for the pastry – STORAGE: 1 day in the refrigerator
DIFFICULTY: 🎩 🎩

SWEET PASTRY DOUGH
200 g plain flour
90 g unsalted butter
90 g icing sugar
30 g ground almonds
1 egg (50 g)

Unsalted butter for the tart rings

ALMOND CREAM
80 g unsalted butter
80 g sugar
1 large egg (60 g)
80 g ground almonds
1 vanilla pod

LEMON AND MINT CRÉMEUX
500 ml cream
75 g sugar
Juice and zest of 3 lemons
8 mint leaves
50 g unsalted butter
5½ eggs (270 g)
45 g cornflour

FRESH FRUIT
20 strawberries
10 blackberries
4 kumquats
20 raspberries
30 blueberries
4 bunches redcurrants

EQUIPMENT NEEDED: Ten 8-cm tartlet rings – piping bag – size 8 plain nozzle

Red berries

Strawberries, raspberries, blackcurrants, blueberries, redcurrants and other small fruits all fall under the name 'berries'. These exquisite and refreshing summer fruits are very well suited to pastry-making, and can be used in tarts, entremets and to make jams, among other applications. They can be enjoyed in salads, in fillings and as decorations, and they can be used to make mousses and crémeux. The berry tart, a delight to both the eyes and the palate, is a summer favourite.

FOR THE TARTLET CASES

1 – Lightly flour the work surface and roll out the sweet pastry dough (see pages 488 and 489) to a thickness of about 3 mm. Using a tartlet ring as a guide, cut out ten discs with a diameter 5 cm larger than that of each ring, about 13 cm.
2 – Butter the rings and line with the dough (see page 493).
3 – Use a knife to trim off the excess dough and put the rings on a baking tray lined with baking parchment.

FOR THE ALMOND CREAM

4 – Whisk the butter in a bowl to a creamy consistency in a bowl, then add the sugar and mix. Incorporate the egg, followed by the ground almonds.
5 – Split the vanilla pod, scrape out the seeds with a knife tip and add to the bowl. Mix.
6 – Spread the almond cream into the tartlet cases, filling them three-quarters of the way to the top. Bake for about 20 minutes.
7 – Leave to cool to room temperature, then remove the rings.

FOR THE LEMON AND MINT CRÉMEUX

8 – Combine the cream with half the sugar in a pan and grate over the lemon zest.
9 – Add the mint and blend with a hand-held blender. Strain through a sieve.

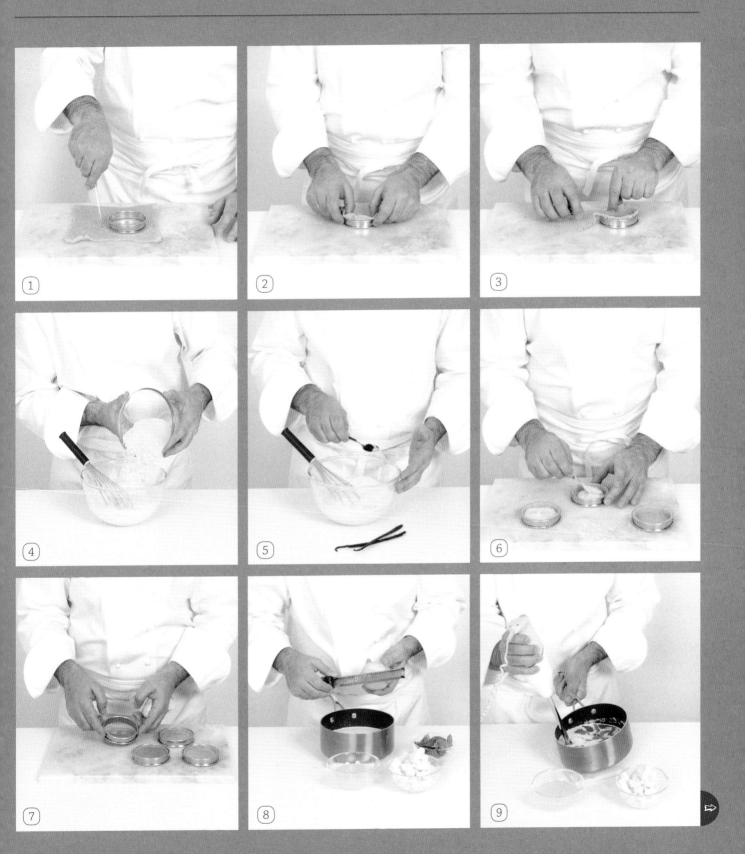

10 – Incorporate the lemon juice, followed by the butter.

11 – Heat to a simmer.

12 – In the meantime, whisk the eggs with the remaining sugar and cornflour, mixing well.

13 – Pour two-thirds of the hot lemon and mint mixture into the egg, sugar and cornflour mixture while whisking briskly.

14 – Return the mixture to the pan and cook gently over a medium heat while stirring constantly with a whisk until thick.

15 – Boil for 1 minute, stirring constantly, until the crémeux thickens. Transfer to a bowl and refrigerate for 30 minutes.

ASSEMBLY AND DECORATION

16 – Whisk the lemon and mint crémeux to smooth. Use a silicone spatula to fill the piping bag fitted with the plain nozzle.

17 – Pipe the crémeux in a spiral in the tartlet cases.

18 – Halve the strawberries and blackberries and finely slice the kumquats. Arrange on the tartlets with the raspberries, blueberries and redcurrants. Refrigerate before serving.

CRÈME BRÛLÉE TARTLETS
with fresh fruit

Makes 10 tartlets

PREPARATION TIME: 45 minutes + 15 minutes for the pastry – BAKING TIME: 55 minutes

CHILLING TIME: 30 minutes + 30 minutes for the pastry + 10 minutes after lining the tartlet rings – STORAGE: 1 day in the refrigerator

DIFFICULTY: ♔ ♔

SWEET PASTRY DOUGH
200 g plain flour
90 g unsalted butter
90 g icing sugar
30 g ground almonds
1 egg (50 g)

20 g unsalted butter for the tartlet rings

CRÈME BRÛLÉE FILLING
420 ml cream
60 g sugar
2 vanilla pods
5 egg yolks (100 g)

FRESH FRUIT
2 mangoes
1 coconut
10 cherries
3 figs
10 physalis

EQUIPMENT NEEDED: Ten 8-cm tartlet rings

Crème brûlée

A popular French dessert, crème brûlée is made using milk, egg yolks and sugar. It is cooked in the oven, and once it has cooled, it is sprinkled with sugar and caramelised in the oven, under a salamander grill or with a chef's blow torch. This caramelised sugar over the cold or warm baked custard cream is the characteristic feature of crème brûlée.

CRÈME BRÛLÉE TARTLETS with fresh fruit

FOR THE TARTLET CASES

1 – Lightly flour the work surface and roll out the sweet pastry dough (see pages 488 and 489) to a thickness of about 3 mm. Using a tartlet ring as a guide, cut out ten discs with a diameter 5 cm larger than that of the ring, about 13 cm.

2 – Butter the rings and line with the dough (see page 493). Trim off the excess dough with a knife.

3 – Preheat the oven to 160°C (gas mark 3). Blind bake the tartlet cases (see page 494) for 15 minutes.

4 – Take out the baking beans, lower the oven temperature to 150°C (gas mark 2) and continue to bake for 10 more minutes.

FOR THE CRÈME BRÛLÉE FILLING

5 – Lower the oven temperature to 100°C (gas mark ¼). Mix the cream with the sugar.

6 – Split the vanilla pod, scrape out the seeds with a knife tip, add to the bowl and mix.

7 – Incorporate the egg yolks and mix.

8 – Use a ladle to pour the mixture into the tartlet cases. Bake for 30 minutes, until the baked custard filling sets. Refrigerate for 30 minutes.

ASSEMBLY AND DECORATION

9 – Cut the mango into dice about 1 cm in size. Break open the coconut and use a vegetable peeler to make shavings. Halve and pit the cherries. Finely slice the figs. Arrange the fruit on top of the tartlets, then decorate with coconut shavings and a physalis.

CHEF'S TIP

Once the tart cases come out of the oven, check that there are no holes in the pastry. If you find any holes, fill them with a little of the raw pastry and return to the oven for 5 more minutes.

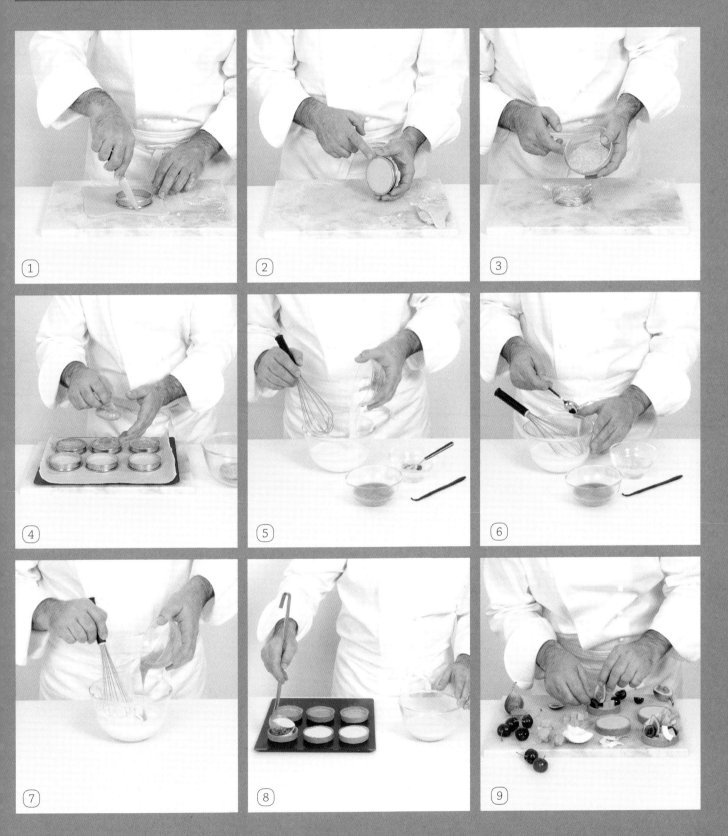

GARIGUETTE STRAWBERRY
and yuzu tart

Serves 6–8

PREPARATION TIME: 30 minutes + 15 minutes for the pastry cream + 15 minutes for the pastry
CHILLING TIME: 30 minutes for the pastry – BAKING TIME: 30 minutes – STORAGE: 2 days in the refrigerator
DIFFICULTY: 🎩 🎩

SWEET PASTRY DOUGH	YUZU PASTRY CREAM
150 g plain flour	170 ml milk
75 g unsalted butter	12 g unsalted butter
75 g icing sugar	1½ egg yolks (35 g)
20 g ground almonds	40 g sugar
½ egg (30 g)	2 tsp plain flour
	1½ tsp cornflour
Unsalted butter for the tart ring	40 g yuzu marmalade

ALMOND AND YUZU CREAM	STRAWBERRIES
60 g unsalted butter	500 g Gariguette strawberries
80 g yuzu marmalade	100 g neutral glaze
60 g ground almonds	
1 large egg (60 g)	DECORATION
	30 g yuzu marmalade

EQUIPMENT NEEDED: 20-cm tart ring – cardboard cake board – pastry brush

Gariguette strawberries

Gariguette strawberries are medium sized and elongated with a reddish-orange colour and a flavour that is both sweet and tart. Their flesh is firm to the touch, but soft and juicy in the mouth. The peak season for Gariguette strawberry production in France is May and June, and this is the earliest variety. It is mainly grown in Brittany and the south of France.

GARIGUETTE STRAWBERRY and yuzu tart

FOR THE SWEET PASTRY DOUGH

1 – Lightly flour the work surface and roll out the sweet pastry dough (see pages 488 and 489) to a thickness of about 3 mm. Using the tart ring as a guide, cut out a disc with a diameter 5 cm larger than that of the ring, or 25 cm.
2 – Line the tart ring with the dough (see page 493) and place on a baking tray lined with baking parchment.

FOR THE ALMOND AND YUZU CREAM

3 – Preheat the oven to 170°C (gas mark 3). Put the butter into a bowl. Add the yuzu marmalade and whisk well, then incorporate the ground almonds.
4 – Add the eggs and whisk well.
5 – Pour the almond and yuzu cream into the tart case and spread uniformly with a silicone spatula. Bake for 30 minutes and leave to cool.

FOR THE YUZU PASTRY CREAM

6 – Make a pastry cream (see page 480) and add the yuzu marmalade. Leave to cool.

ASSEMBLY

7 – Transfer the tart to the cardboard cake board and remove the ring. Whisk the yuzu pastry cream to smooth, then spread over the almond and yuzu cream.
8 – Hull and halve the strawberries. Arrange the strawberry halves over the yuzu pastry cream, starting from the outside and working your way to the centre.
9 – Brush the strawberries with neutral glaze. Decorate the tart with yuzu marmalade.

CHEF'S TIP

You can substitute Gariguette strawberries with any other variety of strawberries, or with raspberries, which also combine very well with the flavour of yuzu.

RHUBARB AND SAFFRON
tart

Serves 8

PREPARATION TIME: 45 minutes + 15 minutes for the pastry – BAKING TIME: 50 minutes

CHILLING TIME: 1 hour for the pastry + 10 minutes after lining the tart ring – STORAGE: 2 days in the refrigerator

DIFFICULTY: 🎩

<u>SWEET PASTRY DOUGH</u>
100 g unsalted butter
100 g icing sugar
1 tbsp ground almonds
210 g plain flour
1 egg (50 g)

Unsalted butter for the tart ring

<u>SAFFRON CREAM FILLING</u>
1½ eggs (80 g)
60 g sugar
4–5 saffron threads
200 ml cream

<u>DECORATION</u>
Icing sugar

<u>COOKED RHUBARB</u>
700 g rhubarb
30 g unsalted butter
50 g sugar

<u>EQUIPMENT NEEDED:</u> 22-cm tart ring – cardboard cake board – pastry brush

Rhubarb

Rhubarb is a summer plant and is grown for its pinkish-red stems, technically leafstalks or petioles. Rhubarb is a very popular ingredient in tarts, compotes and jam, but requires the addition of sugar when cooking to tone down its acidity.

FOR THE TART CASE

1 – Preheat the oven to 170°C (gas mark 3). Lightly flour the work surface and roll out the sweet pastry dough (see pages 488 and 489) to a thickness of about 3 mm. Using the tart ring as a guide, cut out a disc with a diameter 5 cm larger than that of the ring, about 27 cm. Butter the tart ring, line with the dough (see page 493) and place it on a baking tray lined with baking parchment. Refrigerate for 10 minutes.

FOR THE RHUBARB

2 – Blind bake the tart case (see page 494) in the oven for 10 minutes. Keep the oven temperature at 170°C.
3 – Peel the rhubarb and cut into 1.5-cm-thick slices. Heat the butter and sugar in a frying pan and cook the rhubarb over a high heat for 2–3 minutes.

FOR THE SAFFRON CREAM FILLING

4 – Mix the eggs with the sugar in a bowl. Add the saffron threads.
5 – Add the cream and mix.
6 – Fill the tart case to two-thirds with the filling.
7 – Arrange the rhubarb evenly over the filling.
8 – Cover with the remaining saffron cream filling. Bake for 40 minutes.

DECORATING

9 – Leave the tart to cool, then remove the ring. Dust only the very edge of the tart with icing sugar, using a cardboard cake board to cover the remainder of the tart.

FIG TARTLETS
with sugared almonds

Makes 10 tartlets

PREPARATION TIME: 45 minutes + 15 minutes for the pastry – BAKING TIME: 30 minutes
CHILLING TIME: 30 minutes for the pastry – STORAGE: 2 days in the refrigerator

DIFFICULTY: 🎩

SWEET PASTRY DOUGH
200 g plain flour
90 g unsalted butter
90 g icing sugar
30 g ground almonds
1 egg (50 g)

Unsalted butter for the tartlet rings

HAZELNUT CREAM
70 g white sugared almonds
100 g room-temperature unsalted butter
100 g sugar
100 g ground hazelnuts
1½ eggs (85 g)

FIGS
20 figs
35 g unsalted butter, melted
35 g sugar
Knife tip of "fleur de sel" fine sea salt

DECORATION
150 g neutral glaze
80 g white sugared almonds

EQUIPMENT NEEDED: Ten 8-cm tartlet rings – pastry brush

Fig

The fig is a fruit native to Asia that quickly spread throughout the Mediterranean region in ancient times. Figs can only be stored for a short time once picked. When choosing, look for fleshy fruits that are soft to the touch and perfectly ripe. Figs are used for making both desserts and savoury dishes. Dried figs will keep for several months.

FIG TARTLETS with sugared almonds

FOR THE TARTLET CASES

1 – Lightly flour the work surface and roll out the sweet pastry dough (see pages 488 and 489) to a thickness of about 3 mm. Using a tartlet ring as a guide, cut out ten discs with a diameter 5 cm larger than that of the rings, about 13 cm.
2 – Butter the rings and line with the dough (see page 493). Trim off the excess dough with a knife.

FOR THE HAZELNUT CREAM

3 – Crush the sugared almonds with a rolling pin.
4 – Mix the butter with the sugar and ground hazelnuts in a bowl.
5 – Mix in the eggs and incorporate the crushed sugared almonds.

ASSEMBLY AND DECORATION

6 – Preheat the oven to 170°C (gas mark 3). Use a teaspoon to fill the tartlet cases with the hazelnut cream. Use the back of the spoon to spread into a uniform layer.
7 – Finely slice 15 figs and arrange in a rosette on top of the tartlets.
8 – Halve the remaining five figs. Place a fig half in the centre of each tartlet.
9 – Lightly brush the figs with butter, then sprinkle with sugar and "fleur de sel" fine sea salt. Bake for 30 minutes. Leave the tartlets to cool. Brush the figs with neutral glaze. Crush the sugared almonds and sprinkle over the tartlets.

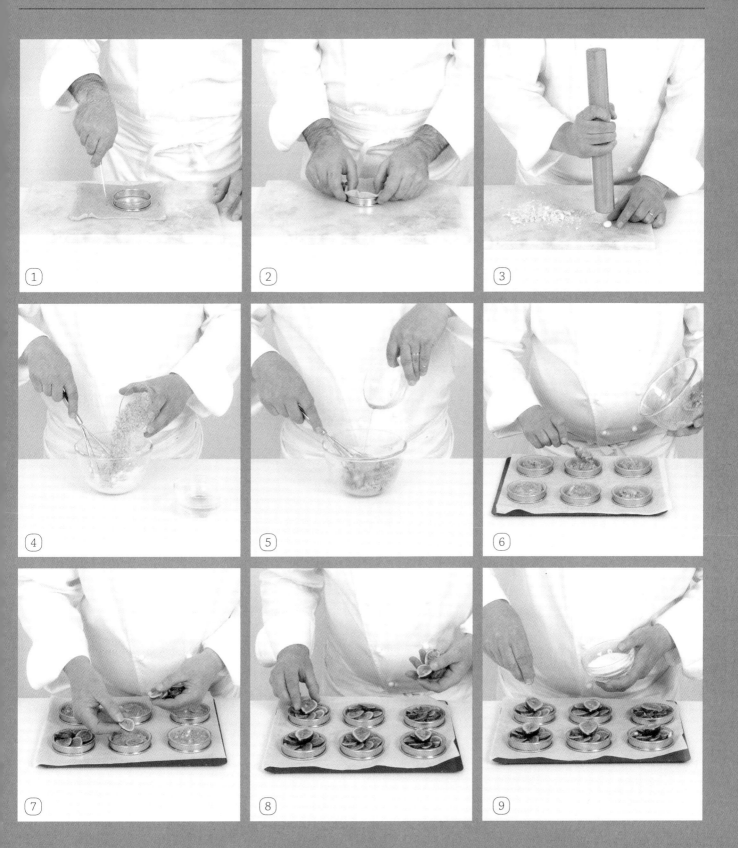

SPECIAL & FESTIVE DESSERTS

CHOCOLATE, TONKA BEAN
and berry prestige

Serves 8–10

PREPARATION TIME: 1 hour 30 minutes – BAKING TIME: 15 minutes – REFRIGERATION TIME: 10 minutes – FREEZING TIME: 5 hours 10 minutes

DIFFICULTY: ♙ ♙ ♙

CHOCOLATE DACQUOISE
2 tsp plain flour
125 g ground almonds
105 g icing sugar
2 tsp unsweetened cocoa powder
4½ egg whites (130 g)
50 g sugar

RED BERRY CRÉMEUX
2 tsp potato starch
30 g sugar
30 g blackcurrant purée
80 g strawberry purée
80 g raspberry purée

SPECULOOS CRISP
80 g speculoos biscuits
30 g dark chocolate
20 g praline paste

CHOCOLATE AND TONKA BEAN MOUSSE
195 g dark couverture chocolate
¾ tonka bean
400 ml cream
2½ egg yolks (70 g)
65 g sugar

GLAZE
3½ gelatine leaves (7 g)
70 ml water
150 g sugar
150 g glucose
Knife tip of red food colouring powder
20 g cocoa butter
180 g milk couverture chocolate
165 ml condensed milk

DECORATION
Strawberries
Raspberries
Icing sugar
Blackberries
1 bunch redcurrants

EQUIPMENT REQUIRED: 2 piping bags – size 12 plain nozzle – 18-cm diameter tart ring
20-cm diameter and 4.5-cm deep entremets ring – Rhodoïd® (acetate) sheet – cardboard cake board – cooking thermometer

Mirror glaze

Pastry chefs often make a mirror glaze, so-called because of its sheen, to finish their entremets. Whether of chocolate or with added food colouring, mirror glaze has to be used at a specific temperature on a frozen entremets so that it will adhere to the surface and set without melting. It should be covered with cling film in direct contact before use to remove any air bubbles. It must be poured over the entremets in one go, and spread over the top and sides, then smoothed for even glazing.

FOR THE CHOCOLATE DACQUOISE

1 – Preheat the oven to 180°C (gas mark 4). Mix the flour, ground almonds, icing sugar and unsweetened cocoa powder in a bowl.
2 – Whisk the egg whites until firm, then incorporate the sugar while whisking to stiff peaks. Fold in the dry ingredients half at a time.
3 – Transfer to a piping bag fitted with the plain nozzle. Draw an 18-cm diameter circle on each of 2 sheets of baking parchment and place each one on a baking tray. Pipe the dacquoise meringue in a spiral inside the circles. Bake for 15 minutes.

FOR THE RED BERRY CRÉMEUX

4 – Mix the potato starch with the sugar in a bowl. Combine the blackcurrant, strawberry and raspberry purées in a pan and bring to the boil. Sprinkle in the starch and sugar mixture. Bring back to the boil while stirring constantly with a whisk, then remove from the heat and leave to cool to room temperature.

FOR THE SPECULOOS CRISP

5 – Use a rolling pin to crush up the biscuits in a bowl.
6 – Melt the chocolate over a bain-marie. Transfer to a bowl and add the praline paste and crushed biscuits.
7 – Lay the tart ring on a sheet of baking parchment. Spread the mixture out inside the ring. Transfer to a baking tray and refrigerate for 10 minutes.
8 – Spread the crémeux over the speculoos crisp and freeze for 10 minutes.

FOR THE CHOCOLATE AND TONKA BEAN MOUSSE

9 – Melt the chocolate in a bowl over a bain-marie. Grate the tonka bean over the chocolate.

• • •

10 – Whip the cream to soft peaks.
11 – Beat the egg yolks with the sugar in a bowl until the mixture turns pale and thickens. Then add to the whipped cream. Mix very gently with the whisk.
12 – Briskly whisk in half the chocolate and tonka bean mixture.
13 – Then fold in the rest of the mixture using a whisk. Finish folding with a silicone spatula, then transfer to a piping bag fitted with the plain nozzle.

ASSEMBLY

14 – Cut out a strip of Rhodoïd® the same size as the circumference and height of the entremets ring. Line the inside of the ring and place over the cardboard cake board. Pipe a ring of chocolate and tonka bean mousse around the inside of the entremets ring.
15 – Place a chocolate dacquoise disc in the centre.
16 – Pipe a spiral of chocolate and tonka bean mousse over the chocolate dacquoise disc.
17 – Pipe a layer of chocolate mousse around the edge and flatten with a palette knife against the sides of the ring to mask well.
18 – Remove the tart ring from the speculoos crisp and crémeux insert and place inside the entremets ring over the chocolate and tonka bean mousse.

• • •

CHEF'S TIP

If you are unable to find a sheet of Rhodoïd® acetate, you can use a sheet of thick plastic such as overhead transparency film or florist film. You only need enough to cut out a strip the length of the circumference of the entremets ring and a width the same as the height of the ring.

19 – Cover with the second chocolate dacquoise disc.

20 – Pipe the remaining chocolate and tonka bean mousse over the chocolate dacquoise disc and smooth with the palette knife. Freeze the entremets for 5 hours.

FOR THE GLAZE

21 – Soften the gelatine leaves in a bowl of cold water.
Combine the water, sugar, and glucose in a pan and heat until the temperature reads 103°C on the cooking thermometer to make a syrup. Add the red food colouring.

22 – Combine the cocoa butter, chocolate, and condensed milk in a bowl. Squeeze the gelatine to drain and incorporate into the mixture in the bowl. Pour in the hot syrup and mix with a silicone spatula.

23 – Blend with a hand-held blender until smooth. Cover the surface of the glaze with a sheet of cling film, then remove immediately to eliminate any bubbles. Leave to cool until the thermometer reads 30°C.

GLAZING AND DECORATING

24 – Remove the entremets ring, then take off the Rhodoïd® strip.

25 – Stand the entremets over a container. Pour all of the glaze over, starting in the centre and moving towards the edges.

26 – Allow the glaze to run over the sides. Lift the entremets and scrape the underside with a palette knife to remove the excess glaze.

27 – Halve the unhulled strawberries and lightly dip the raspberries in icing sugar. Decorate the entremets with the strawberry halves, raspberries, redcurrants and blackberries.

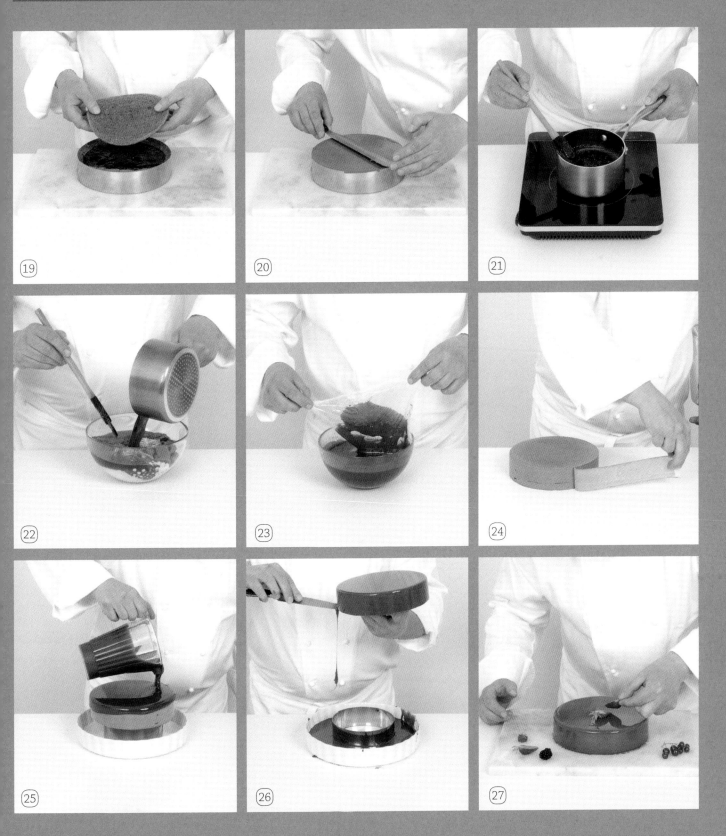

VANILLA CUBES
with sugar-frosted pansies

Makes 6

PREPARATION TIME: 1 hour 30 minutes + 15 minutes for the Joconde "biscuit" sponge – BAKING TIME: about 8 minutes
FREEZING TIME: 12 hours 30 minutes – REFRIGERATION TIME: 12 hours – DRYING TIME: 12 hours – STORAGE: 2 days in the refrigerator.
The sugar-frosted pansies will keep for 1 week in an airtight container.

DIFFICULTY: ♙ ♙

SUGAR-FROSTED PANSIES
100 g sugar
12 fresh pansy flowers
1 egg white (30 g)

VANILLA JOCONDE "BISCUIT" SPONGE
2 eggs (100 g)
70 g ground almonds
60 g unrefined cane sugar
20 g plain flour
Scraped-out seeds from ½ vanilla pod
1 tbsp unsalted butter, melted
----
2 egg whites (60 g)
25 g sugar

Oil for the frames

MASCARPONE MOUSSE
1 vanilla pod
1½ gelatine leaves (3 g)
100 g mascarpone
50 ml cream
20 g sugar
125 ml cream

VIOLET JELLY
5 gelatine leaves (10 g)
100 ml water
50 g sugar
Knife tip of violet food colouring powder
1–2 drops violet extract

WHITE CHOCOLATE GLAZE
125 g white chocolate
2½ gelatine leaves (5 g)
50 ml water
100 g glucose
100 g sugar
2 tsp sparkling silver food colouring
30 g cocoa butter
110 g condensed milk

EQUIPMENT REQUIRED: Six 5-cm square and 3-cm deep entremets frames – size 10 plain piping nozzle
or 1-cm diameter biscuit cutter – 17 x 17 x 3.5 cm baking frame

Pansies

Small, edible flowers, often used as decoration in pastry making and cooking, pansies can enliven your creations in different ways. Sugar-frosted pansies add crunch to your dessert, as well as a colourful, floral touch. They can be substituted by violets when in season, which are prepared in the same way.

FOR THE SUGAR-FROSTED PANSIES

1 – Put the sugar onto a plate. Dip the pansies in the egg white, then dust with the sugar. Shake to remove the excess. Leave to dry in the open air for 12 hours, then store in an airtight container.

FOR THE JOCONDE "BISCUIT" SPONGE

2 – Preheat the oven to 200°C (gas mark 6). Pour the Joconde "biscuit" sponge (see page 485) into a swiss roll tin lined with baking parchment.
3 – Use a silicone spatula to evenly spread the batter to a 1 cm thickness. Bake for 6–8 minutes.
4 – Leave to cool, then use one of the entremets frames to cut out 12 squares.
5 – Use a knife to trim the sponge squares by 5 mm on all four sides.

FOR THE MASCARPONE MOUSSE

6 – Split the vanilla pod and scrape out the seeds with a knife tip. Soften the gelatine leaves in a bowl of cold water. Combine the mascarpone, 50 ml of cream, sugar and vanilla seeds in a pan and heat.
7 – Remove the pan from the heat. Squeeze the gelatine to drain and incorporate into the mixture in the pan.
8 – Whisk the 125 ml of cream to soft peaks. Add a third to the warm mascarpone mixture and whisk. Add the remaining whipped cream and mix well.

ASSEMBLY

9 – Oil the six entremets frames and arrange on a baking tray lined with baking parchment. Put 1 vanilla Joconde "biscuit" sponge square into each frame.

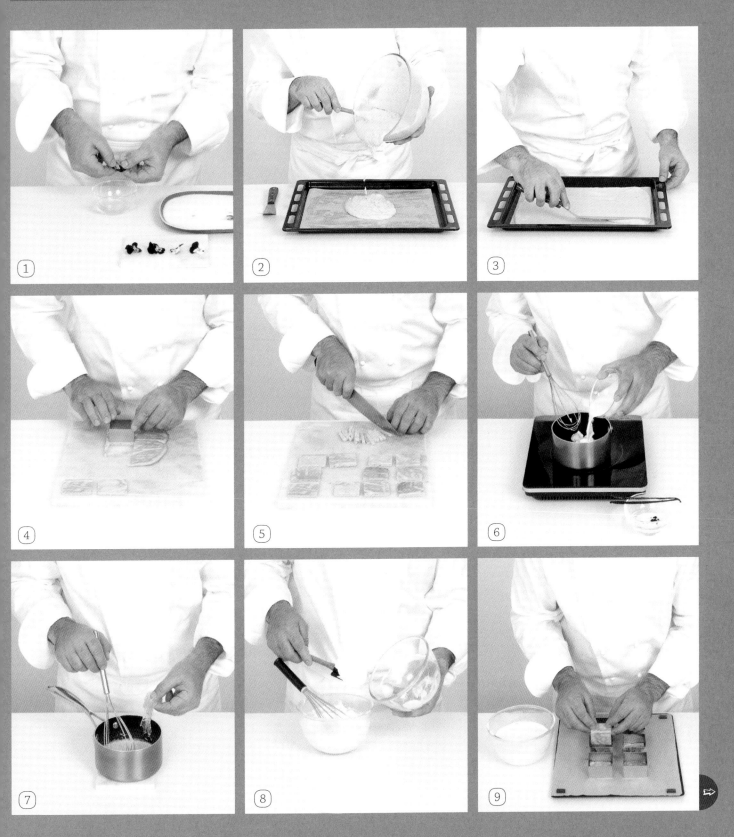

10 – Cover with 1 tablespoon of mascarpone mousse.

11 – Spread the mousse up the sides of the frame to mask.

12 – Put another Joconde "biscuit" sponge square into the frame and press well into the mousse.

13 – Add another tablespoon of the mousse into the frame and spread well with a palette knife to completely cover the Joconde "biscuit" sponge in the mousse. Then smooth the surface. Freeze for 12 hours. Set aside the remaining mousse in the refrigerator.

FOR THE VIOLET JELLY

14 – Lightly heat the large baking frame with a chef's blow torch or put in the oven for a few minutes. Cover the bottom of the frame with cling film and place on a baking tray, then lightly oil the film and insides of the frame (you can also use a swiss roll tin).

15 – Soften the gelatine leaves in a bowl of cold water. Combine the water with the sugar in a pan and bring to the boil to make a syrup, then remove the pan from the heat. Add the violet colouring and the violet extract.

16 – Squeeze the gelatine to drain and add to the syrup.

17 – Pour the syrup into the cling film-covered frame to a depth of 5 mm. Refrigerate for 12 hours.

18 – Warm the entremets frames between your hands and carefully remove from the vanilla cubes. Freeze the cubes for 30 minutes.

• • •

CHEF'S TIP

If the Joconde "biscuit" sponge can still be seen in places after removing the frames from the cubes, use a palette knife to mask well with the remaining mousse, then freeze again.

FOR THE WHITE CHOCOLATE GLAZE

19 – Chop the white chocolate. Soften the gelatine leaves in a bowl of cold water. Heat the water in a pan and dissolve the glucose well. Add the sugar and stir constantly with a whisk until dissolved. Remove the pan from the heat just before it comes to the boil.

20 – Add the sparkling colouring and mix well with a whisk.

21 – Squeeze the gelatine to drain and whisk into the syrup.

22 – Add the cocoa butter and mix well until completely melted.

23 – Transfer the mixture to a bowl and add the white chocolate. Mix until smooth.

24 – Stir in the condensed milk.

GLAZING

25 – Put the cubes on a rack over a container. Use the glaze when it is smooth and a little warm (35°C). Pour the glaze over each cube, covering uniformly. Pass the palette knife under the cubes and slide them across the rack to scrape off the excess glaze, leaving the base smooth. Transfer to a baking tray lined with parchment paper and refrigerate.

26 – Use the plain pastry nozzle to cut out 18 small violet jelly discs.

27 – Arrange 3 on each cube. Serve immediately, decorated with sugar-frosted pansies.

LEMON YULE LOG

Serves 10

PREPARATION TIME: 1 hour 30 minutes + 10 minutes for the meringue – BAKING TIME: About 1 hour 45 minutes
REFRIGERATION TIME – 2 hours – STORAGE: 2 days in the refrigerator

DIFFICULTY: ♙♙

<u>MERINGUE DECORATIONS</u>
1½ egg whites (50 g)
50 g sugar
50 g icing sugar, sifted
Zest of ¼ lemon

<u>LEMON CREAM</u>
1 gelatine leaf (2 g)
5 egg yolks (100 g)
1 egg (50 g)
50 g sugar

110 ml lemon juice
Zest of 1 lemon
250 ml cream

<u>LEMON SYRUP</u>
150 ml water
100 g sugar
30 ml lemon juice

<u>LEMON "BISCUIT" SPONGE</u>
170 g unsalted butter
3 eggs (150 g)

165 g sugar
Zest of 1 lemon
50 ml lemon juice
170 g plain flour
½ tsp baking powder
----
200 g chocolate-hazelnut spread

<u>DECORATION</u>
Unsweetened cocoa powder

<u>EQUIPMENT REQUIRED:</u> 2 piping bags – size 8 plain nozzle – 35 x 7 cm yule log mould – star biscuit cutter
rectangular cardboard cake board – pastry brush

Meringue decorations

Of the three types of meringue – French, Italian and Swiss – French meringue is the easiest to make. Unlike the others, you can use it to make entremets and cake decorations, such as small shells and batons, or use a biscuit cutter to cut out the shapes of your choice. It is a simple way of adding a final flourish to your creations.

FOR THE MERINGUE DECORATIONS

1 – Preheat the oven to 110°C (gas mark ¼). Line a baking tray with baking parchment. Grate the zest and add it to the French meringue (see page 486).
2 – Fill a piping bag fitted with the plain nozzle and pipe lines lengthways over half of the baking tray.
3 – Spread a layer of meringue about 3 mm thick over the other half of the tray. Smooth with a palette knife, then use the biscuit cutter to cut out meringue stars. Bake for 1 hour 15 minutes.

FOR THE LEMON CREAM

4 – Soften the gelatine leaf in a bowl of cold water. Whisk the egg yolks, egg and sugar in a bowl. Add the lemon juice and mix. Transfer to a pan and grate in the lemon zest. Cook, whisking constantly, until the mixture comes to the boil.
5 – Remove the pan from the heat. Squeeze the gelatine to drain and incorporate into the mixture in the pan. Refrigerate for 1 hour.
6 – Whip the cream until it clings to the tip of the whisk. Whisk the lemon cream to smooth, then fold in the whipped cream. Transfer to a piping bag fitted with the plain nozzle.

FOR THE LEMON SYRUP

7 – Combine the water, sugar and lemon juice in a pan and bring to the boil. Leave to cool.

FOR THE LEMON "BISCUIT" SPONGE

8 – Preheat the oven to 180°C (gas mark 4). Melt the butter in a pan. In a bowl, beat the eggs with the sugar and lemon zest until the mixture turns pale and thickens. Add the lemon juice, then the flour and baking powder, mixing well.
9 – Incorporate the warm melted butter.

① ② ③
④ ⑤ ⑥
⑦ ⑧ ⑨

10 – Line the yule log mould with baking parchment and fill with the lemon "biscuit" sponge mixture. Bake for 25–30 minutes. Leave to cool.

ASSEMBLY AND DECORATION

11 – Turn out the log and remove the baking parchment. Slice the lemon "biscuit" sponge across the middle and lay the two halves on a sheet of baking parchment. Brush the surface of both pieces with lemon syrup to imbibe.

12 – Pipe a line of lemon cream on the cardboard cake board and lay the bottom lemon "biscuit" sponge layer on top, with the cut-side facing upwards.

13 – Use a silicone spatula to spread the chocolate-hazelnut spread over the sponge.

14 – Cover with a layer of lemon cream.

15 – Close the log by covering with the other half of the lemon "biscuit" sponge. Imbibe the surface with lemon syrup. Pipe lines of lemon cream lengthways over the entire surface of the log, and mask both ends. Finish by piping three small balls of cream on the surface.

16 – Break the meringue batons into pieces and decorate the yule log.

17 – Put the cocoa powder into a small bowl and use a brush to dust the log.

18 – Arrange the meringue stars over the yule log. Refrigerate for at least 1 hour before serving.

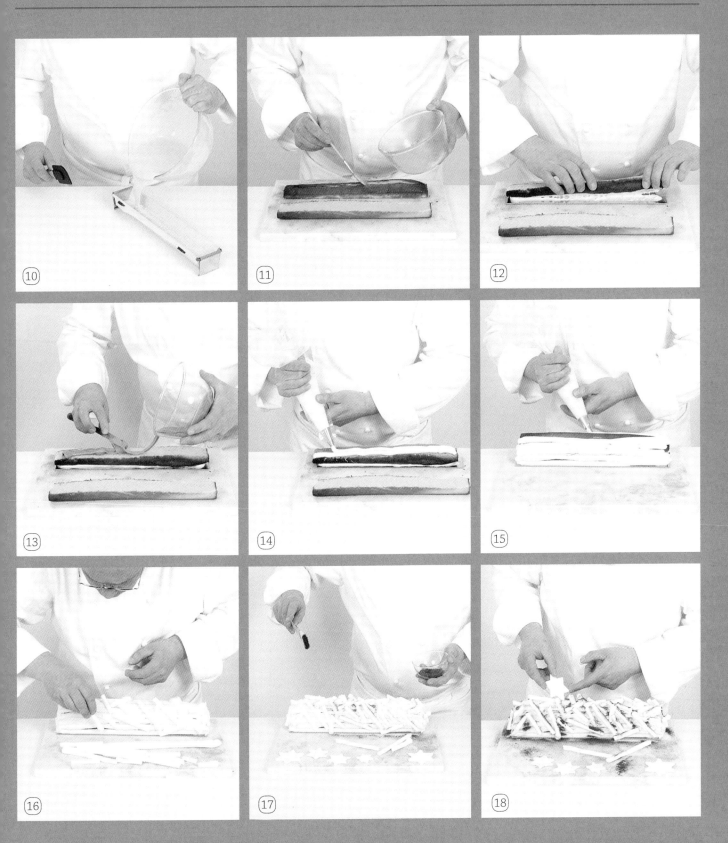

CROUSTI-CHOC ENTREMETS

Serves 12

PREPARATION TIME: 1 hour 30 minutes – BAKING TIME: 20 minutes – REFRIGERATION TIME: 30 minutes – STORAGE: 2 days in the refrigerator

DIFFICULTY: ♙ ♙ ♙

ALMOND MERINGUE
50 g ground almonds
40 g icing sugar
1½ tsp plain flour
2 egg whites (60 g)
30 g sugar

CHOCOLATE MOUSSE
150 g dark chocolate (70% cocoa)
200 ml water
35 g sugar
2 egg yolks (40 g)
250 ml cream

CRISPY PRALINE
150 g praline paste
50 g white chocolate
130 g crushed Gavottes®
crêpes (wafers)

GANACHE GLAZE
25 g dark chocolate (70% cocoa)
25 ml cream
2 tsp sugar
2 tsp water

DECORATION
30 g unsweetened cocoa powder
Edible gold leaf (optional)

EQUIPMENT NEEDED: 2 piping bags – size 12 plain nozzle – paper cone – cooking thermometer

Pâte à bombe

The pâte à bombe technique is used to make creamy and delicious chocolate mousse. It consists of heating sugar and water between 118°C and 120°C, then pouring the syrup over egg yolks and whisking until they cool. As well as guaranteeing your chocolate mousse is a success, it also pasteurises the eggs, extending the time your desserts can be stored.

FOR THE ALMOND MERINGUE

1 – Preheat the oven to 200°C (gas mark 6). Line two baking trays with baking parchment and draw a 15 x 20-cm rectangle on each. Combine the ground almonds, icing sugar and flour in a bowl. Whisk the egg whites until firm, then incorporate the sugar while whisking to stiff peaks.

2 – Fold half of the dry ingredient mixture into the beaten eggs: mix slowly with the silicone spatula, starting at the centre of the mixture and folding the mixture over itself at the edge as though gently kneading a dough, rotating the bowl with your other hand. Then fold in the remainder.

3 – Transfer the almond meringue to a piping bag fitted with the plain nozzle. Pipe a series of touching lines lengthways inside the rectangle on the first baking tray. Bake for 20 minutes, then leave to cool.

FOR THE CRISPY PRALINE

4 – Put the praline paste into a bowl. Melt the chocolate in a bowl over a bain-marie. Pour over the praline paste and mix.

5 – Incorporate the crushed Gavottes® crêpes (wafers).

6 – Use a spoon to spread the mixture inside the rectangle on the second baking tray, then flatten with the back of the spoon.

7 – Lay a second sheet of baking parchment over the top and use a rolling pin to gently roll out the mixture to roughly form a rectangle of at least 15 x 20 cm with a 1 cm thickness. Refrigerate for 10 minutes.

FOR THE CHOCOLATE MOUSSE

8 – Melt the chocolate over a bain-marie. Transfer to a bowl and leave to cool. Make a thick syrup by heating the water and sugar in a pan until the temperature reads 118°C on the cooking thermometer. To make the pâte à bombe, whisk the egg yolks in a bowl. Pour the hot syrup into the yolks while whisking briskly until the mixture turns pale, thickens, and cools down.

9 – Whip the cream to soft peaks in another bowl. Add to the pâte à bombe and mix very gently with a whisk.

• • •

10 – Pour half of this mixture into the warm melted chocolate, mix well, then incorporate the remainder. Transfer to a piping bag fitted with the plain nozzle.

ASSEMBLY

11 – Use a knife to trim the edges of the cake to form a neat rectangle measuring 15 x 20 cm.

12 – Put the almond meringue on top of the crispy praline and cut it to the size of the crispy praline.

13 – Pipe different size balls of chocolate mousse over the top.

14 – Use a teaspoon dipped in hot water to scoop out shallow wells in the largest balls. Refrigerate the entremets for 20 minutes.

FOR THE GANACHE GLAZE

15 – Chop the chocolate and put into a bowl. Use a whisk to mix the cream, sugar and water in a pan and bring to the boil. Immediately pour over the chopped chocolate and mix with a whisk until smooth. Transfer the ganache glaze to a paper cone.

DECORATING

16 – Dust the entremets with unsweetened cocoa powder.

17 – Pipe a little of the ganache glaze into the wells in the chocolate mousse balls.

18 – Optionally, decorate with gold leaf.

PRALINE AND ORANGE CRUNCH
entremets

Serves 8

PREPARATION TIME: 1 hour 30 minutes + 15 minutes for the pastry cream – BAKING TIME: 1 hour 35 minutes

FREEZING TIME: 30 minutes – STORAGE: 3 days in the refrigerator

DIFFICULTY: ♙ ♙

Dried oranges
1 orange

Sugar

Hazelnut macaronnade
190 g icing sugar

80 g ground hazelnuts

40 g ground almonds

3 egg whites (90 g)

25 g sugar

Orange tuiles
120 g icing sugar

50 ml orange juice

Zest of 2 oranges

30 g plain flour

40 g unsalted butter, melted

60 g flaked almonds

Praline and orange cream
Pastry cream
250 ml milk

Zest of 1 orange

1½ egg yolks (30 g)

60 g sugar

1 egg (50g)

30 g cornflour

- - - -

140 g praline paste

130 g room-temperature unsalted butter

Praline and orange crunch
40 g candied orange peel, diced and macerated in 1 tsp Grand Marnier®

150 g orange tuiles

50 g milk chocolate

70 g praline paste

Chocolate glaze
95 g dark chocolate (70% cocoa)

60 g dark chocolate compound coating

60 ml cream

60 ml water

30 g glucose

60 g sugar

EQUIPMENT NEEDED: Cardboard cake board – silicone mat – piping bag – size 12 plain nozzle – 20-cm diameter entremets ring

Orange

Native to China, the orange was introduced into Europe in the fifteenth century. At the time, and for many years, this rare fruit was considered a symbol of wealth. It was often used in table centrepieces on festive occasions and given to children at Christmas. It can be enjoyed as it is, in salads, squeezed into juice, or in marmalade, jelly or syrup. It is one of the most popular fruits in France.

FOR THE DRIED ORANGES

1 – Preheat the oven to 110°C (gas mark ¼). Halve the orange, then finely slice. Lay the slices on a baking tray lined with the silicone mat and dust with sugar. Dry out in the oven for 1 hour. Set aside in a dry place.

FOR THE HAZELNUT MACARONNADE

2 – Raise the oven temperature to 180°C (gas mark 4). Mix the dry ingredients in a bowl. Whisk the egg whites until firm, then incorporate the sugar while whisking to stiff peaks. Use a silicone spatula to fold in the dry ingredients and transfer the mixture to a piping bag fitted with the plain nozzle.
3 – Draw an 18-cm diameter circle on each of 2 sheets of baking parchment and place each one on a baking tray. Pipe the macaronnade inside the circles to form discs and bake for about 20 minutes.

FOR THE ORANGE TUILES

4 – Lower the oven temperature to 160°C (gas mark 3). Mix the icing sugar with the orange juice in a bowl. Grate the orange zest into the bowl. Whisk in the flour and then the melted butter, then fold in the flaked almonds with the spatula.
5 – Spread the mixture over a baking tray lined with a silicone mat. Bake for 15 minutes. Leave to cool, then break the tuile into large pieces.

FOR THE PRALINE AND ORANGE CREAM

6 – Make a pastry cream (see page 480), adding the orange zest to the milk. Once cooked add the praline paste. Leave to cool.
7 – Whisk the butter in a bowl to a creamy consistency, then incorporate into the praline and orange pastry cream, whisking briskly.

FOR THE PRALINE AND ORANGE CRUNCH

8 – Use a rolling pin to crush 150 g of the orange tuiles in a bowl.
9 – Melt the chocolate over a bain-marie. Incorporate the praline paste. Add the crushed orange tuiles and drained candied orange peel.

• • •

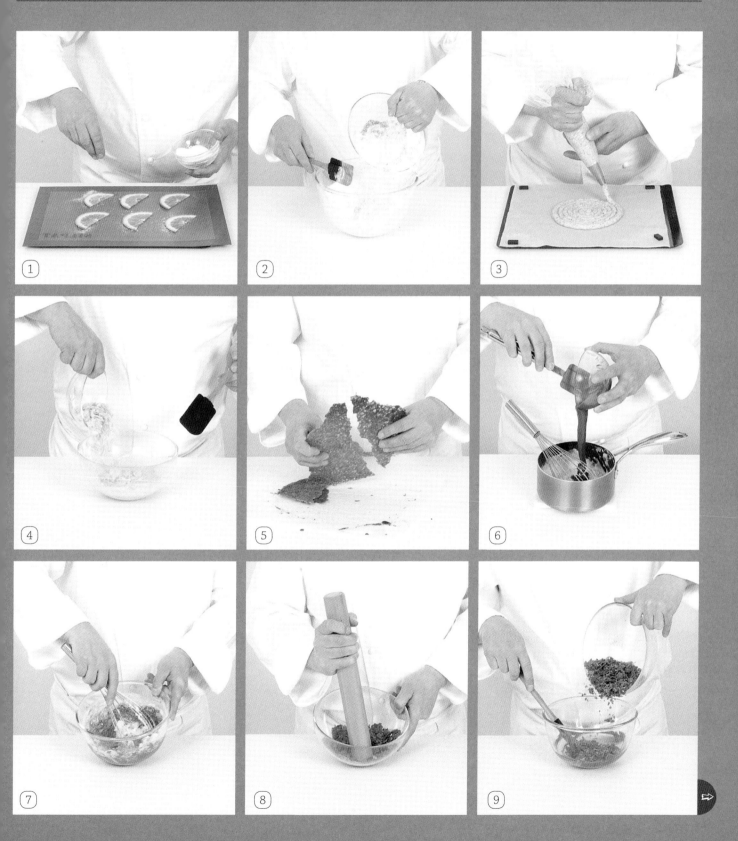

ASSEMBLY

10 – Lay one of the macaronnade discs on a baking tray lined with baking parchment. Spread over with the praline and orange crunch.

11 – Cover the inside of the entremets ring with the praline and orange cream.

12 – Position the ring around the macaronnade disc.

13 – Spread a layer of praline and orange cream inside the ring, over the disc and up the sides.

14 – Cover with the second macaronnade disc and pipe over with the praline and orange cream to the top of the ring. Smooth with a palette knife, then freeze for 30 minutes.

GLAZING AND DECORATION

15 – Chop the chocolate and put into a bowl with the dark chocolate compound coating. Combine the cream, water, glucose and sugar in a pan and bring to the boil. Add to the bowl with the chocolate and mix. Cover with cling film in contact with the glaze and leave to cool.

16 – Cover the work surface with cling film and put a rack on top. Transfer the entremets to the rack. Remove the cling film from the glaze to remove any air bubbles, then pour all the glaze over the entremets at the one time, working your way from the sides into the middle.

17 – Smooth with a palette knife. Transfer the entremets to the cardboard cake board.

18 – Decorate the sides of the entremets with pieces of orange tuile. Pipe three small balls of praline and orange over the entremets and arrange three dried orange slices on top.

NOUGAT AND MANDARIN
yule log

Serves 10

PREPARATION TIME: 2 hours – BAKING TIME: 30 minutes – CHILLING TIME: 30 minutes – FREEZING TIME: 12 hours

STORAGE: 2 days in the refrigerator

DIFFICULTY: ♕ ♕

MANDARIN MARMALADE
3 mandarins
50 ml water
75 g sugar
1 tsp Grand Marnier®

ALMOND "BISCUIT" SPONGE
50 g room-temperature unsalted butter
65 g sugar
Pinch of fine salt
2 eggs (100 g)
100 g ground almonds
2 egg whites (50 g)
1 tsp sugar
1 tbsp flaked almonds

NOUGAT CREAM
1½ gelatine leaves (3 g)
Pastry cream
150 ml cream
75 ml milk
2 egg yolks (50 g)
50 g sugar
25 g cornflour

----

50 g nougat paste
50 g unsalted butter
150 ml cream

WHITE CHOCOLATE AND NOUGAT
50 g white couverture chocolate
50 g nougat paste

DECORATION
150 g neutral glaze
Icing sugar
100 g white couverture chocolate
Unsweetened cocoa powder

EQUIPMENT REQUIRED: Cooking thermometer – 22 x 12 cm silicone yule log mould – 20 x 26 cm Swiss roll tin – pastry brush

Mandarin or clementine

Because both the mandarin and the clementine have the same shape, orange colour and composition, it is always difficult to tell these citrus fruits apart. Native to China, the mandarin is slightly larger, its peel comes away more easily from its flesh, and it contains a lot of seeds. The smaller clementine is a hybrid, created by crossing the mandarin with the Seville orange at the beginning of the twentieth century. It is much more popular in France today than the mandarin.

SPECIAL AND FESTIVE DESSERTS

FOR THE MANDARIN MARMALADE

1 – Peel and cut the mandarins into pieces. Make a thick syrup by heating the water and sugar in a pan until the temperature reads 110°C on the cooking thermometer. Add the mandarin pieces. Cook over a low heat for 20 minutes. Remove from the heat and add the Grand Marnier®.

FOR THE ALMOND "BISCUIT" SPONGE

2 – Preheat the oven to 180°C (gas mark 4). Mix the butter with the sugar and salt in a bowl, then incorporate the eggs and ground almonds.
3 – Whisk the egg whites until firm and they cling to the end of the whisk, then incorporate the sugar while whisking to stiff peaks. Fold into the butter and egg mixture.
4 – Line the Swiss roll tin with baking parchment and fill with the mixture to a depth of 2 cm. Sprinkle the flaked almonds over the top. Bake for 30 minutes.

FOR THE NOUGAT CREAM

5 – Soften the gelatine in a bowl of cold water. Make the pastry cream (see page 480) and incorporate the nougat paste, followed by the butter, while still hot. Squeeze the gelatine to drain and whisk into the pastry cream. Refrigerate for 20 minutes.
6 – Whisk the nougat cream to smooth. Whip the cream until it is firm and clings to the end of the whisk. Add a third of the whipped cream to the nougat cream, whisking to incorporate well, then fold in the rest with a silicone spatula.

FOR THE WHITE CHOCOLATE AND NOUGAT

7 – Melt the white chocolate over a bain-marie. Add the nougat paste and mix.

ASSEMBLY

8 – Cut the almond "biscuit" sponge into three 25-cm long strips – the first 9 cm wide, the second 6 cm wide, and the third 4 cm wide.
9 – Cover the 25 x 9-cm almond "biscuit" sponge strip with a layer of the white chocolate and nougat. Refrigerate for 10 minutes.

● ● ●

10 – Lay the 25 x 4-cm almond "biscuit" sponge strip in the bottom of the mould.

11 – Use a silicone spatula to spread a layer of nougat cream over the sponge and the sides of the mould.

12 – Cover with the 25 x 6-cm almond "biscuit" sponge strip.

13 – Cover with a layer of mandarin marmalade.

14 – Add the rest of the nougat cream to the mould and smooth with a silicone spatula.

15 – Cover with the 25 x 9-cm almond "biscuit" sponge strip, with the white chocolate and nougat facing downwards. Freeze for 12 hours.

DECORATING

16 – Turn out the yule log, brush with neutral glaze and then dust the surface with icing sugar through a sieve.

17 – Temper the white couverture chocolate (see pages 494–495) and spread it out over a cold work surface. Once it begins to harden, while still malleable, scrape with a palette knife to form large curls.

18 – Dust the curls with cocoa powder and decorate the yule log with them.

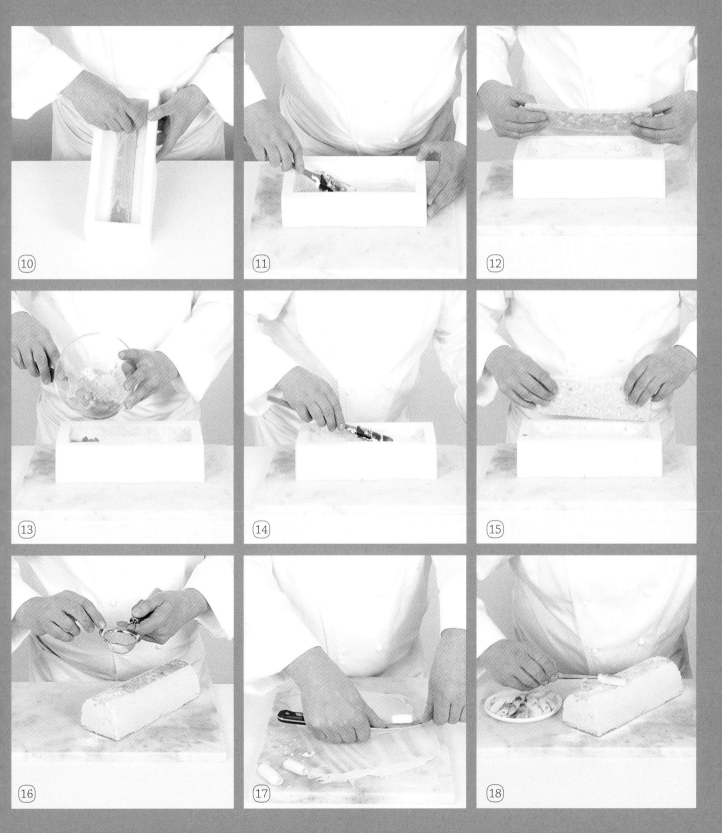

COCONUT AND MANGO
domes

Makes 6

PREPARATION TIME: 2 hours + 15 minutes for the Swiss meringue + 15 minutes for the Joconde "biscuit" sponge + 15 minutes for the crème anglaise + 15 minutes for the pastry – BAKING TIME: about 1 hour 20 minutes – REFRIGERATION TIME: 12 hours 30 minutes – FREEZING TIME: 12 hours

DIFFICULTY: ♙ ♙ ♙

COCONUT MERINGUE BATONS
3 egg whites (90 g)
180 g sugar
Desiccated coconut

JOCONDE "BISCUIT" SPONGE
2 eggs (100 g)
70 g ground almonds
60 g icing sugar
20 g plain flour
½ vanilla pod, split
plus scraped-out seeds
1 tbsp unsalted butter, melted

----

2 egg whites (60 g)
25 g sugar

COCONUT BAVARIAN CREAM
2 gelatine leaves (4 g)
Coconut crème anglaise
1 vanilla pod
170 ml coconut cream
3 egg yolks (60 g)
45 g unrefined cane sugar

----

170 ml cream

DICED MANGO
½ mango

COCONUT SWEET PASTRY DOUGH
½ tbsp ground almonds
½ tbsp desiccated coconut
60 g unsalted butter

Pinch of salt
35 g icing sugar
½ vanilla pod
½ egg (25 g)
100 g plain flour

WHITE CHOCOLATE GLAZE
125 g white chocolate
2½ gelatine leaves (5 g)
50 ml water
100 g glucose
100 g sugar
2 tsp sparkling silver food colouring
30 g cocoa butter
110 g condensed milk

DECORATION (OPTIONAL)
Edible silver leaf

EQUIPMENT REQUIRED: piping bag – size 8 plain nozzle – 6-cm diameter biscuit cutter
4.5-cm diameter biscuit cutter – mould with 7-cm diameter half sphere cavities

White chocolate glaze

If you want to impress your dinner guests, offer them a dessert with a glaze finish. White chocolate glaze is especially elegant and combines perfectly with the tropical flavours of mango and coconut. Follow each step of the process closely to achieve a glaze with the perfect consistency and gloss.

FOR THE COCONUT MERINGUE BATONS

1 – Preheat the oven to 90°C (gas mark ¼). Make a Swiss meringue (see page 487) and fill a piping bag fitted with the plain nozzle.
2 – Pipe long lines of meringue over a baking tray lined with baking parchment.
3 – Dust with desiccated coconut and dry out in the oven for 1 hour.

FOR THE JOCONDE "BISCUIT" SPONGE DISCS

4 – Raise the oven temperature to 200°C (gas mark 6). Pour the Joconde "biscuit" sponge (see page 485) into a Swiss roll tin lined with baking parchment.
5 – Use a silicone spatula to evenly spread the batter to a 1 cm thickness. Bake for 6–8 minutes.
6 – Leave to cool, then use the biscuit cutters to cut out six 6-cm discs and six 4.5-cm discs.

FOR THE COCONUT BAVARIAN CREAM

7 – Soften the gelatine leaves in a bowl of cold water. Make the coconut crème anglaise (see page 481), replacing the milk with the coconut cream. Transfer to a bowl immediately.
8 – Squeeze the gelatine to drain and incorporate into the hot coconut crème anglaise. Refrigerate until cold but still runny (the crème anglaise must not set).
9 – Whip the cream to soft peaks. Refrigerate for 30 minutes. Add a third of the whipped cream to the coconut crème anglaise and whisk briskly until smooth. Then fold in the remaining whipped cream.

ASSEMBLY AND DECORATION

10 – Peel the mango and cut into 5-mm dice.

11 – Oil the mould cavities and put 2 teaspoons of the coconut Bavarian cream into each one, spreading it up the sides of the cavities to completely mask.

12 – Put a 4.5-cm Joconde "biscuit" sponge disc over the coconut Bavarian cream in each cavity.

13 – Cover the coconut Bavarian cream with 1 teaspoon diced mango.

14 – Then fill each cavity with the coconut Bavarian cream, to 5 mm below the rim, leaving space for the larger Joconde "biscuit" sponge disc.

15 – Then insert the 6-cm Joconde "biscuit" sponge discs.

16 – Add 1 spoon of coconut Bavarian cream to the disc and smooth with a palette knife to spread evenly. Freeze for 12 hours for the domes to harden completely.

FOR THE COCONUT SWEET PASTRY DISCS

17 – Make the sweet pastry dough (see pages 488 and 489), mixing the ground almonds with the desiccated coconut. Wrap in cling film and rest in the refrigerator for 12 hours.

18 – Preheat the oven to 150°C (gas mark 2). Roll out the dough to about a 4 mm thickness, then use the 6-cm diameter biscuit cutter to cut out discs. Lay the discs on a baking tray lined with a silicone mat. Bake for 15 minutes, then transfer to a rack to cool.

• • •

CHEF'S TIP

Mango can be a difficult fruit to peel, because its flesh adheres tightly to the stone. Cut the fruit lengthways running the knife as closely as possible to the stone. Then use a vegetable peeler to peel the two halves. Peeling this way is easier if the fruit is not too ripe.

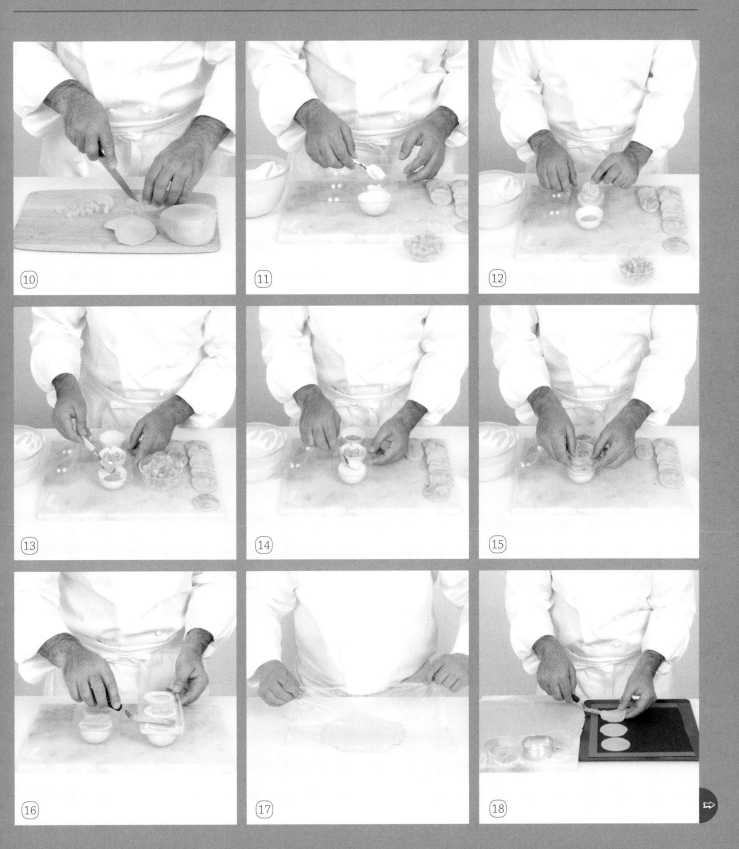

FOR THE WHITE CHOCOLATE GLAZE

19 – Chop the white chocolate. Soften the gelatine leaves in a bowl of cold water. Heat the water in a pan and melt the glucose completely. Add the sugar and stir constantly with a whisk until dissolved. Remove the pan from the heat just before it comes to the boil.

20 – Add the colouring and mix well with a whisk.

21 – Squeeze the gelatine to drain and whisk into the syrup.

22 – Add the cocoa butter and mix well, until completely melted.

23 – Transfer the mixture to a bowl and add the white chocolate. Mix until smooth.

24 – Stir in the condensed milk.

GLAZING

25 – Turn the domes out of the mould and place each one on top of a sweet pastry disc.

26 – Place the domes with its disc on a rack over a container (to collect the excess glaze). Use the glaze when it is smooth and a little warm (35°C). Pour the glaze over each dome, covering uniformly. Pass the palette knife under the dome and slide it across the rack, scraping off the excess glaze and leaving the base smooth.

27 – Refrigerate until it is time to serve. Decorate at the last minute with a coconut meringue baton and a piece of silver leaf.

• • •

CHEF'S TIP

In order to glaze the domes correctly and evenly, like any other pastry, they should be very hard and very cold. The glaze will adhere and harden well.

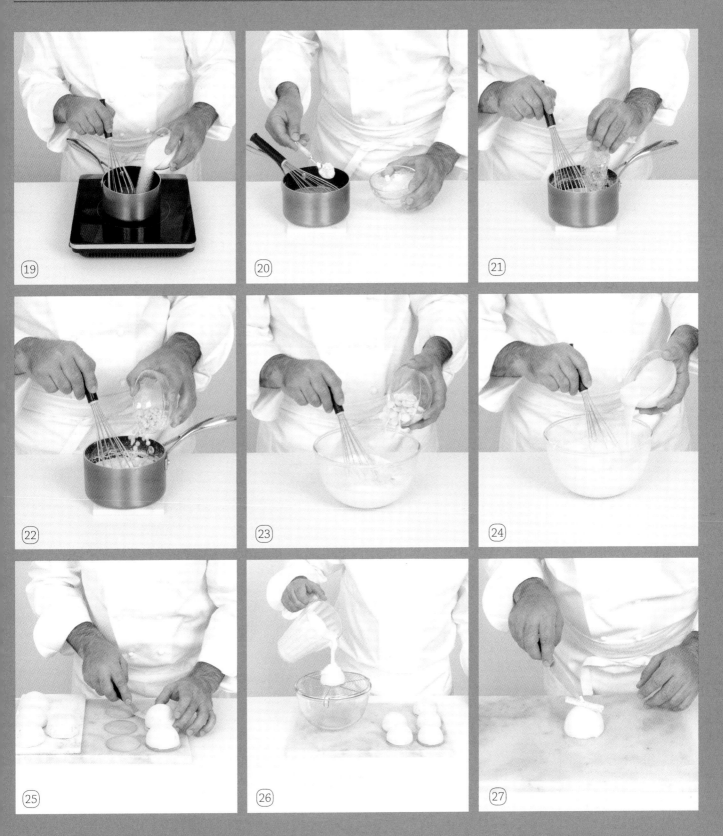

CHOCOLATE AND BLACKCURRANT
domes

Makes 12
———————

PREPARATION TIME: 2 hours + 15 minutes for pastry – BAKING TIME: about 30 minutes – REFRIGERATION TIME: 30 minutes for the pastry
FREEZING TIME: 3 hours 10 minutes – STORAGE: 2 days in the refrigerator
DIFFICULTY: ♧ ♧ ♧

"MI-CUIT" CREAM CHOCOLATE FILLING
1½ eggs (80 g)
65 g sugar
70 g dark chocolate
55 g unsalted butter
1 tsp crème de cassis
1 tsp potato starch

SAVOY "BISCUIT" SPONGE
20 g ground hazelnuts
2 tsp unsweetened cocoa powder
Pinch of baking powder
50 g plain flour
70 g sugar
1½ eggs (80 g)
65 g unsalted butter, melted

BLACKCURRANT COULIS
1½ gelatine leaves (3 g)
140 g blackcurrant purée
1 tablespoon sugar

SYRUP
50 g blackcurrant purée
40 ml water
50 g sugar
2 tsp crème de cassis

CHOCOLATE MOUSSE
170 g dark chocolate
3 egg yolks (60 g)
20 ml water
60 g sugar
300 ml cream

SWEET PASTRY DOUGH
50 g unsalted butter
1 tbsp ground almonds
50 g icing sugar
100 g plain flour
½ egg (25 g)

GLAZE
4½ gelatine leaves (9 g)
150 ml water
80 ml cream
90 g honey
230 g sugar
100 g unsweetened cocoa powder

DECORATION
Apple Blossom micro-greens

EQUIPMENT REQUIRED: 17 x 17 cm baking frame – 6-cm diameter biscuit cutter – 4-cm diameter biscuit cutter
2 piping bags – mould with 7-cm diameter half-sphere cavities – 8-cm diameter biscuit cutter

Micro-greens and flowers for decorating

Use micro-greens and edible flowers to decorate your desserts. They add great originality and a floral touch. They should be used on modern-style pastry creations with clean lines, otherwise their appearance will be overdone. Apple Blossom, with a sharp taste of apple, combines perfectly here with the chocolate and gives the dome a final flourish.

FOR THE "MI-CUIT" CREAM CHOCOLATE FILLING

1 – Preheat the oven to 200°C (gas mark 6). Whisk the eggs with the sugar. Melt the chocolate, add the butter and mix. Incorporate the egg and sugar mixture. Add the crème de cassis and potato starch and mix.

2 – Set the frame on a baking tray lined with baking parchment and fill with the mixture. Spread out well and bake for 5 minutes. Leave to cool.

FOR THE SAVOY "BISCUIT" SPONGE

3 – Keep the oven temperature at 200°C. Mix together the dry ingredients. Whisk the eggs with the sugar in a bowl. Incorporate the dry ingredients, followed by the melted butter.

4 – Spread the mixture over a baking tray lined with baking parchment to form a square about 22 x 22 cm. Bake for 8 minutes and leave to cool.

5 – Lay a sheet of baking parchment over the cold "biscuit" sponge, turn over and and remove the parchment from what was initially the bottom. Use the 6-cm biscuit cutter to cut out 12 discs.

6 – Remove the baking parchment from the "mi-cuit" cream chocolate filling inside the frame and place over another sheet of baking parchment. Run a knife around the inside of the frame to cleanly remove the "mi-cuit" cream chocolate filling from the mould.

7 – Use the 4-cm biscuit cutter to cut out 12 discs.

FOR THE BLACKCURRANT COULIS

8 – Soften the gelatine in a bowl of cold water. Combine the blackcurrant purée with the sugar in a pan and bring to the boil. Remove from the heat, and whisk in the softened gelatine. Refrigerate.

FOR THE SYRUP

9 – Combine the blackcurrant purée, water and sugar in a pan and bring to the boil while stirring with a whisk. Remove from the heat and add the crème de cassis. Transfer to a bowl and refrigerate.

• • •

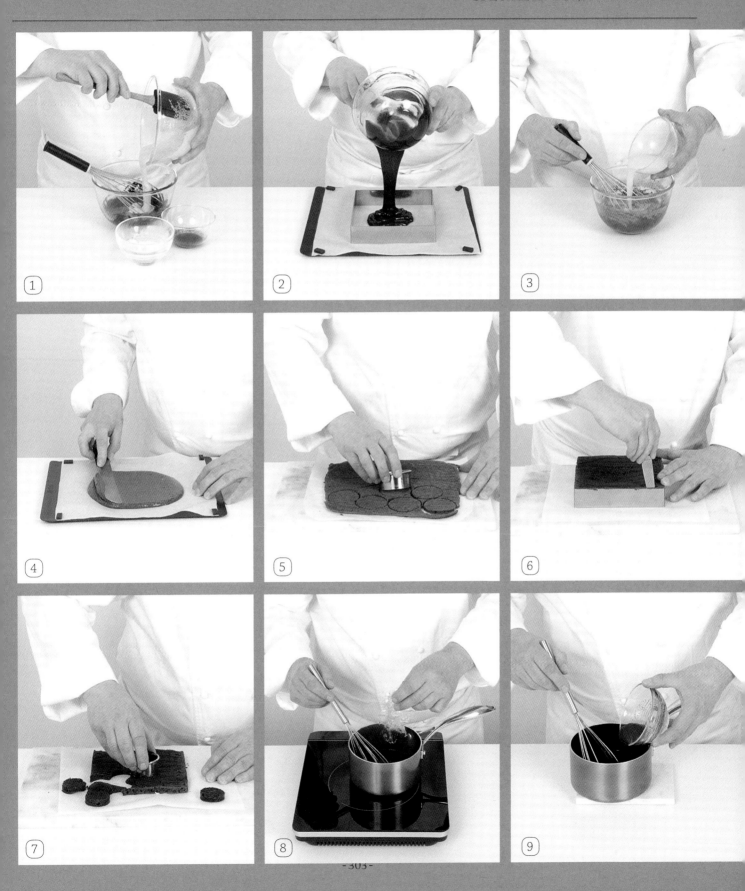

1

2

3

4

5

6

7

8

9

FOR THE CHOCOLATE MOUSSE

10 – Melt the chocolate over a bain-marie. Whisk the egg yolks in a bowl. Make a pâte à bombe by combining the water and sugar in a pan and heating until the temperature reads 118°C on the cooking thermometer. Pour the hot syrup into the egg yolks while whisking briskly until the mixture turns pale, thickens, and cools down.

11 – Whip the cream until it is a little firm and add to the pâte à bombe. Very gently mix.

12 – Pour a third of the mixture into the chocolate and mix with a whisk. Incorporate the remainder and mix until smooth. Transfer to a piping bag.

ASSEMBLY

13 – Pipe chocolate mousse into the mould cavities until one-third full.

14 – Use a tablespoon to spread the mousse over the sides of the cavities, then pipe a ball of mousse into the middle.

15 – Insert a disc of "mi-cuit" cream chocolate filling.

16 – Pipe chocolate mousse all around the disc.

17 – Whisk the blackcurrant coulis to smooth, then fill a piping bag and cut off the end. Pipe a layer of coulis over the "mi-cuit" cream chocolate filling.

18 – Imbibe the Savoy "biscuit" sponge discs with the blackcurrant syrup and insert one into each cavity to close the domes.

• • •

CHEF'S TIP

If you do not have a mould with half-sphere cavities, you can use what you have at home: a muffin tray, cups or small bowls lined with cling film.

19 – Press gently on the Savoy "biscuit" sponge, then smooth with surface with a palette knife to remove the excess mousse. Freeze for 3 hours.

FOR THE SWEET PASTRY DOUGH

20 – Preheat the oven to 170°C (gas mark 3–4). Lightly dust the work surface with flour. Roll out the sweet pastry dough (see pages 488 and 489) to about a 2 mm thickness. Use the 8-cm biscuit cutter to cut out 12 discs. Bake for 15 minutes.

FOR THE GLAZE

21 – Soften the gelatine leaves in a bowl of cold water. Combine the water, cream and honey in a pan and bring to the boil. Mix the sugar and cocoa powder in a bowl, add to the pan and mix. Squeeze the gelatine to drain, whisk into the hot liquid, then pass through a sieve into a bowl.

22 – Cover the surface of the glaze with a sheet of cling film, then remove immediately to eliminate any bubbles. Leave to cool.

23 – Dip the bottom of the mould into a bowl of hot water to remove the domes from the mould, then transfer to a rack. Freeze for 10 minutes, then place the rack over a Swiss roll tin.

24 – Pour the warm glaze over the domes. Pass a palette knife under each dome to remove the excess glaze, leaving a clean base.

FINISHING AND DECORATION

25 – Use a small sieve to dust the pastry discs with icing sugar.

26 – Transfer each dome to a pastry base.

27 – Decorate the domes with Apple Blossom micro-greens.

ALOE VERA AND WILD STRAWBERRY
entremets

Serves 10

PREPARATION TIME: 1 hour 30 minutes – BAKING TIME: 20 minutes – REFRIGERATION TIME: 1 hour – FREEZING TIME: 4 hours
STORAGE: 2 days in the refrigerator

DIFFICULTY: ♟ ♟

HAZELNUT "BISCUIT" SPONGE
4 egg yolks (75 g)
55 g sugar
2½ egg whites (80 g)
20 g sugar
20 g plain flour
35 g potato starch
1 tbsp ground hazelnuts
15 g unsalted butter, melted
30 g chopped hazelnuts

ALOE VERA CRÉMEUX
100 ml cream
2 gelatine leaves (4 g)
200 ml aloe vera juice

Zest of ¼ lemon
1 tablespoon sugar
2 tsp potato starch

ALOE VERA SYRUP
100 ml water
40 ml aloe vera juice
80 g sugar

WILD STRAWBERRY MOUSSE
2 gelatine leaves (4 g)
70 g wild strawberry purée
20 g sugar
1 tsp lemon juice
1 tsp wild strawberry liqueur
200 ml cream

MASCARPONE CHANTILLY CREAM
40 g mascarpone
60 ml cream
2 tsp icing sugar
Knife tip of yellow food colouring

WILD STRAWBERRY GLAZE
5 gelatine leaves (10 g)
150 g fondant
50 g glucose
100 g wild strawberry purée
Knife tip of red food colouring powder

WILD STRAWBERRIES
200 g wild strawberries
50 g neutral glaze

EQUIPMENT REQUIRED: 20-cm diameter and 6-cm deep entremets ring – 18-cm diameter tart ring
10-cm diameter tart ring – piping bag – size 6 plain nozzle

Wild strawberries

Wild strawberries are small red fruit that are a delight to pick in the undergrowth when strolling in the countryside or in a shady corner of the garden. Smaller than strawberries, they are also more fragrant, especially when found in the wild. Wild strawberries can be picked between May and October. The Mara des Bois strawberry is a cultivated variety specifically developed to give 'normal' strawberries a flavour close to that of the wild variety.

FOR THE HAZELNUT "BISCUIT" SPONGE

1 – Preheat the oven to 170°C (gas mark 3–4). Beat the egg yolks with the sugar in a bowl until the mixture turns pale and thickens. Whisk the egg whites until firm enough to cling to the tip of the whisk, then incorporate the sugar while whisking to stiff peaks. Fold in the egg yolk and sugar mixture.
2 – Fold in the dry ingredients, followed by the melted butter and ground hazelnuts.
3 – Place the entremets ring on a baking tray lined with baking parchment and fill with the mixture. Bake for 20 minutes.

FOR THE ALOE VERA CRÉMEUX

4 – Whip the cream to soft peaks. Soften the gelatine leaves in a bowl of cold water. Combine the aloe vera juice with the lemon zest in a pan and heat. Mix the sugar with the potato starch and sprinkle into the pan. Bring to the boil while whisking. Remove the pan from the heat. Squeeze the gelatine to drain and incorporate into the mixture in the pan. Transfer to a bowl, leave to cool a little and fold in the whipped cream.
5 – Cover the bottom of the larger tart ring with cling film and place on the work surface. Use a silicone spatula to spread the aloe vera crémeux evenly inside the ring. Freeze for 2 hours.

FOR THE ALOE VERA SYRUP

6 – Combine the water with the aloe vera juice and sugar in a pan and bring to the boil.

FOR THE WILD STRAWBERRY MOUSSE

7 – Soften the gelatine leaves in a bowl of cold water. Heat the wild strawberry purée with the sugar and lemon juice in a pan. Add the wild strawberry liqueur. Squeeze the gelatine to drain and incorporate. Leave to cool.
8 – Whip the cream to soft peaks and fold half at a time into the wild strawberry mixture.
9 – Slice the hazelnut "biscuit" sponge across the middle into two discs, then trim one of them to be 1 cm smaller than the other.

•••

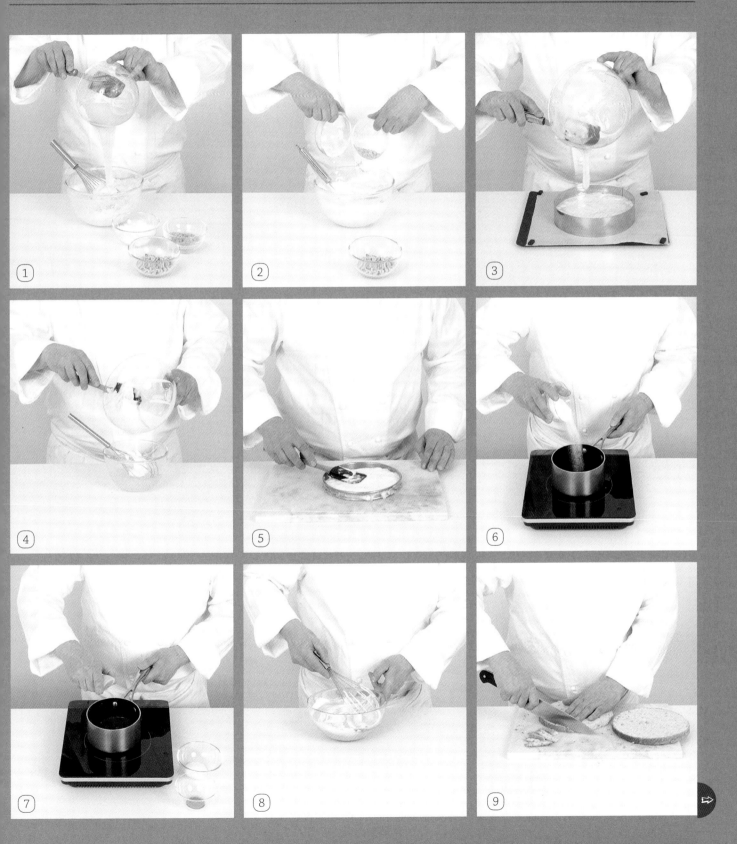

ASSEMBLY

10 – Put the first hazelnut "biscuit" sponge disc inside the entremets ring and brush with the syrup to imbibe. Pipe the wild strawberry mousse around the disc, then over the centre, spreading it evenly and then up the sides to cover completely.

11 – Remove the ring from the aloe vera crémeux and place the insert over the mousse, then add the second hazelnut "biscuit" sponge disc. Imbibe with aloe vera syrup.

12 – Cover with a layer of wild strawberry mousse and smooth with a palette knife. Freeze the entremets for 2 hours.

FOR THE MASCARPONE CHANTILLY CREAM

13 – Whip the mascarpone and cream until firm and clings to the tip of the whisk. Incorporate the sugar, and then the yellow food colouring. Transfer to a piping bag fitted with the plain nozzle.

FOR THE WILD STRAWBERRY GLAZE

14 – Soften the gelatine leaves in a bowl of cold water. Combine the fondant and glucose in a pan and bring to the boil. Add the wild strawberry purée, followed by the red food colouring. Squeeze the gelatine to drain and incorporate into the mixture. Cover with cling film in contact with the glaze and leave to cool.

ASSEMBLY AND DECORATION

15 – Stand the entremets raised over a container. Put the 10-cm tart ring on top, centred. Remove the cling film from the glaze to remove any air bubbles, then pour the glaze over the entremets, around the ring.

16 – Put the wild strawberries into a bowl and mix with a little neutral glaze.

17 – Arrange inside the ring on top of the entremets.

18 – Lift off the ring from around the strawberries and pipe small balls of mascarpone Chantilly cream around them. Refrigerate for 1 hour before serving in order to thaw the entremets.

CHESTNUT, CHOCOLATE
and apricot entremets

Serves 10

PREPARATION TIME: 2 hours – BAKING TIME: 8 minutes – REFRIGERATION TIME: about 45 minutes – FREEZING TIME: 4 hours
STORAGE: 2 days in the refrigerator

DIFFICULTY: 🎩 🎩 🎩

CHESTNUT "BISCUIT" SPONGE
50 g chestnut paste
4½ egg yolks (90 g)
40 g ground almonds
25 g sugar
20 g potato starch
2½ egg whites (80 g)
30 g sugar
1 tbsp unsalted butter, melted
100 g chestnut pieces in syrup

SYRUP
70 ml water
60 g sugar
2 tsp Grand Marnier®

APRICOT CRÉMEUX
130 g sugar
7 g pectin
400 g apricot purée
2 tsp Grand Marnier®

CHESTNUT AND CHOCOLATE GANACHE
50 g chestnut paste
190 ml cream
300 g milk chocolate

GLAZE
2½ gelatine leaves (5 g)
30 ml water
110 g sugar
120 g glucose
130 g milk chocolate
120 g condensed milk
Knife tip of red food colouring
(optional)

DECORATION
50 g chestnut pieces in syrup
3 whole chestnuts in syrup

EQUIPMENT REQUIRED: 20-cm diameter and 4.5-cm deep entremets ring – 18-cm diameter tart ring
piping bag – Rhodoïd® (acetate) sheet

Chestnuts in syrup and candied chestnuts

Either whole or in pieces, chestnuts in syrup are used for entremets and other desserts made with chestnuts. They are preserved in a sugar syrup. Candied chestnuts are chestnuts candied in syrup for 7 days and individually wrapped in gold foil. They first appeared at the court of King Louis XIV, and this confectionery is associated with the end of the year festive celebrations in France.

FOR THE CHESTNUT "BISCUIT" SPONGE

1 – Preheat the oven to 200°C (gas mark 6). Crush the chestnut paste with 1 egg yolk, then loosen. Add the other egg yolks. Incorporate the ground almonds, followed by the 25 g of sugar, then add the potato starch without mixing.

2 – Beat the egg whites, add the 30 g of sugar and mix. Then whisk a third of the egg whites into the chestnut mixture. Incorporate the remaining egg whites and the melted butter.

3 – Using the entremets ring as a guide, spread a 20-cm circle of chestnut "biscuit" sponge mixture on each of two baking trays lined with baking parchment. Sprinkle with the chestnut pieces. Bake for 8 minutes, or until the chestnut "biscuit" sponges are golden.

FOR THE SYRUP

4 – Combine the water and sugar in a pan and bring to the boil. Leave to cool, then add the Grand Marnier®.

FOR THE APRICOT CRÉMEUX

5 – Mix the sugar with the pectin. Warm the apricot purée in a pan, then sprinkle in the sugar and pectin mixture. Bring to the boil, whisking constantly. Leave to cool, then add the Grand Marnier®.

6 – Cover the bottom of the tart ring with cling film and place on a baking tray lined with baking parchment. Pour in the apricot crémeux. Freeze for 1 hour.

FOR THE CHOCOLATE AND CHESTNUT GANACHE

7 – Put the chestnut paste into a bowl. Bring the cream to the boil in a pan, then pour a third into the paste while whisking to loosen. Incorporate the remaining cream.

8 – Add the chopped chocolate and mix with a whisk until the chocolate is fully melted. Refrigerate for 45 minutes.

ASSEMBLY

9 – Turn the "biscuit" sponge discs over onto the work surface and remove the baking parchment. Trim until slightly smaller than the entremets ring. Brush both discs with syrup to imbibe.

• • •

10 – Cut out a strip of Rhodoïd® the same size as the circumference and height of the entremets ring and line the inside of the ring. Place the ring on a cardboard cake board and put one imbibed chestnut "biscuit" sponge disc inside.

11 – Whisk the chocolate and chestnut ganache until emulsified and transfer to the piping bag. Cut off the end of the bag and pipe a ring of ganache around and over the edge of the imbibed chestnut "biscuit" sponge disc.

12 – Use a silicone spatula to spread the chocolate and chestnut ganache up the sides of the entremets ring, then pipe a layer of chocolate and chestnut ganache over the chestnut "biscuit" sponge to halfway up the ring. Smooth with the silicone spatula.

13 – Remove the tart ring from the apricot crémeux and remove the cling film. Put the insert into the entremets ring.

14 – Cover with the second chestnut "biscuit" sponge disc and fill the ring to the top with the remaining chocolate and chestnut ganache. Smooth with a palette knife. Freeze for 3 hours.

FOR THE GLAZE

15 – Soften the gelatine leaves in a bowl of cold water. Combine the water, sugar and glucose in a pan and bring to the boil. Squeeze the gelatine to drain and put into a bowl with the milk chocolate and condensed milk. Pour over the hot liquid. Fold until smooth, then add the food colouring. Cover with cling film in contact with the glaze and leave to cool.

GLAZING AND DECORATING

16 – Remove the ring and the Rhodoïd® strip from the entremets, and transfer to a rack inside a Swiss roll tin. Remove the cling film from the glaze to remove any air bubbles, then pour all the glaze over the entremets, first over the sides and then over the middle. Smooth the surface with the palette knife.

17 – Refrigerate the entremets on the rack for 2 minutes to set the glaze, then lift the entremets and run the palette knife over the bottom to remove the excess glaze, leaving it clean. Put the entremets on a cardboard cake board.

18 – Decorate the base of the entremets with chestnut pieces. Brush the whole chestnuts with a little glaze and arrange on the top of the entremets.

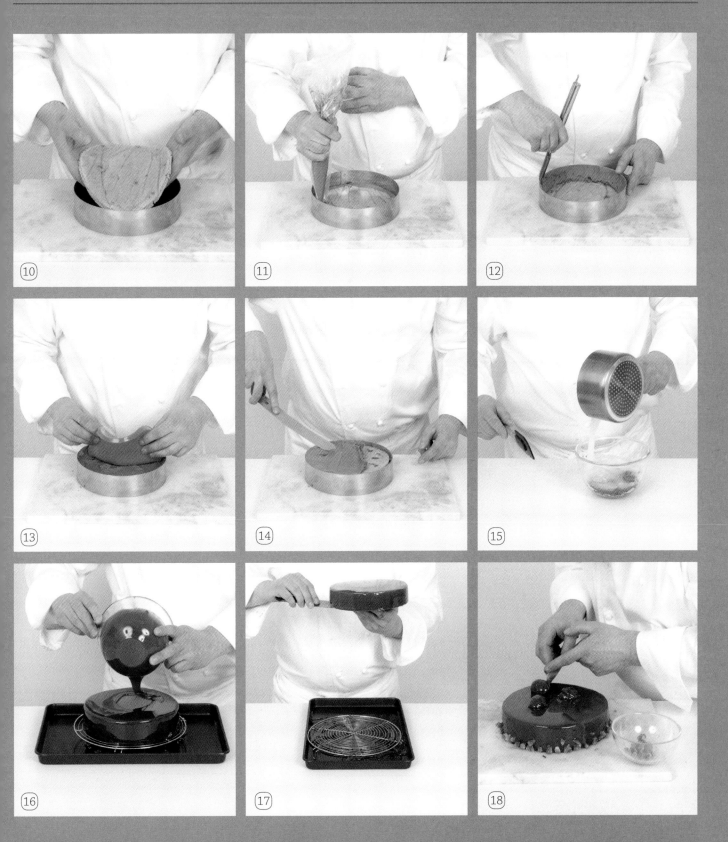

THREE KINGS' CAKE

Serves 10

PREPARATION TIME: 30 minutes + 2 hours 40 minutes for the pastry – REFRIGERATION TIME: 50 minutes – RESTING TIME: 45 minutes
BAKING TIME: 40 minutes – STORAGE: 2 days covered in cling film

DIFFICULTY: ♙ ♙

PUFF PASTRY
300 g plain flour
1½ tsp salt
70 g unsalted butter, melted
160 ml water
250 g dry butter (84% fat)

ALMOND CREAM
70 g unsalted butter
70 g sugar
70 g ground almonds
1 large egg (60 g)
1 tbsp cornflour
1½ tsp rum

1 beaten egg to glaze

SYRUP
25 ml water
25 g sugar

EQUIPMENT REQUIRED: Piping bag – size 10 plain nozzle – 20-cm diameter tart ring
26-cm diameter tart ring – pastry brush

Almond cream or frangipane

Confusion between almond cream and frangipane is quite common, particularly when it comes to the three kings' cake, because both can be used to make this dessert. Almond cream is made from butter, sugar, eggs and ground almonds. Frangipane is almond cream with added pastry cream (about ⅓ pastry cream to ⅔ almond cream).

FOR THE ALMOND CREAM

1 – Whisk the butter in a bowl to a creamy consistency. Add the sugar and whisk well.

2 – Add the ground almonds and mix well.

3 – Incorporate the egg, followed by the cornflour and then the rum and mix. Transfer to a piping bag fitted with the plain nozzle and refrigerate for 20 minutes.

FOR THE SYRUP

4 – Combine the water and sugar in a pan and bring to the boil. Leave to cool.

ASSEMBLY

5 – Make the puff pastry (see page 491).

6 – Roll out the dough to a 1.5-cm thickness and cut into 2 rectangles. Wrap each rectangle in cling film and refrigerate for 30 minutes.

7 – Roll out each rectangle to a 2–3-mm thickness and form two squares about 30 cm.

8 – Lay one dough square over a sheet of baking parchment and lightly press with the 22-cm tart ring to leave a circular impression.

9 – Brush around the marked-out circle with the beaten egg.

• • •

> ### CHEF'S TIP
>
> For maximum enjoyment, the cake should be eaten warm, but it is also delicious served cold.

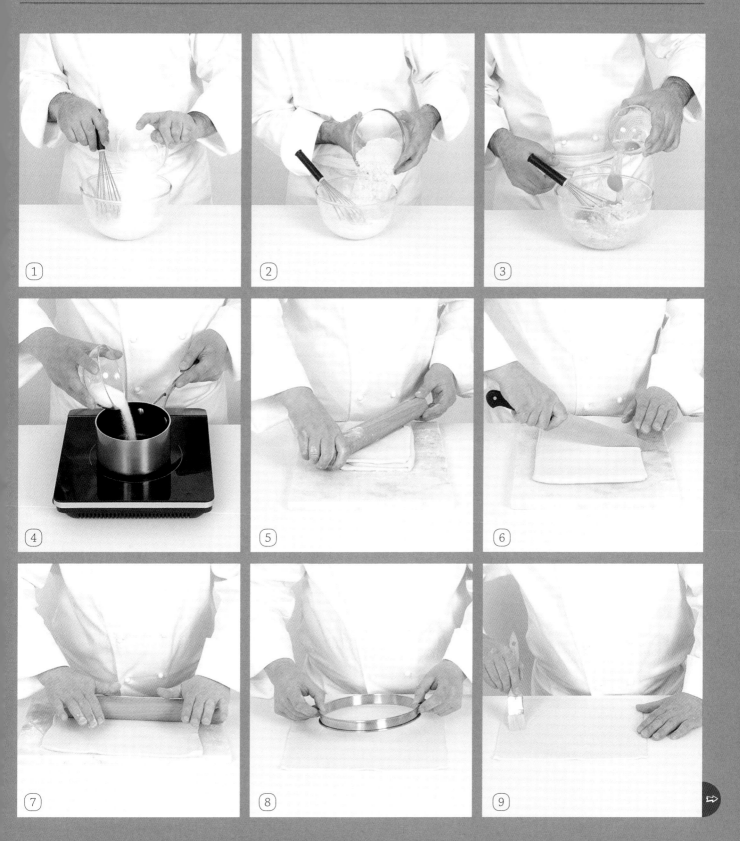

10 – Pipe the almond cream in a spiral inside the marked-out circle, leaving a 2-cm-wide margin.

11 – Slip a porcelain figurine into the almond cream.

12 – Carefully lay the second dough square over the top of the first.

13 – Press down on the edges to encase the cream and remove any air.

14 – Use the 26-cm tart ring to cut out the cake (in order to have a margin of about 2 cm around the almond cream). Remove the excess dough.

15 – Use the back of a knife to crimp the edges.

16 – Transfer the cake to a baking tray. Brush all over with the egg glaze, except for the crimped edge. Rest for 15 minutes, then repeat the process.

17 – Use a knife to score the top of the cake with lines radiating from the centre towards the edges. Rest again for 30 minutes. Preheat the oven to 210°C (gas mark 6–7). Bake for about 15 minutes until the cake is golden, then lower the oven temperature to 180°C (gas mark 4) and bake for 25 more minutes.

18 – When the cake comes out of the oven, brush with the syrup.

CHOCOLATE AND PISTACHIO
opera cake

Serves 8

PREPARATION TIME: 1 hour – BAKING TIME: 20 minutes – REFRIGERATION TIME: 1 hour – STORAGE: 2 days in the refrigerator

DIFFICULTY: ♙ ♙

PISTACHIO JOCONDE "BISCUIT" SPONGE

90 g raw almond paste 50%

45 g pistachio paste

2½ egg yolks (50 g)

½ egg (30 g)

20 g plain flour

20 g unsalted butter, melted and warm

3 egg whites (100 g)

35 g sugar

20 g unsalted butter for the frames

CHOCOLATE GANACHE

200 ml cream

200 g dark couverture chocolate (54% cocoa)

20 g unsalted butter

IMBIBING SYRUP

150 ml water

150 g sugar

30 ml kirsch

PISTACHIO CHANTILLY CREAM

150 ml cream

1 tbsp icing sugar

20 g pistachio paste

1 tsp dessert jelly

DECORATION

Icing sugar

Pistachios

EQUIPMENT NEEDED: Three 17-cm square baking frames – piping bag – pastry brush – size 8 plain nozzle

The opera cake, a French classic

The opera cake is a rectangular chocolate and coffee pastry. This French classic comprises three successive layers of Joconde "biscuit" sponge imbibed with coffee syrup, filled with coffee buttercream and ganache. The French word 'Opéra' is typically piped over the top of the cake.

FOR THE PISTACHIO JOCONDE "BISCUIT" SPONGE

1 – Preheat the oven to 200°C (gas mark 6). Line two baking trays with baking parchment. Butter the three pastry frames. Whisk the almond and pistachio pastes in a bowl.

2 – Add the egg yolks and half egg and mix well. Then incorporate the flour and warm melted butter.

3 – Whisk the egg whites until firm, then incorporate the sugar while whisking to stiff peaks.

4 – Fold the egg whites into the almond and pistachio mixture.

5 – Put two pastry frames on one baking tray and the third on a second baking tray. Pour the mixture into the three frames and smooth with a palette knife.

6 – Bake separately for about 10 minutes. Leave to cool on a rack, then remove the frames.

FOR THE CHOCOLATE GANACHE

7 – Leave the cream to come to room temperature. Melt the chocolate in a bowl over a bain-marie. Pour into the cream and mix.

8 – Add the butter and mix until smooth.

FOR THE SYRUP

9 – Combine the water and sugar in a pan and bring to the boil. Leave the syrup to cool. Add the kirsch.

> ### CHEF'S TIP
>
> To make your own version of the opera cake, feel free to change the flavours, for instance with strawberry, raspberry or passion fruit. You can also replace the buttercream with a flavoured Chantilly cream, piped for a more modern finish.

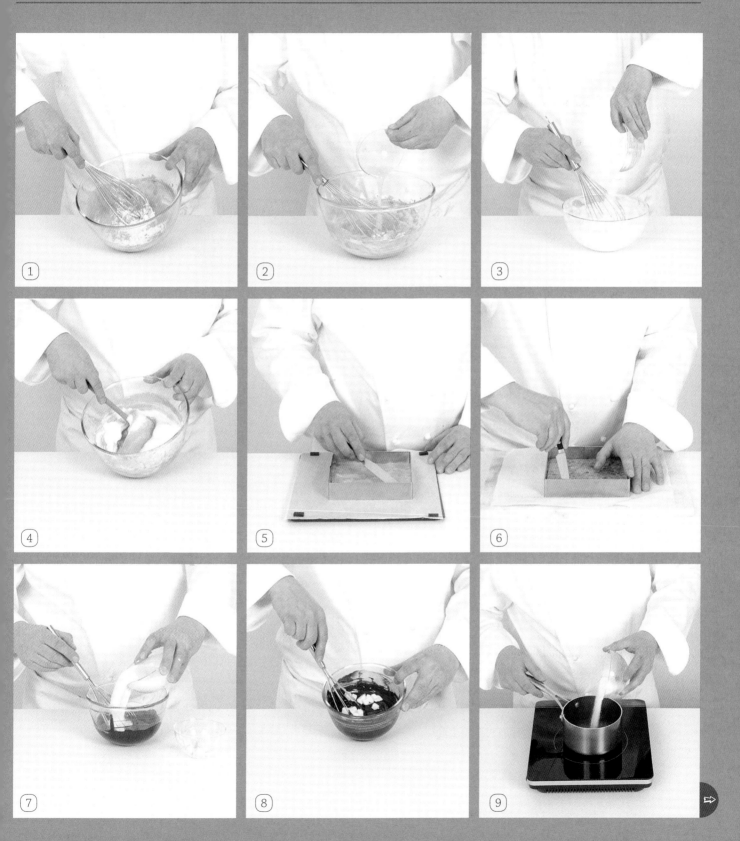

ASSEMBLY

10 – Clean a baking frame and place on a baking tray lined with baking parchment. Lay one of the pistachio Joconde "biscuit" sponges inside the frame and brush with syrup to imbibe.

11 – Pour in a layer of chocolate ganache and smooth with a palette knife.

12 – Cover with the second Joconde "biscuit" sponge and brush with the syrup.

13 – Pour in another layer of chocolate ganache and smooth with the palette knife.

14 – Cover with the third Joconde "biscuit" sponge.

FOR THE PISTACHIO CHANTILLY CREAM

15 – Whip the cream with the icing sugar, pistachio paste and dessert jelly until it is firm and clings to the tip of the whisk. Transfer to the piping bag fitted with the plain nozzle.

ASSEMBLY AND DECORATION

16 – Remove the frame from the entremets (lightly heat the frame with a chef's blow torch to make the operation easier). Cut off the tip of the piping bag and spread a layer of Chantilly cream over the top of the entremets. Smooth with the palette knife.

17 – Make another layer of Chantilly cream by piping a line from side to side over the entire surface.

18 – Refrigerate for 1 hour, dust the opera cake with icing sugar and decorate with pistachios before serving.

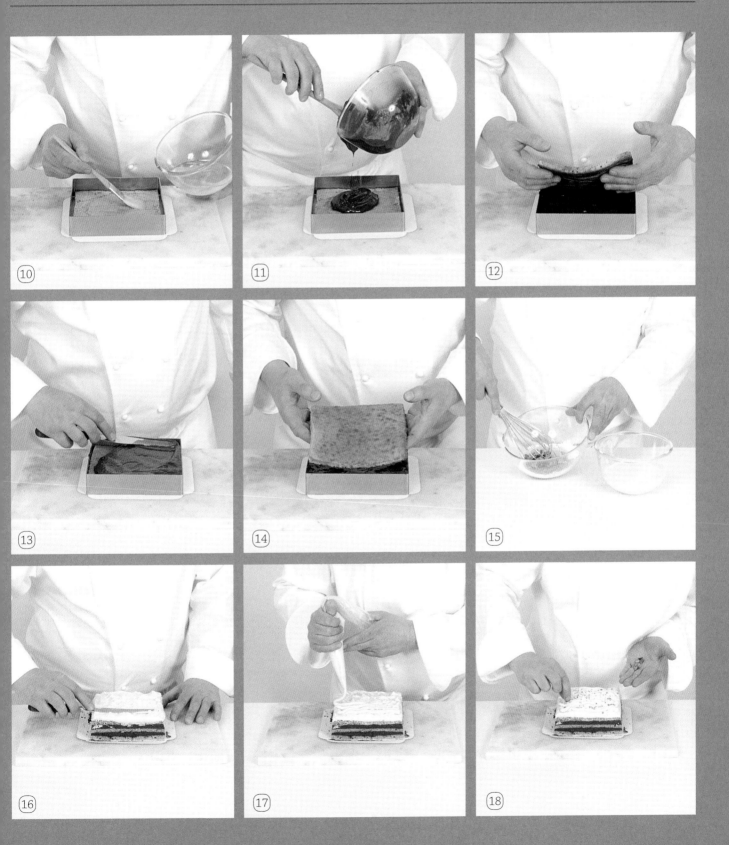

CHOCOLATE AND BERRY
tart

Serves 6–8

PREPARATION TIME: 2 hours + 15 minutes for the pastry – REFRIGERATION TIME: 30 minutes for the pastry + 10 minutes after lining the tart ring – BAKING TIME: 35 minutes – FREEZING TIME: 3 hours – STORAGE: 2 days in the refrigerator

DIFFICULTY: 🎩 🎩

SWEET PASTRY DOUGH
150 g plain flour
75 g unsalted butter
75 g icing sugar
20 g ground almonds
1 small egg (30 g)

Unsalted butter for the mould

ALMOND CREAM
50 g unsalted butter
Zest of ¼ lemon
40 g sugar

50 g ground almonds
1 small egg (40 g)

120 g raspberries

CHOCOLATE AND BERRY MOUSSE
30 g blackcurrant purée
50 g wild strawberry purée
40 g raspberry purée
2 tsp sugar
1 tbsp dessert jelly
70 g milk chocolate
200 ml cream

CHOCOLATE GLAZE
2½ gelatine leaves (5 g)
55 g unsweetened cocoa powder
40 ml water
50 g glucose
50 ml cream
110 g sugar

DECORATION
250 g raspberries

EQUIPMENT REQUIRED: 20-cm diameter tart ring – 16-cm diameter plastic mould

Chocolate glaze

Commonly used by professionals for its stunning appearance, chocolate glaze is the perfect finishing touch for desserts, even the simplest. Also known as 'mirror glaze', it gives a smooth and glossy aspect to entremets, yule logs and individual pastries, as well as a melt-in-the-mouth texture and intense cocoa flavour that delight the palate.

CHOCOLATE AND BERRY tart

FOR THE TART CASE

1 – Lightly flour the work surface and roll out the sweet pastry dough (see pages 488 and 489) to about a thickness of 3 mm. Using the tart ring as a guide, cut out a disc with a diameter 5 cm larger than that of the ring, 25 cm.
2 – Preheat the oven to 180°C (gas mark 4). Butter the tart ring, line with the dough (see page 493) and place it on a baking tray lined with baking parchment. Refrigerate for 10 minutes.
3 – Blind bake the tart case (see page 494) for 10 minutes.

FOR THE ALMOND CREAM

4 – Lower the oven temperature to 170°C (gas mark 3–4). Whisk the room temperature butter in a bowl to a creamy consistency, then whisk in the lemon zest, sugar and ground almonds. Finally, incorporate the egg.
5 – Pour the almond cream into the tart case and smooth using the back of a tablespoon.
6 – Insert raspberries into the almond cream and bake for 25 minutes.

FOR THE CHOCOLATE AND BERRY MOUSSE

7 – Combine the three purées in a pan and heat, then add the sugar and dessert jelly together. Heat to a simmer, stirring constantly with a whisk.
8 – Chop the chocolate and place in a bowl, pour the hot purée mixture over it. Mix well until smooth. Leave to cool a little.
9 – Whisk the cream to soft peaks, then fold into the chocolate and berry mixture.

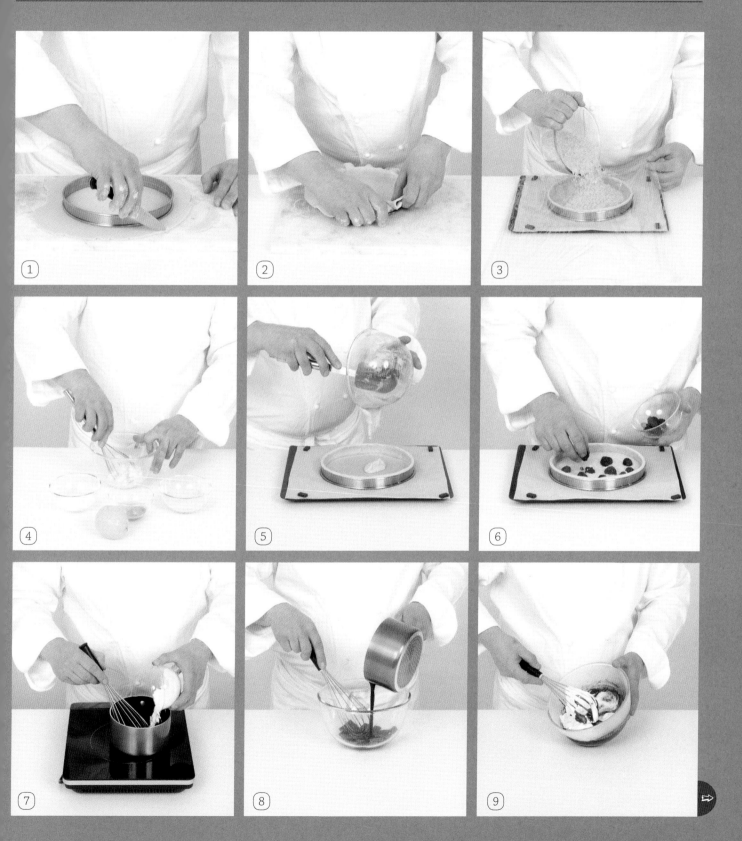

ASSEMBLY

10 – Fill the plastic mould to the top with the chocolate and berry mousse.

11 – Smooth with a palette knife, then freeze for 3 hours for the mousse to harden completely.

12 – Spread the remaining mousse inside the tart case, over the almond cream.

CHEF'S TIP

To glaze the mousse insert, you can also place it on a rack on a Swiss roll tin or other container, which will allow the excess glaze to be collected easily and the work surface kept clean.

FOR THE CHOCOLATE GLAZE

13 – Soften the gelatine leaves in a bowl of cold water. Squeeze to drain and combine with the cocoa powder in another bowl. Combine the water, glucose, cream and sugar in a pan and bring to the boil, then pour into the bowl.

14 – Mix to a very smooth consistency, pass through a sieve and cover with cling film in direct contact with the glaze. Leave to cool.

GLAZING AND DECORATING

15 – Turn out the frozen mousse insert by cutting away the plastic in several places.

16 – Cover the work surface with cling film. Put the mousse on a cardboard cake board and place on a bowl to raise above the work surface. Remove the cling film from the chocolate glaze to remove any air bubbles, then pour all the glaze evenly over the mousse insert.

17 – Run a palette knife between the mousse and the cardboard, then transfer the mousse to the tart case. Collect the surplus glaze and set aside for the decoration.

18 – Decorate around the insert with raspberries. Put the glaze into a paper cone and use it to fill the raspberries.

CHOCOLATE AND COFFEE
macaronnade

Serves 8

PREPARATION TIME: 1 hour 30 minutes – FREEZING TIME: 3 hours 10 minutes – BAKING TIME: 30 minutes

DIFFICULTY: ♙ ♙ ♙

FLOURLESS CHOCOLATE "MI-CUIT"
1 large egg (60 g)
60 g sugar
1½ tsp Trablit® coffee extract
55 g dark chocolate (55% cocoa)
55 g unsalted butter

COFFEE MACARONNADE
2 egg whites (60 g)
A few drops of lemon juice
1 tbsp sugar
1½ tsp Trablit® coffee extract
120 g icing sugar
85 g ground almonds

COFFEE CRÉMEUX
1¾ gelatine leaves (3.5 g)
80 ml cream
2 egg yolks (40 g)
40 g sugar
1 tbsp Trablit® coffee extract
100 ml cream

GLAZE
1¾ gelatine leaves (3.5 g)
60 g white couverture chocolate
55 g condensed milk
1 tbsp cocoa butter
25 ml water
50 g glucose
50 g sugar
2 tsp Trablit® coffee extract

MASCARPONE AND COFFEE CREAM
70 g mascarpone
200 ml cream
1 tbsp icing sugar
1½ tsp Trablit® coffee extract

DECORATION
20 g white chocolate

EQUIPMENT REQUIRED: 2 piping bags – size 12 plain nozzle – two 20-cm diameter tart rings – cardboard cake board cooking thermometer – Saint-Honoré nozzle

Coffee extract

Stimulating to drink, and to eat, coffee comes in many different forms and it has been used to flavour desserts for many years. In the form of coffee extract, it adds intensity to entremets and combines well with chocolate, enhancing its flavours. Its unique aromas arouse the taste buds and heighten every creation to which it is added.

FOR THE FLOURLESS CHOCOLATE "MI-CUIT"

1 – Preheat the oven to 220°C (gas mark 7). Mix the egg with the sugar and coffee extract in a bowl. Melt the chocolate over a bain-marie, then add the butter and mix well. Incorporate into the egg and sugar mixture.
2 – Set one of the tart rings on a baking tray lined with baking parchment and fill with the mixture.
3 – Use a silicone spatula to spread well to a uniform thickness. Bake for 5 minutes. Leave to cool, then freeze for 10 minutes to make it easier to turn out of the ring.

FOR THE COFFEE MACARONNADE

4 – Lower the oven temperature to 170°C (gas mark 3–4). Whisk the egg whites with the lemon juice to firm peaks that cling to the tip of the whisk. Incorporate the sugar and coffee extract.
5 – Mix the icing sugar with the ground almonds in a bowl, then fold into the beaten egg whites half at a time. Mix without working the meringue.
6 – Transfer to a piping bag fitted with the plain nozzle. Draw a 22-cm diameter circle on a sheet of baking parchment and lay on a baking tray. Pipe the macaronnade mixture in a spiral inside the circle. Bake for 25 minutes.

FOR THE COFFEE CRÉMEUX

7 – Soften the gelatine leaves in a bowl of cold water. Make a coffee crème anglaise (see page 481), adding the coffee extract to the blanched egg and sugar mixture.
8 – Squeeze the gelatine to drain and incorporate into the hot coffee crème anglaise. Leave to cool.
9 – Whip the cream until it is firm and clings to the end of the whisk. Add a little to the coffee crème anglaise and mix well. Gradually fold in the remainder.

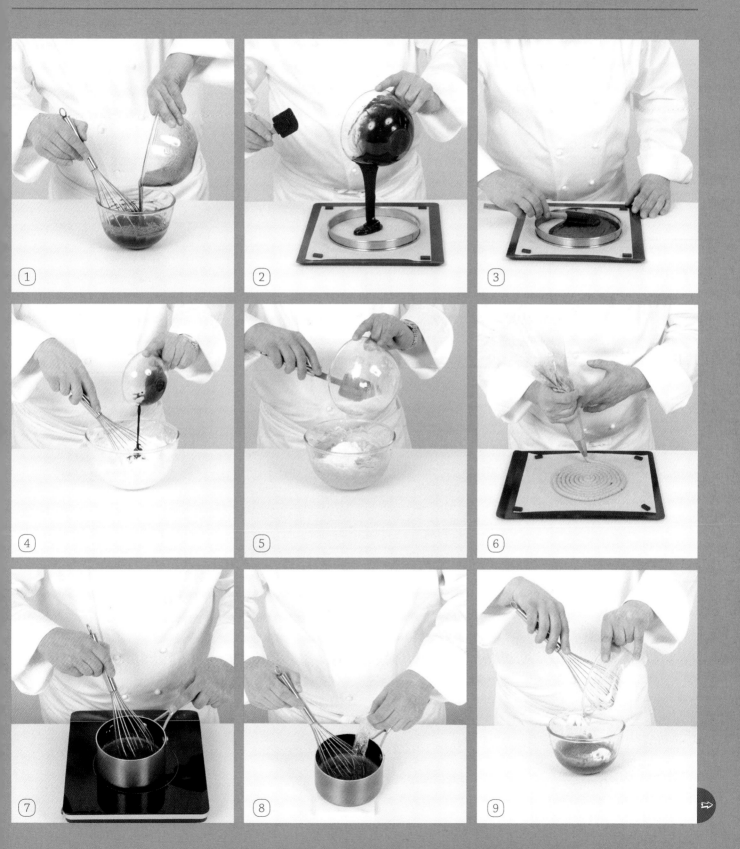

10 – Cover the bottom of the second tart ring with cling film and place on a cardboard cake board. Pour the coffee crème anglaise into the ring. Freeze for 3 hours.

FOR THE GLAZE

11 – Soften the gelatine leaves in a bowl of cold water. Put the white couverture chocolate, condensed milk and cocoa butter in a bowl. Combine the water, glucose, sugar and coffee extract in a pan and bring to the boil, then pour into the bowl.

12 – Squeeze the gelatine to drain and incorporate. Cover the glaze with cling film in direct contact with the glaze. Leave to cool until the cooking thermometer reads 25°C.

FOR THE MASCARPONE AND COFFEE CREAM

13 – Put the mascarpone into a bowl. Pour in a little of the cream and whisk to soften the mascarpone. Pour in the remaining cream and whisk until soft. Fold in the icing sugar and coffee extract with a whisk. Transfer to a piping bag fitted with the Saint-Honoré nozzle.

ASSEMBLY AND DECORATION

14 – Put the flourless chocolate "mi-cuit" disc on top of the frozen coffee crémeux disc.

15 – Cover the work surface with cling film, then turn the tart ring over onto a rack. Remove the cling film from the crémeux, and then the tart ring. Remove the cling film from the glaze to remove any air bubbles. Pour all the glaze over the entremets, then smooth with a palette knife to remove the excess, leaving a uniform surface.

16 – Quickly place the entremets on the coffee macaronnade disc.

17 – Melt the white chocolate and transfer to a paper cone. Decorate the top of the entremets with streaks of melted white chocolate.

18 – Pipe coffee mascarpone cream around the side of the entremets, over the exposed part of the coffee macaronnade.

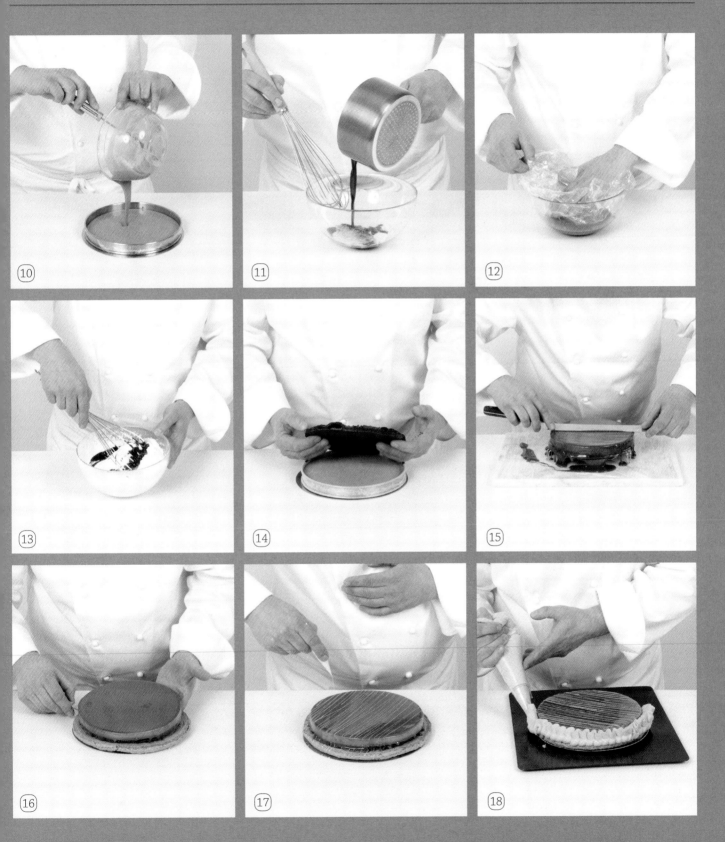

BISCUITS & SMALL CAKES

COCONUT-RASPBERRY
financiers

Makes 20 financiers

PREPARATION TIME: 20 minutes – COOKING TIME: 15 minutes – STORAGE: 2 days in an airtight container

DIFFICULTY: ♙

<u>FINANCIER MIXTURE</u>
140 g unsalted butter
260 g icing sugar
9 egg whites (270 g)
60 g ground almonds
40 g desiccated coconut
20 g honey
100 g plain flour
1 tsp baking powder
250 g raspberries

<u>DECORATION</u>
30 g desiccated coconut

<u>EQUIPMENT NEEDED:</u> Piping bag - silicone financier mould 7.5 x 4 cm

Financiers

A small oval or rectangular cake, perfect for teatime, the financier is known for its soft texture and delicate almond flavour. It is made with ground almonds, egg whites, flour, sugar and melted butter; nut brown butter may be used give the financier an additional dimension of flavour. Easy and quick to prepare, they can be made miniature and with different flavours.

FOR THE FINANCIER MIXTURE

1 – Preheat the oven to 180°C (gas mark 4). Melt the butter in a saucepan. Put the icing sugar in a bowl, add the egg whites, and whisk.

2 – Add the ground almonds.

3 – Add the desiccated coconut and mix well.

4 – Add the honey and mix.

5 – Mix in the flour and baking powder.

6 – Finally, add the melted butter and mix.

ASSEMBLY AND DECORATION

7 – Transfer the mixture to a piping bag, cut off the end and pipe into the imprint, filling each three-quarters full.

8 – Press 2 raspberries into the mixture in each imprint.

9 – Sprinkle with a little desiccated coconut. Bake for 15 minutes, or until the financiers are golden brown.

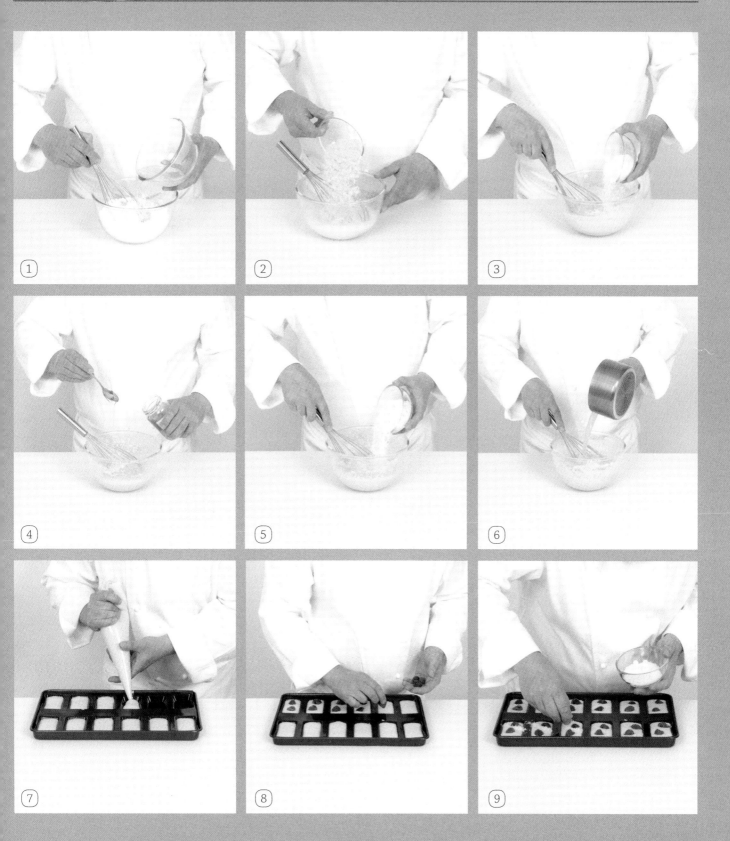

COCONUT MACARONS

Makes 20 macarons

PREPARATION TIME: 1 hour – COOKING TIME: 18 minutes – CHILLING TIME: 1 hour + overnight – STORAGE: 3 days in the refrigerator

DIFFICULTY: ♢

MACARON MIXTURE
4 egg whites (130 g)
60 g sugar
Knife tip of brown food colouring
180 g ground almonds
320 g icing sugar

COCONUT FILLING
90 ml cream
130 ml coconut milk
1 tbsp cream
1 tbsp potato starch
95 g white chocolate
2 tbsp Malibu®
110 g unsalted butter

EQUIPMENT NEEDED: 2 piping bags – size 8 star nozzle

Colour the macarons

You may use liquid, powder or gel food colouring to bring a little colour to your macaron shells. The colour is usually mixed in once the whites have been whisked and made into a meringue. A wide variety of food colourings are available, allowing you to colour your macarons however you wish. If you're just starting out, opt for a powder, as unlike liquid food colouring, these will not change the consistency of the mixture.

COCONUT MACARONS

FOR THE MACARON MIXTURE

1 – Whisk the egg whites until firm, then incorporate the sugar to make a meringue. Add the food colouring and mix well, distributing the colour evenly.

2 – Sift the dry ingredients together, then add to the meringue.

3 – Incorporate the dry ingredients using a silicone spatula, mix slowly, cutting straight down to the bottom of the bowl and lifting up the contents. Bring the spatula up the side of the bowl and fold back to the centre while giving the bowl a quarter turn with your other hand. Continue to fold until the meringue loses volume and becomes smooth and shiny (*Macaronnage*), transfer to a piping bag fitted with the plain nozzle.

4 – Line a baking tray with baking parchment and pipe balls about 4 cm in diameter onto the tray, in staggered rows to keep separate. Tap the base of the tray lightly to remove any air bubbles from the mixture. Leave to crust for 30 minutes. Preheat the oven to 170°C (gas mark 3-4) and bake for 18 minutes.

FOR THE COCONUT FILLING

5 – In a saucepan, combine the 90 ml cream and the coconut milk and bring to the boil. Separately, mix the tablespoon of cream with the potato starch, then add to the saucepan. Bring to the boil, whisking constantly.

6 – Pour the mixture over the white chocolate, add the Malibu® and whisk together.

7 – Leave the mixture to cool, then add the butter in pieces. Mix the coconut filling with a hand-held blender and refrigerate for 1 hour.

ASSEMBLY

8 – Transfer the coconut filling to a piping bag with the star nozzle and pipe a small ball on half of the macaron shells.

9 – Next, top each piece with another macaron shell and press together gently. Refrigerate the macarons overnight before serving.

SPICED MANGO MACARONS

Makes 20 macarons

PREPARATION TIME: 45 minutes – COOKING TIME: 18 minutes – CHILLING TIME: 1 hour + overnight
STORAGE: 3 days in the refrigerator

DIFFICULTY : 🎩 🎩

MACARON MIXTURE	SPICED MANGO FILLING
4 egg whites (130 g)	60 ml cream
60 g sugar	130 g mango purée
Knife tip of yellow food colouring	Knife tip of quatre-épices spice blend
180 g ground almonds	Knife tip of vanilla powder
320 g icing sugar	Zest of ¼ lime
	30 ml cream
	25 g potato starch
	100 g white chocolate
	110 g unsalted butter

EQUIPMENT NEEDED: 2 piping bags – size 8 plain nozzle

"Macaronnage"

Essential step for obtaining smooth and shiny shells, the macaronnage consists of decreasing the volume of the egg white meringue. This technical gesture is done by hand and will enable air bubbles to escape from the preparation ensuring that the macarons are smooth and homogeneous once removed from the oven.

SPICED MANGO MACARONS

step-by-step

FOR THE MACARON MIXTURE

1 – Whisk the egg whites until firm, then add the sugar to make a meringue. Add the food colouring and mix well to distribute the colour evenly.

2 – Sift the dry ingredients together, then add to the meringue.

3 – Incorporate the dry ingredients using a silicone spatula, mix slowly, cutting straight down to the bottom of the bowl and lifting up the contents. Bring the spatula up the side of the bowl and fold back to the centre while giving the bowl a quarter turn with your other hand. Continue to fold until the meringue loses volume and becomes smooth and shiny (*Macaronnage*), transfer to a piping bag fitted with the plain nozzle.

4 – Line a baking tray with baking parchment and pipe balls about 4 cm in diameter onto the tray, in staggered rows to keep separate. Tap the base of the tray lightly to remove any air bubbles from the mixture. Leave to crust for 30 minutes. Preheat the oven to 170°C (gas mark 3-4) and bake for 18 minutes.

CHEF'S TIP

You can add a knife tip of cream of tartar or a few drops of lemon juice to the egg whites to stabilise them.

FOR THE SPICED MANGO FILLING

5 – In a saucepan, combine the 60 ml cream with the mango purée, quatre-épices spice blend, vanilla powder and lime zest. Separately, mix the 30 ml cream with the potato starch, then add to the saucepan. Bring to the boil, whisking constantly.

6 – Pour the mixture over the white chocolate and whisk together.

7 – Leave the mixture to cool, then add the butter. Blend the spiced mango filling using a hand-held blender and refrigerate for 1 hour.

ASSEMBLY

8 – Transfer the spiced mango filling to a piping bag with the plain nozzle and pipe a small ball on half of the macaron shells.

9 – Next, top each piece with another macaron shell and press together gently. Refrigerate the macarons overnight before serving.

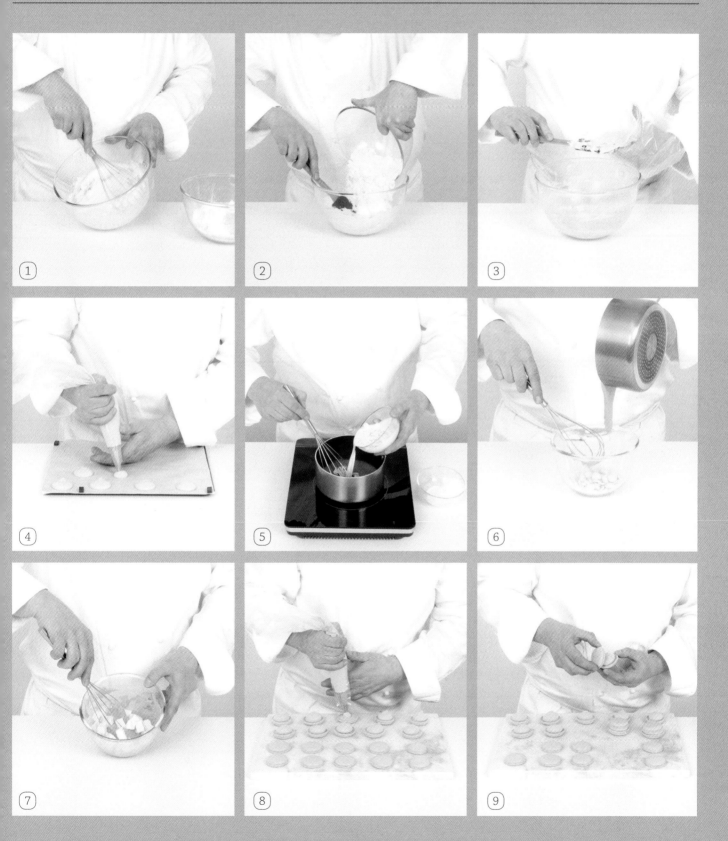

CHOCOLATE
financiers

Makes 10 financiers

PREPARATION TIME: 45 minutes – COOKING TIME: 10 minutes – FREEZING TIME: 1 hour

DIFFICULTY: 🎩

CHOCOLATE FINANCIER MIXTURE
130 g icing sugar
50 g ground almonds
20 g unsweetened cocoa powder
2 tsp honey
4½ egg whites (135 g)
30 g plain flour
Pinch of baking powder
70 g unsalted butter, melted

CHOCOLATE GANACHE
150 g dark chocolate (70% cocoa)
150 ml cream

COATING
300 g chocolate compound coating

EQUIPMENT NEEDED: 2 piping bags – silicone financier mould 7.5 x 4 cm – paper cone

Decorating with a paper cone

A simple way to give an elegant finish to cakes both big and small is to decorate them with melted chocolate or ganache: stripes, writing or other designs. To do so, make a small paper cone, pour in the melted chocolate and decorate your creation however you like. This decoration will be even more refined if you first coat your cake with tempered chocolate or chocolate compound coating.

CHOCOLATE financiers

FOR THE CHOCOLATE FINANCIER MIXTURE

1 – Preheat the oven to 200°C (gas mark 6). In a bowl, combine the icing sugar, ground almonds, unsweetened cocoa powder and honey.
2 – Add the egg whites, half at a time, whisking well between additions.
3 – Mix in the flour and baking powder, then add the melted butter.
4 – Transfer the mixture to a piping bag, cut off the end and distribute the mixture among the moulds, filling them three-quarters full. Bake for 10 minutes, then turn the financiers out of the moulds.

FOR THE CHOCOLATE GANACHE

5 – Chop the chocolate into a bowl. In a saucepan, bring the cream to the boil. Pour the hot cream immediately over the chocolate. Let the chocolate melt and mix with a silicone spatula until smooth. Leave to cool.
6 – Transfer the ganache to a piping bag, cut off the tip and pipe the ganache into the same mould, filling each case halfway.
7 – Set a financier into each case, rounded side against the ganache. Freeze for 1 hour.

GLAZING AND DECORATING

8 – Melt the chocolate compound coating. Turn the chocolate financiers out of the mould. Place the point of a knife into the centre of the chocolate financier and dip the ganache side into the chocolate compound coating.
9 – Transfer the remaining ganache to a small cone and drizzle stripes over the financiers.

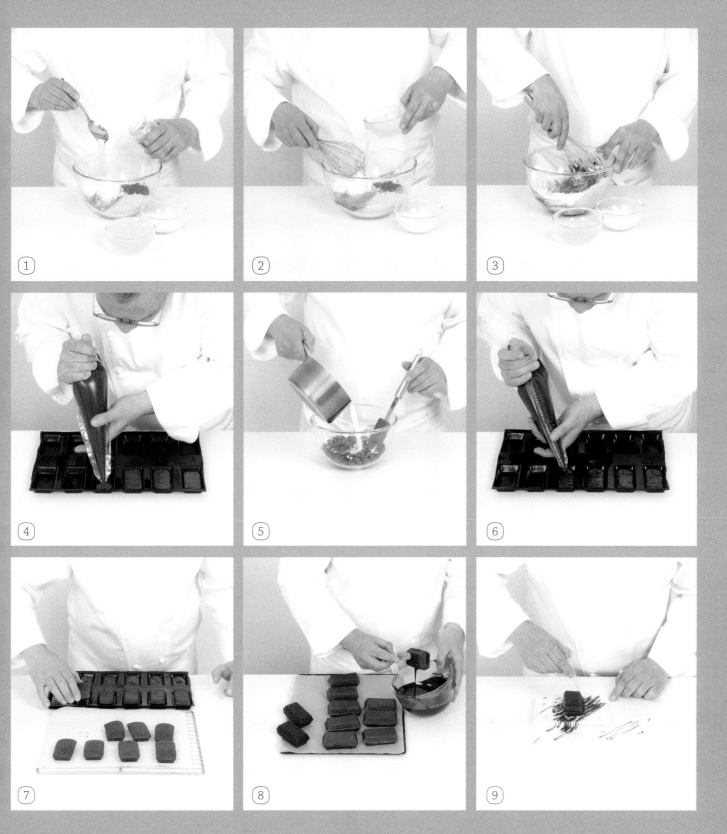

RASPBERRY MACARONS

Makes 20 macarons

PREPARATION TIME: 45 minutes – COOKING TIME: 18 minutes – CHILLING TIME: 30 minutes + overnight
STORAGE: 3 days in the refrigerator
DIFFICULTY : 🍳

MACARON MIXTURE	RASPBERRY FILLING
4 egg whites (130 g)	70 g glucose
60 g sugar	65 g sugar
Knife tip of red food colouring	20 ml water
180 g ground almonds	20 g sugar
320 g icing sugar	1 tsp pectin
	220 g raspberries

EQUIPMENT NEEDED: 2 piping bags – size 8 plain nozzle - cooking thermometer

Raspberries

A small rosy red or yellow berry, the raspberry is sweet, very flavourful and delicately tart. Raspberries grown in greenhouses can be found in French markets beginning in April, but field-grown raspberries do not appear until mid-June. They are used in a number of pastries, including macarons, tarts, entremets, ice creams and charlottes.

FOR THE MACARON MIXTURE

1 – Whisk the egg whites until firm, then add the sugar to make a meringue.

2 – Add the food colouring, then mix until evenly distributed.

3 – Sift the dry ingredients together, then add to the meringue bowl.

4 – Incorporate the dry ingredients using a silicone spatula, mix slowly, cutting straight down to the bottom of the bowl and lifting up the contents. Bring the spatula up the side of the bowl and fold back to the centre while giving the bowl a quarter turn with your other hand. Continue to fold until the meringue loses volume and becomes smooth and shiny (*Macaronnage*), transfer to a piping bag fitted with the plain nozzle.

5 – Line a baking tray with baking parchment and pipe balls about 4 cm in diameter onto the tray, in staggered rows to keep separate. Tap the base of the tray lightly to remove any air bubbles from the mixture. Leave to crust for 30 minutes. Preheat the oven to 170°C (gas mark 3-4) and bake for 18 minutes.

FOR THE RASPBERRY FILLING

6 – In a saucepan, heat the glucose, 65 g sugar and water. Mix together the 20 g sugar and pectin, then tip slowly into the saucepan, whisking constantly.

7 – Continue to heat until the temperature reads 110°C on the cooking thermometer, then add the raspberries. Bring to the boil, then leave to cool. Pour into a bowl and refrigerate for 30 minutes.

ASSEMBLY

8 – Transfer the raspberry filling to a piping bag with the nozzle and pipe a small ball on half of the macaron shells.

9 – Next, top each piece with another macaron shell and press together gently. Refrigerate the macarons overnight before serving.

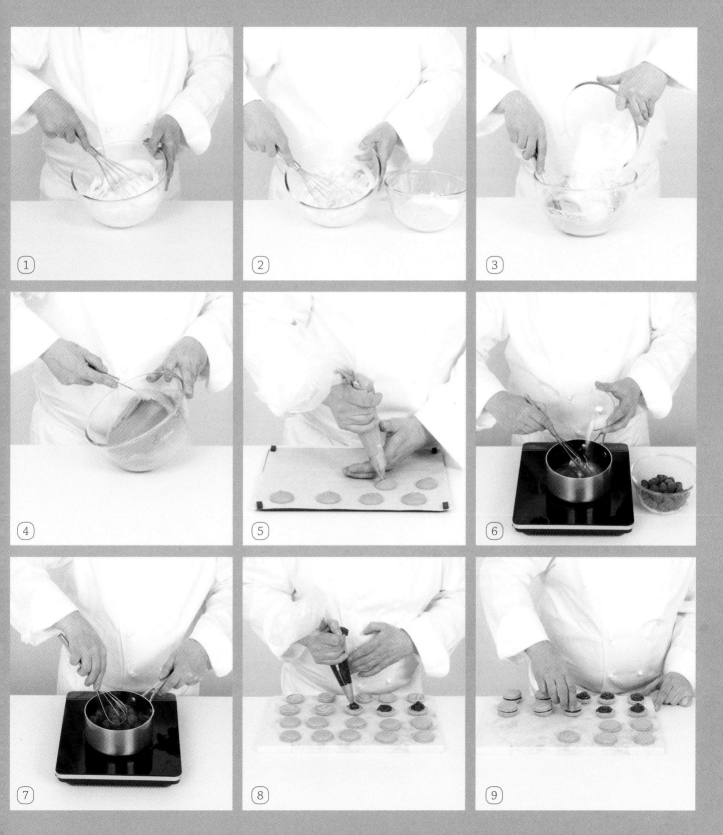

BROWNIE

Serves 10–12

PREPARATION TIME: 30 minutes (to be started the previous day) – COOKING TIME: 30 minutes – SETTING TIME: 12 hours

DIFFICULTY: ♢

BROWNIE MIXTURE	CHOCOLATE GANACHE
100 g unsalted butter	60 g dark chocolate (55% cocoa)
85 g chocolate (65% cocoa)	145 g dark chocolate (70% cocoa)
35 g cocoa mass (100% cocoa)	250 ml cream
1 vanilla pod	25 g glucose
2 eggs (90 g)	35 g unsalted butter, cut into cubes
100 g sugar	
35 g plain flour	
Pinch of salt	
½ tsp baking powder	
45 g dark chocolate chips (55% cocoa)	
35 g walnuts, chopped	

Oil for the pastry frame

EQUIPMENT NEEDED: Square pastry frame 17 x 17 x 3.5 cm – piping bag – size 12 plain nozzle

Brownies

The brownie, a cake rich in chocolate and studded with walnuts, is an American culinary speciality. Its name refers to its brown colour. Its moist inside is due to its high sugar and butter content. Traditionally, it is cut into squares. In this recipe, the brownie is topped with a chocolate ganache to create a combination of textures and intensify the chocolate taste.

THE PREVIOUS DAY, MAKE THE BROWNIE MIXTURE

1 – Preheat the oven to 160°C (gas mark 3). Over a bain-marie, melt the butter with the chocolate and cocoa mass.

2 – Split the vanilla pod in two and scrape with the tip of a knife. In a bowl, whisk together the eggs, sugar and vanilla seeds.

3 – Mix the flour with the salt and baking powder. Add to the egg-sugar-vanilla mixture.

4 – Mix in the warm melted chocolate. Add the chocolate chips, then the nuts.

5 – Oil the pastry frame, then place it on a baking tray lined with baking parchment. Tip in the mixture and bake for 25-30 minutes. Leave to cool, then refrigerate for 12 hours.

FOR THE GANACHE

6 – Chop the two types of chocolate into a bowl. Heat the cream; just before it reaches the boil, remove from heat and mix in the glucose. Pour over the chocolates and mix well.

7 – Add the butter and mix until smooth. Cover with cling film and leave to stand at room temperature for 12 hours.

THE FOLLOWING DAY

8 – Run the blade of a knife around the edge of the frame, then turn the brownie out of the frame. Trim 3 mm from each edge of the brownie to expose the inside.

9 – Transfer the ganache to a piping bag fitted with the plain nozzle and pipe small balls over the top of the brownie.

CHEF'S TIP

If you want to ensure that the top of the brownie remains flat while baking, place a baking tray on top halfway through the baking time.

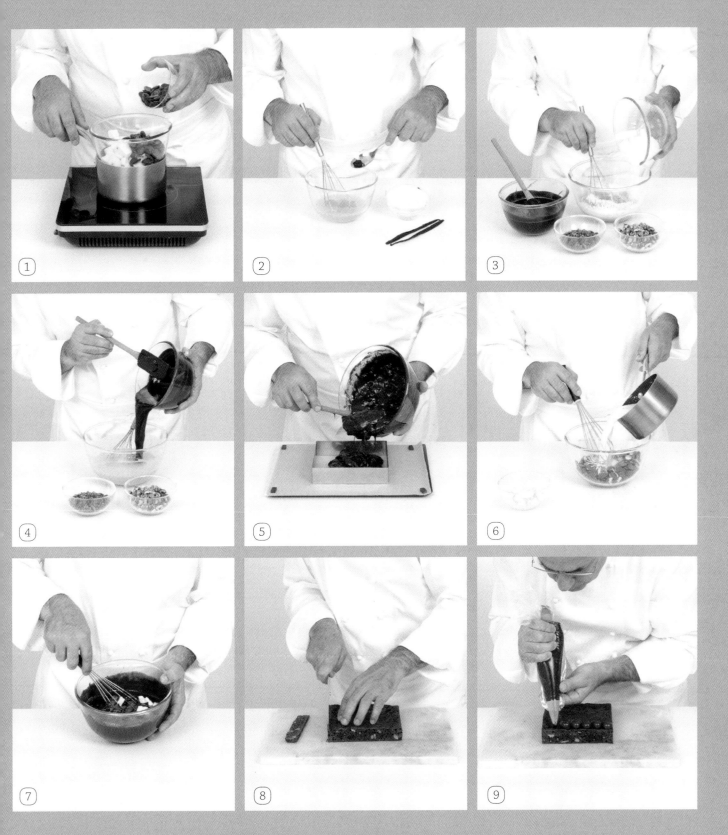

MINI SICILIAN
pistachio-cherry financiers

Makes 35 financiers

PREPARATION TIME: 20 minutes – COOKING TIME: 10 minutes

DIFFICULTY: ♙

<u>FINANCIERS</u>

40 g ground almonds

110 g icing sugar

1 tbsp coloured pistachio paste

2 tsp honey

4 egg whites (115 g)

45 g plain flour

Pinch of baking powder

65 g unsalted butter, melted

20 Amarena cherries

<u>EQUIPMENT NEEDED:</u> Silicone mini financier mould – piping bag

Sicilian pistachios

Sicilian pistachios, or *Pistacchio verde di Bronte,* come from the small village of Bronte at the foot of Mount Etna in Sicily. The unique nature of the land, bathed in lava and continually fertilised by volcanic ash, allows the production of an exceptionally green pistachio with a strong taste that will flavour your baked creations.

FOR THE FINANCIERS

1 – Preheat the oven to 180°C (gas mark 4). In a bowl, combine the ground almonds, icing sugar, pistachio paste and honey.

2 – Gradually add the egg whites, whisking constantly.

3 – Mix well until smooth.

4 – Add the flour and baking powder. Mix well.

5 – Last, add the melted butter.

6 – Transfer the mixture to a piping bag.

7 – Cut off the end and pipe the mixture into the moulds.

8 – Cut the Amarena cherries in half.

9 – Press one cherry half into the top of the mixture in each imprint. Bake for 10 minutes, then turn the financiers out of the moulds.

CHOCOLATE CHIP-WALNUT
cookies

Makes 12 cookies

PREPARATION TIME: **15 minutes** – CHILLING TIME: **12 hours** – COOKING TIME: **7 minutes**

DIFFICULTY: ◇

COOKIE DOUGH	
100 g unsalted butter	150 g plain flour
100 g unrefined raw sugar	Pinch of salt
40 g icing sugar	Pinch of baking powder
1 small egg (40 g)	100 g shelled walnuts, chopped
	100 g chocolate chips

EQUIPMENT NEEDED: bread knife

Cookies

Originally from the United States, the treat that Europeans call a 'cookie' is a flat biscuit traditionally flavoured with the addition of dark chocolate chips. In English-speaking countries, this is known as a 'chocolate chip cookie', as the general term 'cookie' can refer to any kind of biscuit. It comes from the Dutch word *koekje*, which means 'biscuit'.

FOR THE COOKIE DOUGH

1 – Place the butter in a bowl and mix with the unrefined raw sugar using a silicone spatula.

2 – Mix in the icing sugar.

3 – Add the egg and mix.

4 – Add the flour, salt and baking powder. Mix well until a smooth dough comes together.

5 – Add the chopped walnuts and mix.

6 – Lastly, add the chocolate chips.

7 – Lay a sheet of cling film on the work surface and place the cookie dough on top.

8 – Wrap the cling film around the dough and roll into a log about 7 cm in diameter. Refrigerate for 12 hours.

THE FOLLOWING DAY

9 – Preheat the oven to 190°C (gas mark 5). Remove the cling film and use the bread knife to cut the log into rounds 7 mm thick. Place on a baking tray lined with baking parchment. Bake for 7 minutes.

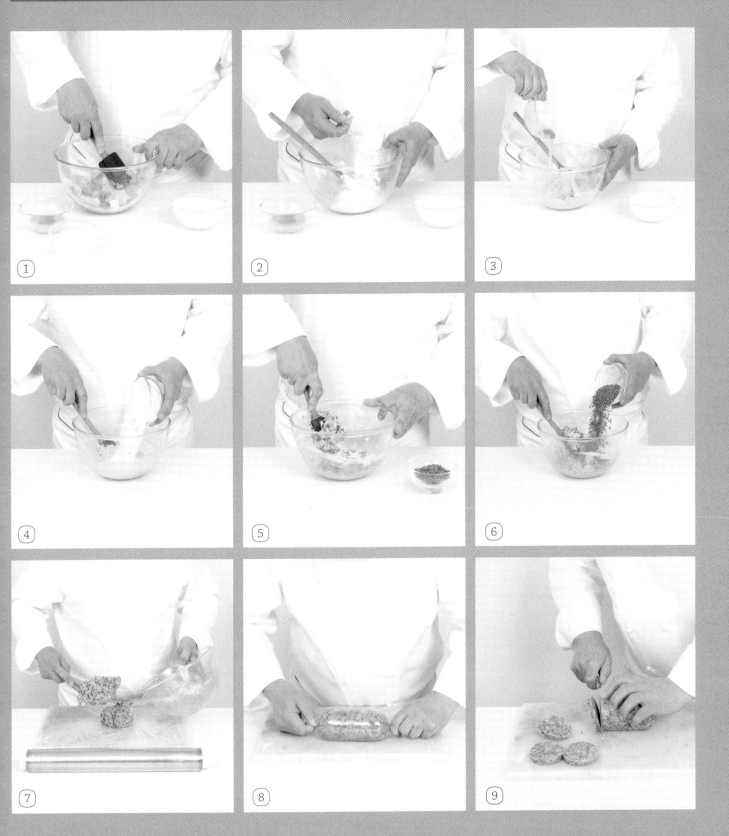

LARGE MADELEINES

Makes 12 madeleines

PREPARATION TIME: 30 minutes – COOKING TIME: 10 minutes – CHILLING TIME: 30 minutes

STORAGE: 2-3 days in an airtight container in the refrigerator

DIFFICULTY: 🎩

MADELEINE MIXTURE
2 small eggs (80 g)
65 g sugar
20 g honey
1 vanilla pod
30 ml milk
100 g plain flour
1 tsp baking powder
100 g unsalted butter, melted

50 g unsalted butter for the tin
Plain flour for the tin

EQUIPMENT NEEDED: Madeleine tin for large madeleines – piping bag – size 10 plain nozzle

Proust's madeleine

Very widespread in France and the pride of the town of Commercy in Lorraine, the madeleine has won literary fame through the work of the author Marcel Proust. The famous 'Proust's Madeleine' is a reference to the first volume of his work *In search of lost time*. It evokes an experience of taste, smell and touch that bring back a memory permanently loaded with feeling.

FOR THE MADELEINES

1 – Preheat the oven to 200°C (gas mark 6). In a bowl, whisk together the eggs and sugar. Add the honey.

2 – Scrape the inside of the vanilla pod with the point of a knife and add the seeds to the bowl.

3 – Add half of the milk and whisk.

4 – Mix the flour and baking powder and add to the mixture.

5 – Add the rest of the milk and mix well. Mix in the melted butter. Refrigerate the madeleine mixture for 30 minutes.

6 – Use a brush to butter the cases of the madeleine tin.

7 – Flour the tin, then turn it over and tap to remove any excess flour.

8 – Transfer the madeleine mixture to a piping bag fitted with the plain nozzle. Fill the cases almost to the brim with madeleine mixture.

9 – Put the tin in the oven and immediately lower the temperature to 160°C (gas mark 3). Bake for about 10 minutes or until the madeleines are a light golden brown. Check that they are done by piercing the centre of one with the tip of a knife: the blade should come out clean. Immediately turn the madeleines out of the tin and leave to cool before serving.

CHEF'S TIP

The milk is incorporated in two additions to prevent lumps from forming.

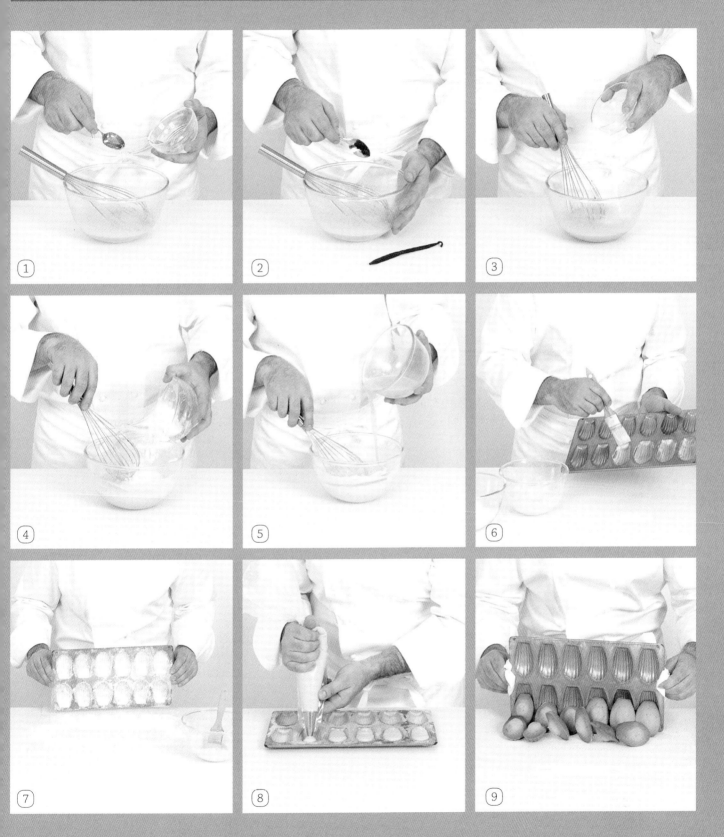

MANGO MUFFINS
with chocolate chips

Makes 10 muffins

PREPARATION TIME: 20 minutes – COOKING TIME: 20 minutes – Storage: 3 days in an airtight container

DIFFICULTY: ♙

MUFFIN MIXTURE | ½ tbsp lemon juice
225 g mango | 145 g plain flour
3 eggs (150 g) | 1 tsp baking powder
210 g sugar | 65 g unsalted butter
½ tsp salt | 75 g chocolate chips
70 g crème fraîche |

EQUIPMENT NEEDED: 7.5 cm x 4 cm muffin cases

The muffin's key ingredient

Often eaten in English-speaking countries at breakfast and for afternoon tea, muffins are a moist cake that come in an endless variety of flavours. These are traditionally made with sour cream, which is difficult to find in France, but can be made by mixing crème fraîche with a few drops of lemon juice.

FOR THE MUFFINS

1 – Preheat the oven to 180°C (gas mark 4). Peel the mango and cut into small dice.

2 – Whisk together the eggs, sugar and salt until the mixture begins to become pale and thick.

3 – Add the crème fraîche and lemon juice, whisking constantly.

4 – Whisk in the flour and baking powder.

5 – Mix well until the mixture is just smooth.

6 – Melt the butter and add it to the mixture.

7 – Add the diced mango, then the chocolate chips. Mix.

8 – Transfer the mixture to a piping bag, then cut off the tip.

9 – Distribute the muffin mixture between the cases, then bake for 20 minutes. Leave the muffins to cool before serving.

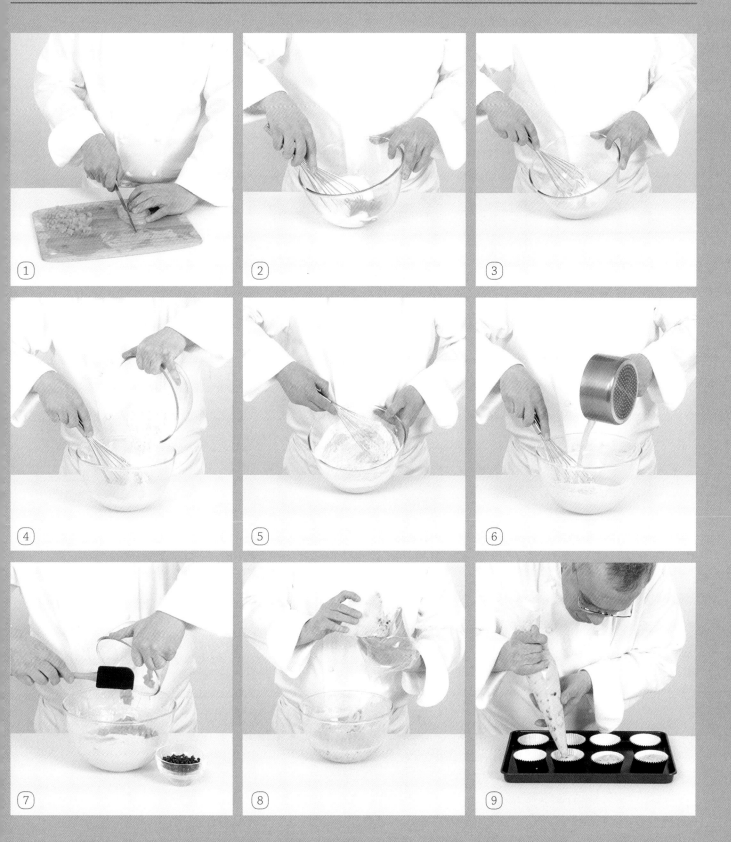

APRICOT SHORTBREAD
biscuits

Makes 20 shortbread biscuits

PREPARATION TIME: 30 minutes – COOKING TIME: 10 minutes

DIFFICULTY: 🎩

SHORTBREAD DOUGH	FILLING
200 g plain flour	150 g apricot jam
120 g unsalted butter	Icing sugar
65 g icing sugar	
Pinch of salt	
25 g ground almonds	
1 small egg (40 g)	

EQUIPMENT NEEDED: 7-cm fluted round biscuit cutter – 2.5-cm plain round biscuit cutter

Shortbread biscuits

Very easy to make, and can be made any size and shape you like with a biscuit cutter. For a more attractive result, try cutting your dough with a fluted biscuit cutter and filling your shortbread biscuits with jam or ganache, cutting a hole in the biscuit to let the filling peek through.

APRICOT SHORTBREAD biscuits

FOR THE SHORTBREAD DISCS

1 – Preheat the oven to 170°C (gas mark 3-4). On a lightly floured work surface, roll out the shortbread dough (see page 489) to a thickness of 3 mm.
2 – Cut out 40 discs with the 7-cm fluted biscuit cutter.
3 – Take half the discs and cut out their centres with the 2.5-cm plain cutter. Bake all the discs for 10 minutes. Leave to cool.

ASSEMBLY

4 – In a saucepan, heat the apricot jam.
5 – Brush the whole shortbread discs with the jam.
6 – Sprinkle the shortbread discs with the centres removed with icing sugar.
7 – Set one of these sugared discs on top of every whole shortbread disc glazed with apricot jam.
8 – Strain the jam through a sieve to obtain a smooth texture.
9 – Use a teaspoon to fill the depression in the top of the shortbread discs to the brim with jam.

CHEF'S TIP

You can replace the apricot jam with any other fruit jam. This is a very easy way to change the flavour and colour of your shortbread biscuits.

SANDWICH-STYLE
chocolate biscuits

Makes approximately 10 biscuits

PREPARATION TIME: 30 minutes – COOKING TIME: about 15 minutes – SETTING TIME: 12 hours

DIFFICULTY: ♙

SWEET PASTRY DOUGH	GANACHE
200 g plain flour	200 g chocolate (65% cocoa)
120 g unsalted butter	225 ml cream
25 g ground almonds	22 g glucose
65 g icing sugar	35 g unsalted butter
2 g salt	
1 small egg (40 g)	

EQUIPMENT NEEDED: 7-cm biscuit cutter – 2-cm biscuit cutter – 12-mm biscuit cutter
piping bag – size 12 star nozzle

Chocolate ganache

Ganache is an equal or nearly equal mixture of cream and chocolate.
This soft substance is used as a centre for "biscuit" sponges, coating for cakes
and a filling for tarts. By raising the proportion of chocolate in relation to
cream, you can obtain a firmer ganache perfect for making truffles or other
sweets.

FOR THE SWEET PASTRY DOUGH DISCS

1 – Preheat the oven to 150°C (gas mark 2). Roll out the sweet pastry dough (see page 488) to a thickness of 4 mm.
2 – Use the 7 cm biscuit cutter to cut out 20 discs and place on a baking tray lined with a silicone baking mat.
3 – Take 10 discs and cut out 'eyes' with the 12-mm biscuit cutter and a 'mouth' with the 2-cm cutter. Bake for 12-15 minutes, until the discs are golden brown.

FOR THE GANACHE

4 – Chop the chocolate into a bowl. Heat the cream; just before it reaches the boil, remove from heat and mix in the glucose.
5 – Pour the hot liquid over the chocolate and mix well.
6 – Mix in the butter. Cover with cling film and let stand at room temperature for 12 hours.

ASSEMBLY

7 – Transfer the ganache to a piping bag fitted with the star nozzle.
8 – Pipe a swirl of ganache onto each of the whole biscuit discs.
9 – Top each of the ganache disc with a 'face' round, pressing them together gently to make the ganache come up through the eyes and mouth.

CHOCOLATE-BANANA
two-tone macarons

Makes 20 macarons

PREPARATION TIME: 45 minutes – COOKING TIME: 18 minutes – CHILLING TIME: 30 minutes + overnight
STORAGE: 3 days in the refrigerator

DIFFICULTY: ♙

MACARON MIXTURE	CHOCOLATE-BANANA FILLING
4 egg whites (130 g)	150 g bananas
60 g sugar	20 g unsalted butter
180 g ground almonds	70 g honey
320 g icing sugar	2 tsp rum
Knife tip of brown food colouring	100 ml cream
Knife tip of yellow food colouring	130 g milk chocolate
	80 g dark chocolate (70% cocoa)

EQUIPMENT NEEDED: 2 piping bags – 1 size 8 plain nozzle

The macaron

Macarons are a mignardise 3 to 5 cm in diameter, very crisp on the outside but moist on the inside, made from a delicate mixture of egg whites, sugar and ground almonds. The famous Parisian macaron, made from two smooth macaron shells and a ganache, cream or jam filling, comes in all colours and flavours. In France there are also other types of macaron, such as Nancy and Comery macarons, which do not have a filling.

FOR THE MACARON MIXTURE

1 – Whisk the egg whites until firm, then add the sugar to make a meringue. Meanwhile, sift the dry ingredients together.

2 – Add the dry ingredients to the meringue and mix gently.

3 – Place the two food colourings in separate bowls. Divide the macaron mixture between the two bowls.

4 – Incorporate the dry ingredients into both bowls using a silicone spatula. Mix slowly, cutting straight down to the bottom of the bowl and lifting up the contents. Bring the spatula up the side of the bowl and fold back to the centre while giving the bowl a quarter turn with your other hand. Continue to fold until the meringue loses volume and becomes smooth and shiny (*Macaronnage*).

5 – Transfer the two macaron mixtures into the same piping bag fitted with the plain nozzle, trying not to mix them.

6 – Line a baking tray with baking parchment and pipe balls about 4 cm in diameter onto the tray, in staggered rows to keep separate. Tap the base of the tray lightly to remove any air bubbles from the mixture. Leave to crust for 30 minutes. Preheat the oven to 170°C (gas mark 3-4) and bake for 18 minutes.

FOR THE CHOCOLATE-BANANA FILLING

7 – Cut the bananas into round slices. In a frying pan, heat the butter and honey, then add the banana slices. Cook for 2 minutes, then pour in the rum. Tip in the cream and continue to cook for 2 minutes.

8 – Chop the two chocolates, place into a bowl and tip the hot banana mixture over the top. Mix, then blend with a hand-held blender until smooth. Refrigerate for 30 minutes.

ASSEMBLY

9 – Transfer the chocolate-banana filling to a piping bag fitted with the plain nozzle, then pipe onto half of the macaron shells, pressing down lightly. Top each piece with another macaron shell. Refrigerate the macarons overnight before serving.

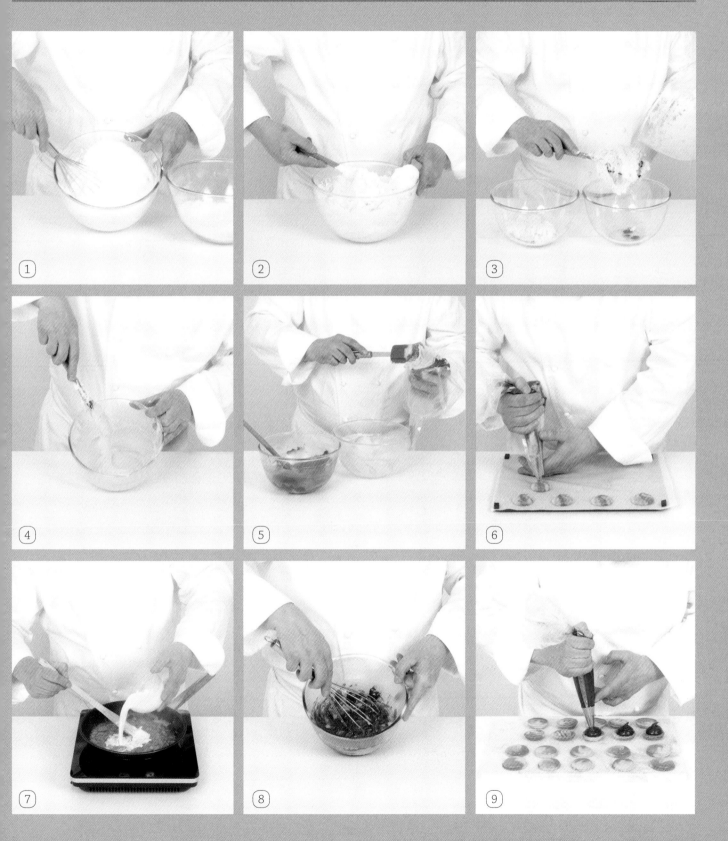

Sweets &
Little Treats

CHOCOLATE, RASPBERRY
and lemon lollipops

Makes 18 lollipops

PREPARATION TIME: 1 hour – FREEZING TIME: 3 hours – STORAGE: 10 days in an airtight container

DIFFICULTY: ♙ ♙

CANDIED LEMON	CHOCOLATE-RASPBERRY GANACHE
1 lemon	225 g dark chocolate
Pinch of salt	150 ml cream
75 ml water	1 or 2 drops raspberry flavouring
75 g sugar	40 g honey
	1 tsp room-temperature unsalted butter

LEMON ALMOND PASTE	
65 g ground almonds	COATING
40 g icing sugar	400 g white chocolate compound coating (pâte à glacer)
1 tbsp cocoa butter	Yellow coloured cocoa butter
Knife tip of yellow food colouring	Red coloured cocoa butter
45 g candied lemon, chopped	White coloured cocoa butter

EQUIPMENT NEEDED: 2 piping bags – silicone mould with 18 3.5-cm spherical cases – 18 wooden sticks

Chocolate compound coating

Chocolate compound coating (also called pâte à glacer) is made of cocoa powder, sugar and dairy products, finely ground and mixed with a vegetable fat. It is used to cover entremets and other pastry products to create the desired shine and crunchy finish. When a white chocolate compound coating is used, it can be coloured however you like to brighten up and decorate your creations.

FOR THE CANDIED LEMON

1 – In a saucepan of boiling water with the salt, blanch the whole lemon. Change the water and repeat.

2 – Cut the lemon into quarters, then slices. Remove the seeds. In a saucepan, bring the water and sugar to the boil, add the lemon slices and simmer over low heat for 30 minutes. Drain the candied slices in a colander, then chop into small pieces.

FOR THE LEMON ALMOND PASTE

3 – Mix the ground almonds, icing sugar, cocoa butter and yellow food colouring. Add the candied lemon pieces. Transfer this paste to a piping bag.

FOR THE CHOCOLATE-RASPBERRY GANACHE

4 – Melt the dark chocolate over a bain-marie. Let the cream come to room temperature. Mix with the raspberry flavouring and tip over the melted chocolate along with the honey. Add the room-temperature butter and mix. Transfer the ganache to a piping bag.

ASSEMBLY AND DIPPING

5 – Cut the end from the piping bag containing the almond paste and use to fill the depressions in the first half-sphere mould to the brim.

6 – Place the second half-sphere mould on top of the first.

7 – Cut the end from the piping bag filled with the chocolate-raspberry ganache and use to fill the cases through their holes.

8 – Insert the sticks into the holes. Freeze for 3 hours.

9 – Gently remove the lollipops from the mould. Melt the chocolate compound coating and pour into a bowl. Add the yellow cocoa butter, then the red and white cocoa butters. Stir briefly with a lollipop stick to swirl them together. Dip the lollipops very gently into the coating, twisting as you lift to create a swirl of colours on the surface of each lollipop.

CHOCOLATE TRUFFLES

Makes 45 truffles

PREPARATION TIME: 1 hour + 30 minutes to temper the chocolate – CHILLING TIME: 5 minutes
STORAGE: 15 days in an airtight container

DIFFICULTY: 🎩 🎩

CHOCOLATE GANACHE	COATING
150 ml cream	250 g dark couverture chocolate (70% cocoa)
100 g milk chocolate	100 g unsweetened cocoa powder
110 g dark chocolate (70%)	
55 g honey	
12 g unsalted butter	

EQUIPMENT NEEDED: Cooking thermometer – piping bag – size 12 plain nozzle – plastic gloves

Truffles

These sweets, a particular favourite during the (end of year) festive season, are made of chocolate, cream (or butter) and sugar. Truffles may be flavoured with cinnamon, coffee, vanilla, rum, lemon, tea, etc. Essentially the ganache is shaped into a ball. They may be coated with chocolate and then rolled in unsweetened cocoa powder.

FOR THE CHOCOLATE GANACHE

1 – Let the cream come to room temperature. Melt the chocolates over a bain-marie, then add the honey.

2 – Add the cream.

3 – Whisk together gently.

4 – Delicately whisk in the butter, then continue to mix gently with a silicone spatula until the mixture is smooth. Leave the ganache to thicken, then transfer it to a piping bag fitted with the plain nozzle.

5 – On a baking tray lined with baking parchment, pipe balls 2 cm in diameter. Refrigerate for 5 minutes.

6 – Put on the plastic gloves and roll each truffle between your hands to make it completely round.

COATING

7 – Temper the dark chocolate (see pages 494-495). Tip the unsweetened cocoa powder onto a plate.

8 – Using a fork, dip the ganache balls one by one into the tempered chocolate.

9 – Next, working quickly, roll them in the unsweetened cocoa powder. Leave to cool in the cocoa powder.

CHEF'S TIP

If you do not want to temper the chocolate, you can skip this step and roll the ganache balls directly in the unsweetened cocoa powder.

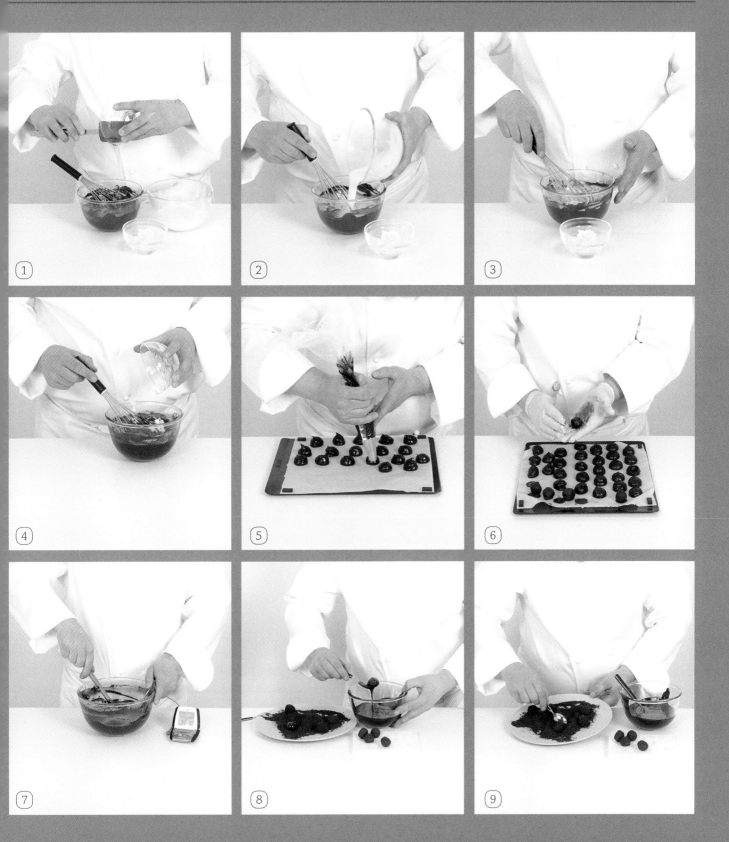

① ② ③ ④ ⑤ ⑥ ⑦ ⑧ ⑨

MANGO FRUIT JELLIES

Makes about 65 fruit jellies

PREPARATION TIME: 30 minutes – SETTING TIME: 4 hours – STORAGE: 6 days in an airtight container

DIFFICULTY: ♙

MANGO FRUIT JELLIES
200 g mango purée
150 g apricot purée
1½ tsp yellow pectin
35 g sugar
100 g glucose
375 g sugar
1½ tsp liquid tartaric acid in solution

DECORATION
Sugar

EQUIPMENT NEEDED: Cooking thermometer – silicone mould with 4-cm round imprints

Yellow pectin: perfect for fruit jellies

Yellow pectin is typically used to make fruit jellies, as its slow set is good for gelling acidic substances high in sugar. It also provides a fairly firm texture that gives fruit jellies good stability while still maintaining the yielding texture characteristic of these confectioneries.

FOR THE MANGO FRUIT JELLIES

1 – Heat the mango purée with the apricot purée. Mix the yellow pectin and 35 g sugar.

2 – Sprinkle the sugar-pectin mix over the warm purée.

3 – Add the glucose.

4 – Bring the mixture to the boil, then add 375 g sugar.

5 – Continue cooking, stirring continuously with a silicone spatula, until the temperature reads 105°C on the cooking thermometer.

6 – The consistency should be somewhat thick and heavy.

7 – Turn off the heat and add the tartaric acid, stirring in with the silicone spatula.

8 – Distribute the mixture between the imprints of the mould with a tablespoon. Leave to set for 4 hours at room temperature.

9 – Turn the fruit jellies out the mould. If you wish, tip a little sugar into a container and dip the jellies in it.

CHEF'S TIP

You can replace the tartaric acid with a few drops of lemon juice.

MENDIANT-STYLE
caramel-chocolate fingers

Makes 10 fingers

PREPARATION TIME: 1 hour + 30 minutes to temper the chocolate – CHILLING TIME: 2 hours 15 minutes

SETTING TIME: 15 minutes – STORAGE: 1 week in an airtight container

DIFFICULTY: ♙ ♙

CARAMEL
½ vanilla pod
150 ml cream
110 g sugar
40 ml water
100 g sugar
100 g glucose
55 g unsalted butter

CHOCOLATE GANACHE
150 ml cream
90 g milk chocolate
115 g dark chocolate (70% cocoa)
40 g honey
12 g unsalted butter

COATING
500 g dark couverture chocolate (70% cocoa)

DECORATION
Blanched almonds
Skinned hazelnuts
Candied orange
Pistachios

EQUIPMENT NEEDED: Cooking thermometer – Cacao Barry® polycarbonate mould (11 x 2.3 x 1.4 cm) – 3 piping bags – small paper cone

Mendiants

The term *mendiant*, French for 'mendicant', originally meant a mix of almonds, hazelnuts, raisins and figs whose colours represented the robes of the monks belonging to the mendicant orders. Combined with chocolate, this became a prized and classic end of year festive treat. Everyone can express their creative side and use other candied fruit and nuts, such as pistachios, oranges or apricots.

FOR THE CARAMEL

1 – Split the vanilla pod half in two and scrape with the tip of a knife.
In a saucepan, bring the cream to the boil with 110 g sugar and the vanilla seeds. Remove from heat.
2 – In another saucepan, heat the water with 100 g sugar. Add the glucose.
3 – Leave to caramelise without stirring.
4 – Once the caramel turns brown, add the butter and whisk together.
5 – Quickly tip in the hot cream-sugar-vanilla mixture, whisking constantly. If the sugar sets on the whisk, bring back to the boil. Remove from heat and leave the caramel to cool, then transfer to a piping bag.

FOR THE CHOCOLATE GANACHE

6 – Bring the cream to room temperature. Melt the two chocolates over a bain-marie and add the honey. Next, add the cream and whisk gently.
7 – Gradually whisk in the butter, then continue to mix gently with a silicone spatula until the mixture is smooth. Leave to cool, then transfer the ganache to a piping bag.

COATING AND ASSEMBLY

8 – Temper the chocolate (see pages 494-495). Transfer to a piping bag, cut off the end and fill the imprints in the mould with chocolate.
9 – Tap the mould on the work surface to remove any air bubbles.

① ② ③

④ ⑤ ⑥

⑦ ⑧ ⑨

10 – Turn the mould over and tap it on the bottom so the chocolate runs down the sides of the imprints, then with the mould still upside down, scrape its surface. Only a thin layer of chocolate lining the imprints should remain.

11 – Scrape the surface clean with a plastic dough scraper. Leave to set for 15 minutes. Keep the tempered chocolate at 32°C by placing it over a gentle bain-marie (take care to ensure that the temperature does not exceed 32°C).

12 – Take the piping bag with the ganache, cut off the end and fill the imprints two-thirds full.

13 – Take the piping bag with the caramel, cut off the end and pipe over the ganache, leaving 3 mm of space at the top of each imprint. Refrigerate for 15 minutes.

14 – Use the piping bag of tempered chocolate to seal off the fingers in the mould.

15 – Immediately cover with a thick acetate or guitar sheet and press down over each case to press the chocolate inside.

16 – Scrape the surface with a plastic dough scraper to remove any excess chocolate. Refrigerate for 2 hours.

DECORATE

17 – Once the chocolate-caramel fingers have set completely, turn them out of the mould. Make a small paper cone and fill it with the remaining ganache.

18 – Pipe a few dots of ganache onto the top of each stick, using them to stick down the nuts and candied fruit.

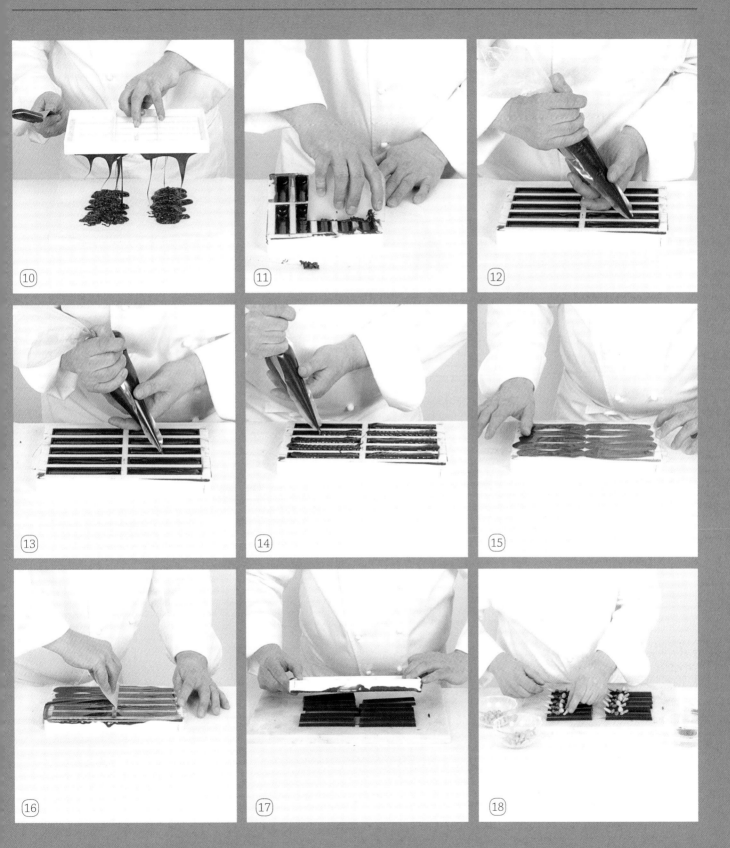

LITTLE TOFFEE APPLES

Makes 10 toffee apples

———————

PREPARATION TIME: **30 minutes**

DIFFICULTY: ♙

APPLES	RED CARAMEL
1 lemon	500 g sugar
10 apples	150 ml water
	80 g glucose
	Knife tip of raspberry red food colouring
	3 vanilla pods

EQUIPMENT NEEDED: 10 wooden skewers – cooking thermometer

Toffee apples

Queen of the fair, the toffee apple, or 'love apple' in French, is an apple covered in crunchy red caramel and skewered on a stick. The caramel may be flavoured with vanilla or cinnamon. This confectionery takes its name from the tomato, once called the 'love apple', which it resembles in both shape and colour. For something different than the traditional Golden Delicious, try using smaller apple varieties to make little toffee apples.

FOR THE APPLES

1 – Squeeze the lemon juice into a large bowl of water.

2 – Remove stems and peel the apples, dropping them immediately into the acidulated water to keep them from turning brown.

FOR THE RED CARAMEL

3 – Pour the sugar and water into a saucepan. Mix to dissolve the sugar, then add the glucose.

4 – Bring to the boil, skimming off any impurities with a tablespoon.

5 – Add the food colouring and continue to boil.

6 – Split the vanilla pods in two and scrape with the tip of a knife. Add the vanilla seeds to the caramel and mix.

7 – Heat until the temperature reads 160°C-170°C on the cooking thermometer.

COAT THE APPLES

8 – Drain the apples on paper towels or a clean, dry tea towel, then skewer each one with a wooden skewer.

9 – Once the caramel has reached the proper temperature, remove the saucepan from the heat. Immediately dip the apples in the caramel, placing them quickly on a sheet of baking parchment. Leave to harden.

CHEF'S TIP

You can leave the apples unpeeled if you wish. In you do so, there will be no reason to place them in a bowl of acidulated water.

PASSION FRUIT-CHOCOLATE
bars

Makes 10 bars

———————

PREPARATION TIME: 1 hour + 30 minutes to temper the chocolate

FREEZING TIME: 1 hour – CHOCOLATE SETTING: 1 hour – STORAGE: 5 days in an airtight container

DIFFICULTY: ♙ ♙

PASSION FRUIT ALMOND PASTE
60 g passion fruit purée

1 tbsp cocoa butter

85 g ground almonds

50 g icing sugar

20 g potato starch

PASSION FRUIT GANACHE
30 g passion fruit purée

2½ tsp sugar

2 tsp glucose

120 g milk chocolate

20 g dark chocolate (70% cocoa)

400 ml cream

6 g unsalted butter

COATING
350 g milk couverture chocolate

EQUIPMENT NEEDED: 1 Silikomart® Mini Pick mould – 10 wooden sticks – 1 transfer sheet for chocolate

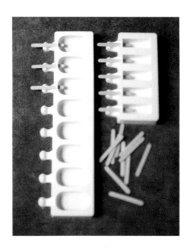

Lollipop moulds

To make your own lollipops - a confection that delights young and old alike - find a special mould that will let you make original shapes: sticks, hearts, stars or rounds are all easy to use and will make your lollipops turn out even.

PASSION FRUIT-CHOCOLATE bars

FOR THE PASSION FRUIT ALMOND PASTE

1 – In a saucepan, reduce the passion fruit purée by half, then while still hot, add the cocoa butter.

2 – Combine the ground almonds and icing sugar in a bowl, then tip the hot liquid over the top.

3 – Mix well to make a paste.

4 – With a little potato starch, roll out the passion fruit almond paste into a thin layer about 3 mm thick.

5 – Cut into 6 x 4 cm rectangles.

6 – Sprinkle with potato starch.

7 – Lay the rectangles starch side-down into the mould imprints. Press down to line the cases well.

FOR THE PASSION FRUIT GANACHE

8 – In a saucepan, reduce the passion fruit purée by half, add the sugar and glucose and heat. Chop the chocolates and place in a bowl.

9 – Add the cream and heat, stirring constantly.

•••

CHEF'S TIP

You can replace the passion fruit with another tart fruit that will pair well with chocolate, such as raspberry, pineapple or blackcurrant. The combination of a little tartness with the chocolate will ensure that your confection remains light.

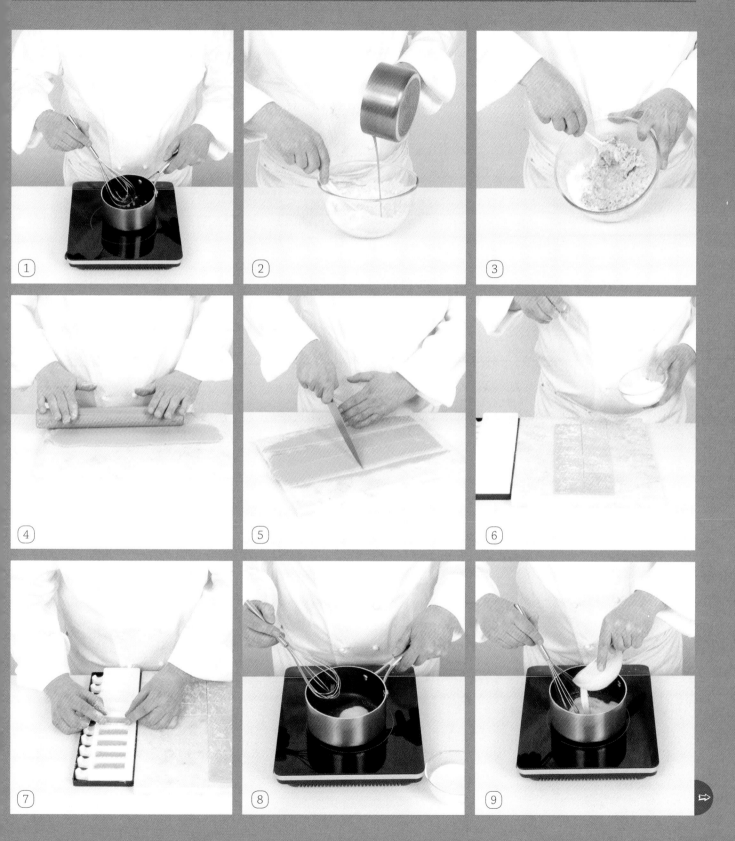

10 – Pour the mixture over the chopped chocolates and mix well.

11 – Mix in the butter. Transfer the passion fruit ganache to a piping bag.

12 – Fill the imprints three-quarters full with passion fruit ganache.

13 – Insert the sticks into the passion fruit ganache.

14 – Continue filling the imprints with passion fruit ganache to the brim.

15 – Scrape the surface with a spatula to remove any excess passion fruit ganache. Leave to set for 1 hour at room temperature, then freeze for at least 1 hour until the bars are completely set.

16 – Turn the bars out of the mould onto a sheet of baking parchment.

COATING AND DECORATING

17 – Temper the milk couverture chocolate (see pages 494-495).

18 – Set the transfer sheet on your work surface. One by one, dip the bars in the chocolate, then place immediately on the transfer sheet. Leave to set.

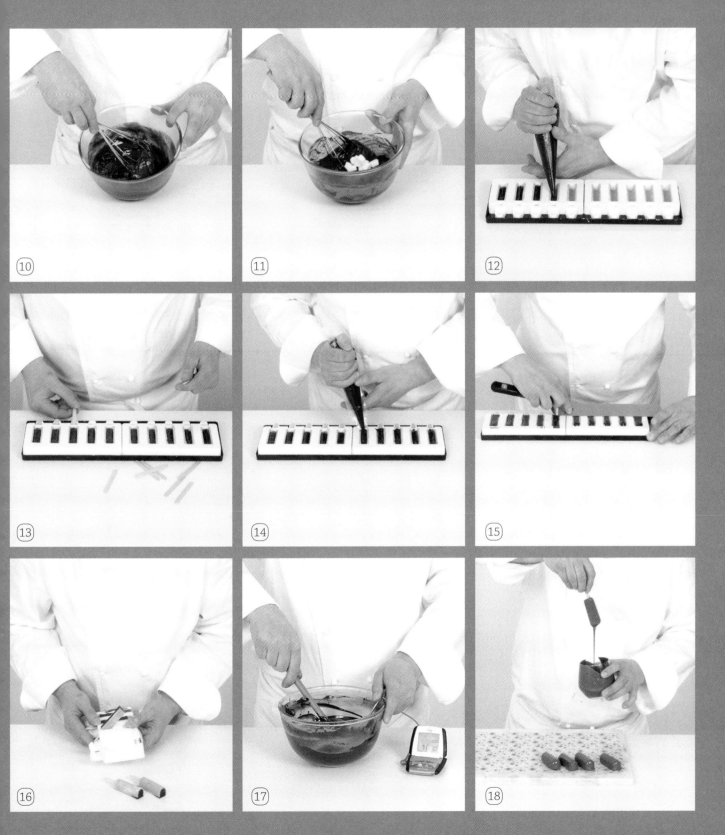

CHOCOLATE-ORANGE
bâtonnets

Makes 8 bâtonnets

PREPARATION TIME: 1 hour 30 minutes – COOKING TIME: 10 minutes – TEMPERING TIME: 30 minutes

CHILLING TIME: 1 hour 5 minutes – FREEZING TIME: 2 hours – STORAGE: 8 days in an airtight container

DIFFICULTY: ♙ ♙

CRUNCHY ALMONDS
1 tbsp water
1 tbsp sugar
50 g slivered almonds
Sugar

PRALINE-ORANGE CRUNCH
12 g milk chocolate
50 g praline
20 g unsalted butter
10 g candied orange peel
25 g crushed Gavottes® crêpes (wafers)

PRALINE GANACHE
100 ml cream
25 g honey
220 g milk chocolate
80 g praline
1 tbsp Cointreau®

COATING
300 g milk couverture chocolate

EQUIPMENT NEEDED: 1 Silikomart® Mini Classic mould – 1 piping bag – 12 wooden bâtonnets

Using tempered chocolate several times in the same recipe

To be able to use the same tempered chocolate for all three stages of this recipe, you must keep it at the proper temperature (between 28°C and 30°C) until the final step of the coating is complete to ensure that it maintains the same colour and shine. To do so, briefly place it over a bain-marie from time to time.

FOR THE CRUNCHY ALMONDS

1 – Preheat the oven to 150°C (gas mark 2). Bring the water and sugar to the boil. Tip into a bowl with the slivered almonds, stir and sprinkle with sugar.

2 – Bake for 10-15 minutes. Turn them halfway through baking.

FOR THE PRALINE-ORANGE CRUNCH

3 – Melt the chocolate over a bain-marie. Mix in the praline, then the butter.

4 – Add the orange peels, then the crushed Gavottes® crêpes (wafers).

5 – Spread the mixture onto a sheet of baking parchment. Set another sheet of baking parchment on top and roll out with a rolling pin to a thickness of about 4 mm. Refrigerate for 30 minutes.

6 – Remove the sheets of baking parchment and cut into 6 x 3 cm rectangles.

FOR THE PRALINE GANACHE

7 – In a saucepan, bring the cream and honey to the boil. Melt the milk chocolate over a bain-marie.

8 – Pour the hot liquid over the chocolate and whisk gently.

9 – Mix in the praline, then the Cointreau®. Refrigerate for 30 minutes.

● ● ●

> ### CHEF'S TIP
>
> To insert the bâtonnets correctly, make sure that the chocolate is soft and find the right place: don't stick it in too far or not enough. You'll soon get the hang of it.

ASSEMBLY AND DIPPING

10 – Temper the milk couverture chocolate (see pages 494-495).
Use a brush to coat the imprints of the mould with the tempered chocolate.
Refrigerate for 5 minutes until the chocolate has set. Keep the tempered
chocolate at 28-30°C.

11 – Whisk the ganache briskly to emulsify and lighten it. Transfer
to a piping bag.

12 – Pipe the ganache into the chocolate-lined imprints, filling them halfway.

13 – Insert the bâtonnets at the level marked in the mould.

14 – Place a rectangle of praline-orange crunch in each imprint.

15 – Use the piping bag to fill the imprints the rest of the way to the brim with
ganache.

16 – Scrape the surface of the mould with a spatula to remove any excess
ganache.

17 – Pour a little tempered chocolate over the imprints and scrape immediately
with the spatula. Freeze for 2 hours. Keep the tempered chocolate at 28-30°C.

18 – Turn the bâtonnets out of the mould and dip them one by one in the
tempered chocolate. Leave to drain, then place the bâtonnets on a clean work
surface. Immediately sprinkle with crunchy almonds.

CHOCOLATE MARSHMALLOWS

Makes about 65 marshmallows

PREPARATION TIME: 30 minutes – RESTING TIME: 24 hours – STORAGE: 3 days in an airtight container

DIFFICULTY: 🎩

CHOCOLATE MARSHMALLOWS
11 gelatine leaves (22 g)
70 ml water
175 g sugar
75 g glucose
100 g Trimoline® (inverted sugar)

110 g Trimoline® (inverted sugar)
45 g cocoa mass
150 g icing sugar
150 g potato starch

Unsalted butter for the frame

EQUIPMENT NEEDED: Cooking thermometer – 16 x 16 cm pastry frame – pastry brush

Marshmallow

The word 'marshmallow' originally referred to a plant sold at chemist's shops for its medicinal properties; these were often rendered into a paste. It was this texture that gave this well-known confectionery its name. Marshmallows are generally made of syrup, sugar and gelatine and are often coloured. The famous round marshmallows of the English-speaking world are one variety.

FOR THE CHOCOLATE MARSHMALLOW
(THE PREVIOUS DAY)

1 – Soften the gelatine leaves in a bowl of cold water. Heat the water, sugar, glucose and 100 g Trimoline® until the temperature reads 113°C on the cooking thermometer.

2 – Squeeze the gelatine leaves to drain and place them in a bowl with 110 g Trimoline®. Tip in the syrup and mix with an electric whisk until the mixture begins to turn white and holds soft peaks.

3 – Melt the cocoa mass and add to the mixture.

4 – Butter the pastry frame, then place on a baking tray lined with baking parchment. Tip in the marshmallow mixture.

5 – Mix together the icing sugar and potato starch and sprinkle over the marshmallow. Let the marshmallow set at room temperature for 24 hours.

THE FOLLOWING DAY, TURN OUT
THE MARSHMALLOW AND DECORATE

6 – Run a knife around the edge of the frame to unstick the marshmallow from the sides.

7 – Turn the marshmallow out onto another tray lined with baking parchment, then remove the baking parchment from the bottom of the marshmallow.

8 – Sprinkle with the icing sugar-potato starch mix, then use the pastry brush to brush off any excess.

9 – Cut into 2 cm strips, then the strips into 2 cm cubes.

CHEF'S TIP

You can replace the Trimoline® with set honey.

NOUGAT

Makes 1 kg nougat

PREPARATION TIME: 45 minutes – COOKING TIME: 35 minutes – Storage: 10 days in an airtight container

DIFFICULTY: ♟ ♟

NOUGAT MIXTURE
100 g skinned hazelnuts
200 g blanched almonds
100 g blanched pistachios
1½ egg whites (50 g)
20 g sugar
215 g honey

----

250 g sugar
100 g glucose
70 ml water

Oil for the silicone mats

EQUIPMENT NEEDED: Cooking thermometer – 2 silicone mats

Making nougat

Nougat, a confectionery made of sugar and honey, must contain 15% nuts. Its texture may be hard or soft depending on how it is cooked. It may also contain candied fruit. Many regions of France produce nougat, but the town most famous for this product is Montélimar, the historical capital of the confectionery. Nougat made there contains at least 30% nuts, which include almonds and pistachios.

FOR THE NOUGAT

1 – Preheat the oven to 160°C (gas mark 3-4). Place the hazelnuts, almonds and pistachios on a baking tray and bake for 15 minutes. In a large bowl, whisk the egg whites with an electric whisk until firm. Add the sugar to make a meringue. At the same time, heat the honey in a saucepan until the temperature reads 140°C on the cooking thermometer.

2 – Once the temperature reaches 140°C, immediately tip the honey over the meringue and mix gently with an electric whisk.

3 – In a saucepan, heat the sugar, glucose and water until the temperature reads 175°C on a cooking thermometer while continuing to whisk the meringue mixture.

4 – Tip immediately into the meringue mixture and continue to mix until the texture becomes uniform.

5 – Place the bowl over a bain-marie and heat for 10 minutes until the mixture becomes thick and fairly firm.

6 – Remove the bowl from the bain-marie and incorporate the nuts with a wooden spatula.

7 – Set a silicone mat on your work surface and turn the nougat out onto it. Set another oiled silicone mat on top and press down with the palm of your hand.

8 – Flatten gently with a rolling pin to obtain a uniform thickness of 1.5-2 cm. Leave to cool to room temperature.

9 – Cut neat strips of nougat, then cut the strips into small pieces.

RASPBERRY-ALMOND
fruit jellies

Makes about 65 fruit jellies

PREPARATION TIME: 45 minutes – SETTING TIME: 4 hours – STORAGE: 6 days in an airtight container

DIFFICULTY: 🎩

<u>RASPBERRY FRUIT JELLIES</u>
300 g raspberry purée
1 tsp yellow pectin
30 g sugar
80 g glucose
295 g sugar
1 tsp tartaric acid in solution

<u>ALMOND PASTE</u>
200 g white almond paste

<u>DECORATION</u>
Sugar

<u>EQUIPMENT NEEDED:</u> Cooking thermometer – 16 x 16 cm pastry frame

Fruit jellies

Originally from Auvergne, fruit jellies are confectionery made from fruit, sugar and a gelling agent, usually yellow pectin. Their intense fruity flavour comes from the fruit purée they contain, which is their main ingredient. This confectionery comes in as many flavours as there are fruit: raspberry, strawberry, mango, apricot, quince, plum etc.

FOR THE RASPBERRY FRUIT JELLIES

1 – In a saucepan, heat the raspberry purée. Combine the yellow pectin and 30 g sugar, then sprinkle the mixture over the warm purée. Add the glucose.

2 – Bring the mixture to the boil, then add 295 g sugar.

3 – Continue cooking, whisking constantly, until the temperature reads 104°C on the cooking thermometer.

4 – Remove from the heat and add the tartaric acid.

5 – Set the frame on a baking tray lined with baking parchment and fill with the raspberry mixture. Leave to set for 4 hours at room temperature.

6 – Roll out the almond paste very finely. Peel the baking parchment off the base of the fruit jelly and place the jelly, still in its frame, on top of the almond paste. Trim off the excess almond paste so that the edges align. Set the trimmings aside.

7 – Run a knife blade around the inside of the frame to loosen the fruit jelly, then remove the frame. Collect the almond paste trimmings into a ball. Roll out very finely and place on top of the fruit jelly. Trim off the excess almond paste so that the edges align.

8 – Cut into 2-cm strips, then the strips into 2 x 2 cm cubes.

9 – Tip a little sugar onto a plate and sugar two sides of each fruit jelly.

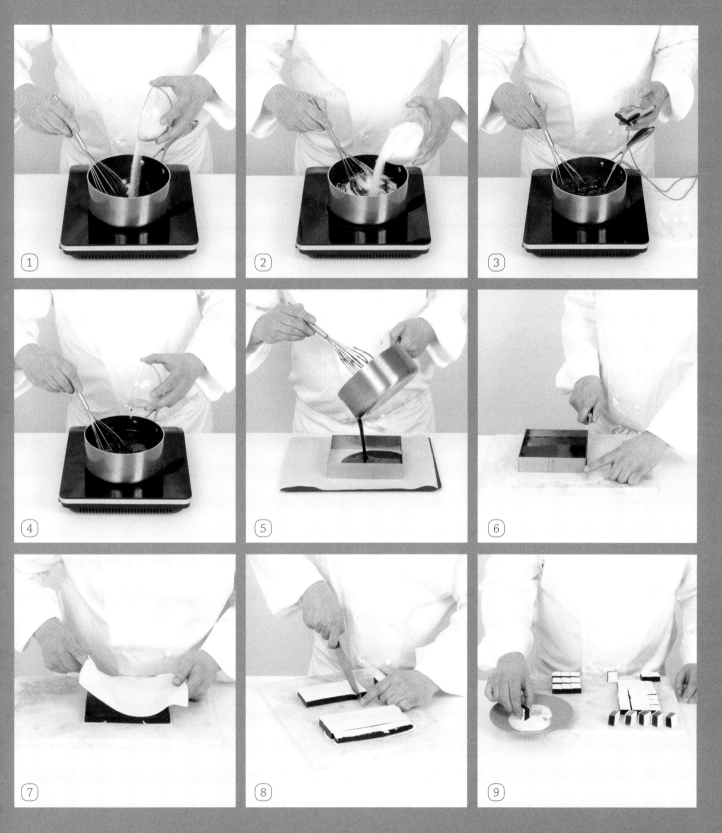

BLACKCURRANT-PRALINE
lollipops

Makes 20 lollipops

PREPARATION TIME: 1 hour + 30 minutes to temper the chocolate – CHILLING TIME: 15 minutes

SETTING TIME: 1 hour – STORAGE: 1 week in an airtight container

DIFFICULTY: 🎩

BLACKCURRANT-PRALINE PASTE
200 g milk chocolate
60 g dark chocolate (70% cocoa)
120 g blackcurrant purée
20 g sugar
1 tsp pectin
180 g praline paste
Icing sugar

COATING
400 g dark couverture chocolate (70% cocoa)

EQUIPMENT NEEDED: 20 wooden sticks – transfer sheet for chocolate – round 5-cm biscuit cutter

Transfer sheets for chocolate

Easy to use, transfer sheets let you embellish your chocolate confectionery or desserts and give them a professional finish. They come in a multitude of patterns to let you imprint the design of your choice on your creations. Carefully spread a layer of chocolate on the transfer sheet, and you'll be all set!

FOR THE BLACKCURRANT-PRALINE PASTE

1 – Chop the two types of chocolate and place into a bowl. In a saucepan, warm the blackcurrant purée. Mix together the sugar and pectin, then sprinkle over the blackcurrant purée.

2 – Bring to the boil for a few seconds, then pour over the chopped chocolate and mix.

3 – Mix in the praline paste, then leave to cool to room temperature, until the mixture has the texture of a paste.

4 – Sprinkle a sheet of baking parchment with icing sugar, set the ball of paste on top and sprinkle all over with icing sugar. Place another sheet of baking parchment on top.

5 – Roll out with a rolling pin to a thickness of 1 cm. Transfer to a baking tray and refrigerate for 15 minutes.

6 – Cut 20 lollipops out of the blackcurrant-praline paste using the biscuit cutter.

7 – Insert the sticks into the lollipops.

COATING AND DECORATION

8 – Temper the dark chocolate (see pages 494-495) and transfer to a bowl. Lay a sheet of baking parchment on your work surface. Cut the transfer sheet to make 20 squares about 6 x 6 cm in size.

9 – One by one, dip each lollipop into the tempered chocolate, let any excess drip off, then place on the baking parchment. Immediately set a square of transfer sheet on top. Leave to set for 1 hour at room temperature.

RASPBERRY AND SPECULOOS
caramels

Makes 40 caramels

PREPARATION TIME: 30 minutes – SETTING TIME: 12 hours – STORAGE: 1 week in an airtight container

DIFFICULTY: ♙ ♙

<u>RASPBERRY AND SPECULOOS CARAMELS</u>

100 g speculoos biscuits

360 ml cream

200 g sugar

50 g glucose

Small pinch of bicarbonate of soda

60 g Trimoline® (inverted sugar)

160 g raspberry purée

30 g lightly salted butter

20 g cocoa butter

Pinch of soy lecithin

<u>EQUIPMENT NEEDED:</u> Cooking thermometer – 16 x 16 cm pastry frame – round 4-cm biscuit cutter

Biscuit cutters

Whether smooth, fluted, round, square or another shape, biscuit cutters are utensils whose purpose is to cut precise shapes out of a rolled-out paste or dough of any kind. Made of tin, stainless steel or plastic, biscuit cutters are widely used in pastry making and can be employed to make biscuits or treats in all kinds of shapes.

FOR THE RASPBERRY AND SPECULOOS CARAMELS

1 – Reduce the speculoos biscuits into crumbs.

2 – In a large saucepan, combine the cream, sugar, glucose and bicarbonate of soda. Cook until the temperature reads 118°C on the cooking thermometer, stirring constantly with a silicone spatula.

3 – Once the mixture reaches 118°C, add the Trimoline®, then the raspberry purée. Stir constantly and gently until the temperature returns to 118°C.

4 – Mix in the butter, cocoa butter and soy lecithin, then remove from heat immediately.

5 – Add the crumbled speculoos biscuits.

6 – Set the pastry frame on a baking tray lined with baking parchment and fill with the caramel. Spread the layer out evenly with a silicone spatula. Leave to set for 12 hours at room temperature.

7 – Once the caramel is completely set, run a knife blade around the inside of the pastry frame and gently remove it.

8 – Cut off two 2-cm strips, then cut the strips into 4-cm rectangles.

9 – Cut out the rest of the caramels with a round biscuit cutter.

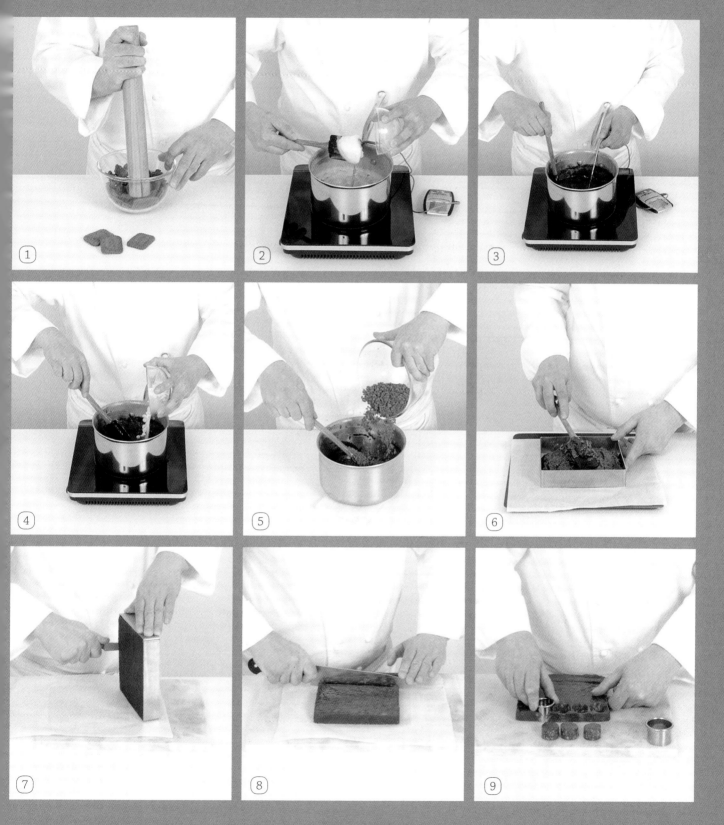

MATCHA TEA BITES

Makes 40

PREPARATION TIME: 30 minutes + 15 minutes for the pastry – CHILLING TIME: 3 hours + 30 minutes for the pastry
COOKING TIME: 10 minutes – Storage: 2 days in the refrigerator

DIFFICULTY: 🎩

WHITE CHOCOLATE GANACHE
270 g white chocolate
100 ml cream
20 g unsalted butter

MATCHA TEA JELLY
1 tsp matcha green tea powder
½ tsp agar-agar powder
30 g sugar
400 ml water
50 g honey

SWEET PASTRY DOUGH
80 g unsalted butter
50 g icing sugar
Pinch of salt
80 g plain flour
½ egg (20 g)

DECORATION
40 strawberries
Icing sugar

EQUIPMENT NEEDED: Silicone mould with 4-cm round imprints – 5-cm round biscuit cutter
piping bag – size PF16 star nozzle

Matcha green tea

Imported from China, matcha is an aromatic green tea sold as a fine
powder. It is made by grinding dried green tea leaves. Highly prized in
Japan for the famous tea ceremony, matcha tea is made by adding hot - but
not boiling - water to matcha powder. The preparation is then emulsified
with a bamboo whisk until it becomes a uniform jade green blend capped
with a light layer of foam.

MATCHA TEA BITES

FOR THE WHITE CHOCOLATE GANACHE

1 – Melt the white chocolate over a bain-marie. Bring the cream and butter to the boil, then pour immediately over the white chocolate. Mix until smooth. Refrigerate for 1 hour.

FOR THE MATCHA TEA JELLY

2 – Mix together the matcha green tea powder, agar-agar and sugar. In a saucepan, combine the water and honey, then add the dry ingredients.
3 – Bring the mixture to the boil, whisking constantly.
4 – Tip into a bowl, leave to cool, then pour into the mould, filling each imprint to the brim. Refrigerate for 2 hours.

FOR THE SWEET PASTRY DOUGH DISCS

5 – Preheat the oven to 170°C (gas mark 3-4). Roll out the sweet pastry dough (see pages 488 and 489) to a thickness of 3 mm, then cut out the discs using the biscuit cutter. Place on a baking tray lined with baking parchment. Bake for 10 minutes.

ASSEMBLY AND DECORATION

6 – Turn the matcha jellies out of the mould and place each one on top of a pastry disc.
7 – Whisk the white chocolate ganache. Transfer to a piping bag fitted with the star nozzle, then pipe out swirls of ganache onto a sheet of baking parchment.
8 – Sprinkle the raspberries with icing sugar, then set them on top of the ganache swirls.
9 – Top each matcha jelly-pastry disc with a ganache swirl.

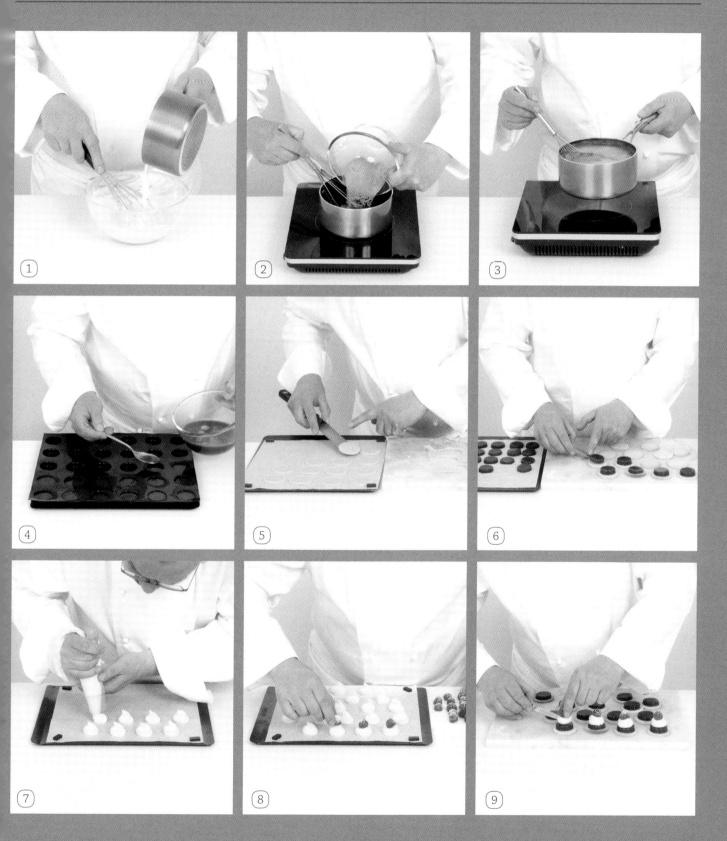

LEMON TART CARAMELS

Makes about 40 caramels

———————

PREPARATION TIME: 1 hour – SETTING TIME: 12 hours – STORAGE: 1 week in an airtight container

DIFFICULTY: 🎩 🎩

CARAMEL
115 g Brittany shortbreads
300 ml cream
Zest of 1 lemon
150 g sugar
50 g honey

Pinch of bicarbonate of soda
60 g pear purée
50 g Trimoline® (inverted sugar)
25 g unsalted butter
20 g white chocolate (31% cocoa)

EQUIPMENT NEEDED: Cooking thermometer – 6 x 16 cm pastry frame

Lemon tart caramels

You will find the delicious flavour of a lemon tart in this tangy, refreshing caramel. It perfectly re-creates the taste of the French culinary classic with a mix of Brittany shortbread, cream and lemon zest. Crunchy and melt-in-the-mouth, these caramels will satisfy any sweet tooth.

FOR THE LEMON TART CARAMELS

1 – In a bowl, crush the Brittany shortbreads to make crumbs.

2 – Pour the cream into a saucepan. Grate the lemon zest and add.

3 – Add the sugar, honey and bicarbonate of soda.

4 – Cook until the temperature reads 118°C on a cooking thermometer, stirring constantly with a silicone spatula.

5 – Once the mixture reaches 118°C, mix the pear purée and Trimoline® and add. Cook, continuing to stir gently, until the temperature returns to 118°C on the cooking thermometer.

6 – Remove from the heat and add the butter and white chocolate, then the crushed Brittany shortbread.

7 – Place the pastry frame on a baking tray lined with baking parchment and fill with the caramel. Spread the layer out evenly with a silicone spatula. Leave to set for 12 hours at room temperature.

8 – Once the caramel is completely set, remove the frame by running a knife blade around the inside edge.

9 – Cut into 2-cm strips, then cut the strips into 3-cm rectangles.

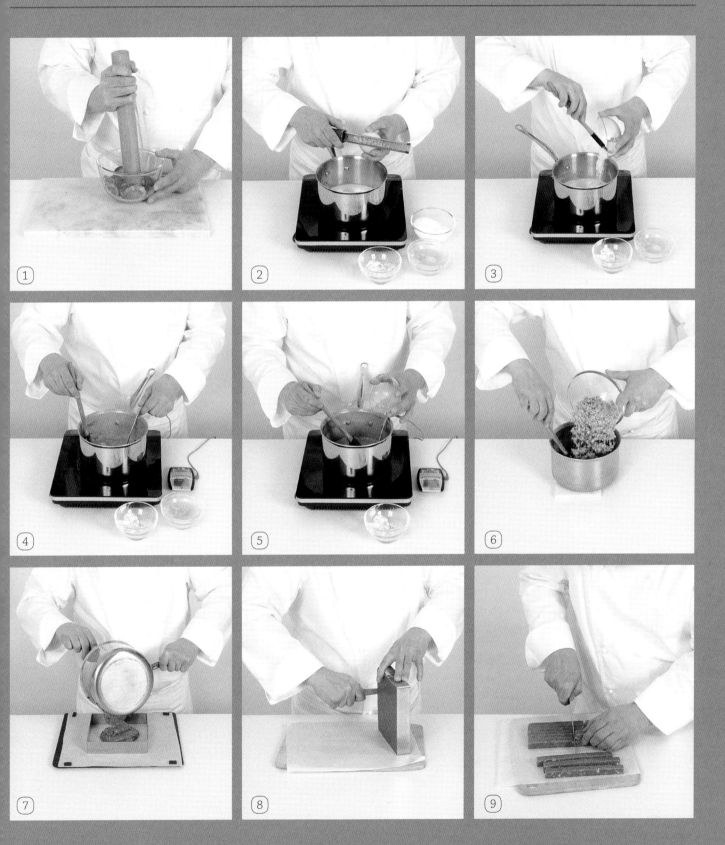

PASTRY
BASICS

UTENSILS

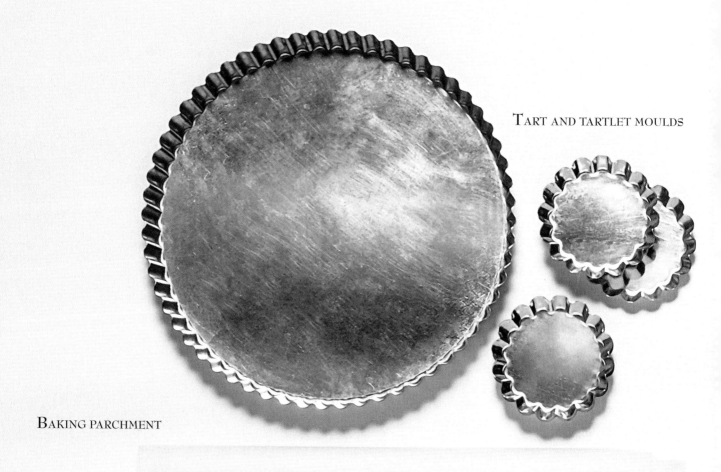

Tart and tartlet moulds

Baking parchment

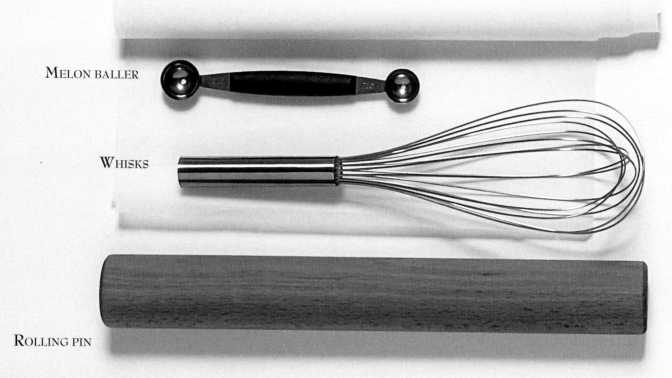

Melon baller

Whisks

Rolling pin

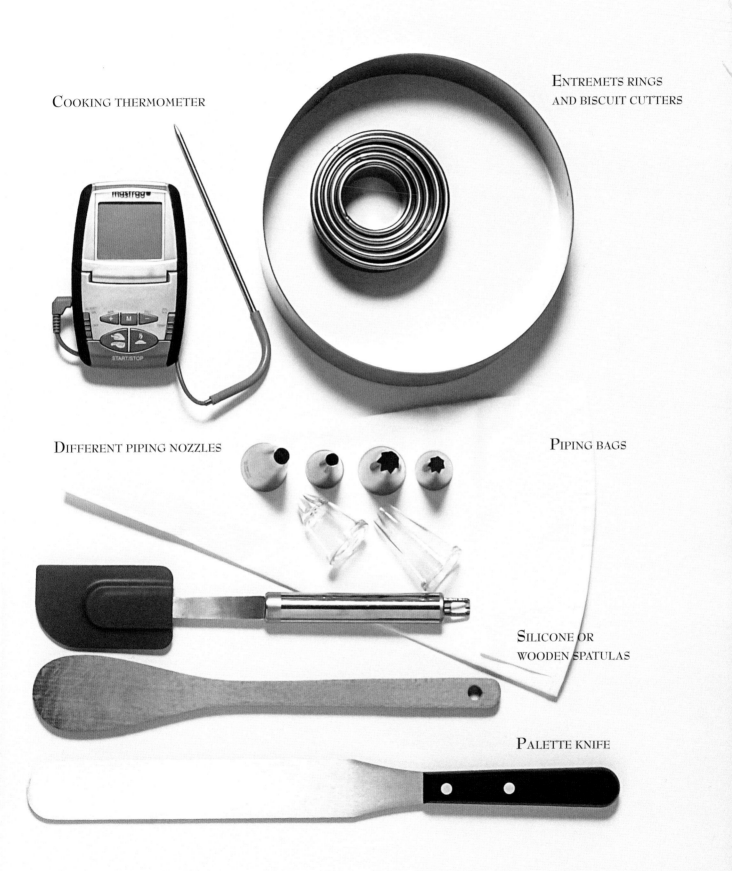

COOKING THERMOMETER

ENTREMETS RINGS
AND BISCUIT CUTTERS

DIFFERENT PIPING NOZZLES

PIPING BAGS

SILICONE OR
WOODEN SPATULAS

PALETTE KNIFE

INGREDIENTS

Cocoa powder

Flour

Icing sugar

Milk

Glucose

Sugar

VANILLA PODS

GELATINE

CORNFLOUR

NATURAL
FLAVOURINGS

JASMIN

COUVERTURE
CHOCOLATE

EGGS

BUTTER

THE UTENSILS
for pastry making

WHISKS

The whisk is a kitchen utensil used to beat or mix a preparation while incorporating air. It is indispensable when making many different pastry creations, such as Chantilly cream, whisked egg whites or sabayons. There are many different types of whisks, made in different shapes to suit different purposes. On one end of the spectrum, there is the 'balloon' whisk: the wires of this whisk, which may come in varying thicknesses, curve to a rounded end. This whisk is used for preparations where more air must be incorporated, such as egg whites or whipped cream. On the other, we find the sauce (or emulsion) whisk, which is more elongated and has stiffer wires. It is used for egg-based mixes, and its ergonomic shape helps keep egg-based sauces from coagulating. Lastly, we should also mention electric whisks. Widely used today, these can be set to many speeds and allow all types of preparations to be whisked efficiently.

SILICONE OR WOODEN SPATULAS

The spatula is a kitchen utensil used to gently mix delicate preparations. For example, it is used when folding egg whites and whipped cream to prevent them from deflating. It is also used to scrape the bottoms of containers and make it easier to get all of the preparation into a piping bag or mould. Different types of spatulas are used for different purposes: for delicate preparations that must be mixed or scraped out gently, silicone spatulas are used, recognisable for their long handle and rectangular end topped with a round, flexible silicone head. If you simply need to mix or flip ingredients, a more rigid wooden spatula will do just fine. There are also spatulas more commonly found in professional or semi-professional contexts, such as triangle spatulas, Exoglass® spatulas or angled spatulas, used for glazing and icing.

TART AND ENTREMETS RINGS

Tart and entremets rings are rings with no base, most often made of stainless steel, that come in a variety of depths and diameters. Although home bakers most often use cake and tart tins, professionals prefer rings, as these allow perfect entremets to be made, as well as being more practical during the delicate stage of turning a preparation out of the mould. Rings help prevent damage to preparations during this process.

BISCUIT CUTTERS

Biscuit cutters are a kitchen utensil, most often made of metal or plastic, made to precisely 'cut' all sorts of doughs in order to give them a special shape. Biscuit cutters come in all shapes and sizes, from the most simple to the most extravagant.

PASTRY FRAMES

Pastry frames are a kitchen utensil that are the square or rectangular version of tart or entremets rings. It is a mould without a base, most often made of stainless steel, for baking pastry cases and Génoise sponges. It can also be used to give a clean, neat look to desserts by 'framing' them. Frames have the advantage of sometimes being expandable, and can therefore be adapted to the recipe and desired number of portions. They are also very practical when it comes to the always-delicate operation of turning the preparation out of the mould; with traditional tins, this runs the risk of damaging the baked goods.

Piping bags

A piping bag (or pastry bag) is a cone-shaped pouch with a hole in the end in which a nozzle is placed. Used to decorate or fill preparations, the piping bag is an indispensable pastry making tool. It can be made of different materials: silicone, food-grade polyurethane or even single-use plastic. For a last-minute decoration, you can even make you own home-made piping bag by folding some baking parchment into a cone. Using a piping bag is simple, but requires a certain knack that comes with experience. To use it correctly, fill the bag with a spatula, pushing the mixture down to fill the end of the bag; you will also need to twist the top of the bag to close it and to be able to squeeze the preparation out.

Different piping nozzles

A pastry making essential, a piping nozzle is the end that is fitted to a piping bag to let you pipe out or decorate preparations. There are many kinds of nozzles, ranging from the fantastical (shaped like stars, flowers, leaves, etc.) to the classic (plain, star, etc.). You should choose the right nozzle for the decoration or piping you

want to do. Today, these may be made of polycarbonate or stainless steel. The most commonly used nozzles are plain, star and Saint-Honoré nozzles. These come in a wide range of diameters. The plain nozzle is typically used to make decorations or pipe into cavities. The star, whose aperture is conical and toothed, is used to make decorations and pipe meringues. Lastly, the Saint-Honoré nozzle has a diagonally-cut end that is perfect for decorating desserts with Chantilly cream, such as Saint-Honoré cakes or religieuses.

Baking parchment and silicone mats

Very frequently used in pastry making, baking parchment and mats are used for baking many types of preparations without requiring the addition of grease. Widely familiar to the general public, baking parchment is paper coated with a fine layer of silicone to make it waterproof and heat-resistant. There are also silicone baking mats, once used only by professional bakers, but now beginning to appear in home kitchens. These are most often called Silpat® after the brand that sells them. It is a non-stick baking mat made from a fibreglass weave impregnated with silicone. These baking mats are primarily used to bake preparations such as macarons, meringues and doughs.

Rolling pin

The rolling pin is a cylindrical cooking utensil, most often fitted with two handles, used to roll out dough. Traditionally made of wood, versions made of other materials can now be found (such as silicone, plastic and stainless steel). In baking and in pastry making, it is absolutely indispensable for making different pastries: puff, shortcrust, sweet pastry dough, etc.

To prevent the dough from sticking to the rolling pin and deforming, you must flour the pin before using it.

BRUSH

The pastry brush is a kitchen utensil used to finish pastry preparations. It can be used to glaze, brush or decorate. According to the surface you are working with, you can choose a larger or smaller brush. Pastry brushes are made from different materials: bristles (boar bristles) or synthetic or silicone fibres (more practical for applying fatty substances). They are very easy to use: you need only avoid over-saturating them to obtain a clean, neat result.

MELON BALLER

A melon baller is a small, round deep cutter used to cut small balls of fruit or vegetables. This utensil is often used to make balls of melon for fruit dishes and drinks, hence its name. To use a melon baller, you must dig it into the flesh of the fruit or vegetable and rotate it to extract a round ball.

COOKING THERMOMETER

Indispensable to the careful cook or pastry chef, the cooking thermometer is a kitchen utensil that allows you to find the exact temperature of a foodstuff or preparation while it is cooking. Used in pastry making for the preparation of pâte à bombe, caramel or fruit jellies, thermometers with a probe are preferable, as they are easy to use.

RHODOÏD® SHEETS

Rhodoïd® (acetate) sheets are plastic squares or bands used to line entremets rings during the preparation of mousses or creams. They are also used for working with chocolate decorations. With their smooth, shiny surface, Rhodoïd® sheets make turning desserts out of their moulds easier and create neat, clean edges. Originally, Rhodoïd® was the name of the brand that sold these sheets, but with time, it has come to be a term in its own right in pastry making. Rhodoïd® sheets come in many sizes. They are most often sold in rolls in specialised shops or on the Internet.

THE INGREDIENTS
for pastry making

FLOUR

Flour is a powder made by grinding grains or other solid food products. The most well-known is wheat flour, most often used to make bread and both savoury and sweet pastries. There are many types of flour, classified by how finely they are milled: in the French system, the higher the number following the T, the more of the bran is kept (the closer it is to wholemeal). The most widespread are T45 for pastry making and T55 for all uses, particularly bakery bread. These days, a number of gluten-free flours are in fashion: flours made from rice, chestnut, chickpeas, corn, etc. These cannot be made into bread - they are unsuitable for leavened doughs - but can be used mixed with wheat flour or to make certain cakes and desserts.

MILK

When we talk about milk, we're talking about cow's milk, as many other kinds exist. Very commonly used in pastry making, cow's milk has a rich composition (contains water, fats, lactose, proteins, caseins, minerals, etc.). The first standard used to classify milk is its fat content: full-fat milk, semi-skimmed milk and skimmed milk. It is often recognised by the colour of the cap, however the colours differ from country to country. There are many ways of preserving milk: pasteurisation, which involves heating the milk and holding it for 20 seconds between 72 and 85°C; sterilisation, which involves holding the milk for 15 to 20 minutes at 115°C; and UHT sterilisation (ultra-high-temperature processing), which involves heating the milk to between 140 and 150°C for a few seconds. Depeding on the method used, milk can be kept for between 7 and 150 days.

CREAM

Cream is made by skimming milk: the goal is to separate cream from milk using a separator-centrifuge that spins the milk at a high speed. The cream leaves the machine through the top, while the skimmed milk leaves through the bottom. The types of cream are distinguished by three criteria: shelf-life treatment, fat content and consistency. Like milk, to extend its shelf life, cream can be pasteurised, sterilised or UHT-sterilised. In terms of consistency, it can be liquid, semi-thick or thick; these are useful in different pastry preparations. Cream must contain 35% fat in order to be whipped.

SUGAR AND ICING SUGAR

The taste of pleasure bar none, sugar is made from sugar cane or sugar beet. There are many different kinds of sugar, which are the results of different production methods: unrefined cane sugar, organic white sugar, light or dark brown sugar, candy sugar or icing sugar. Each one has a specific colour and flavour. Frequently used in pastry making, icing sugar is made by grinding granulated sugar and adding starch or silica to prevent lumps from forming.

BUTTER

A pastry making essential, butter is made from milk fat, which is then churned. In France, the apellation 'butter' is protected by law: to merit the name, butter must contain at least 82% fat (80% for lightly salted butter), and at most 16% water and 2% milk solids. Usually yellow, butter can also be more white depending on the source of the milk used to make it. Another kind of butter, called 'dry butter' or 'laminating unsalted butter' in French, is also very commonly used in baking and pastry making. At least 84% fat, it is firmer and easier to work in hot conditions. It is also exceptionally plastic. Dry butter is primarily used to make puff pastry and the related yeast-based pastries: croissants, pain au chocolat, etc.

EGGS

Low in calories and rich in protein, chicken eggs are the most commonly used in pastry making. In general terms, eggs serve to bind things together, but it is important to distinguish the uses of the yolk from those of the white in pastry making. The yolk acts as a thickener when heated (in a cream, for example); it also serves as an emulsifier when air is beaten in, as well as binding together a cake batter which, thanks to its high fat content, will be moist. The white brings solidity to a dough and, when whisked, lightens doughs and mousses.

VANILLA

Originally from Mexico, where it has been grown since Aztec times, vanilla is a classic pastry spice. Today, the vast majority of production comes from islands in the Indian ocean: Madagascar, Réunion, Mauritius, etc.

Vanilla is sold in different forms, each with its own use in cookery: whole vanilla pods which should be split before use; vanilla powder, the result of grinding dried vanilla pods (it can be either pure or sweetened); and vanilla extract (liquid or dry), which is made by macerating vanilla in alcohol, then filtering it and infusing it into a sugar syrup.

COUVERTURE CHOCOLATE

Couverture chocolate is a high-quality chocolate used by chocolatiers and pastry makers: whether dark or milk, it should contain at least 32% cocoa butter, giving fluidity and letting it melt more easily. Due to its properties, it is couverture chocolate that is used to temper chocolate, make chocolate sweets and produce chocolate decorations. This allows the fat crystals to set and give the qualities of a well-finished chocolate: shiny and with a perfect snap once it is fully set.

BAKING POWDER

Baking powder is a mix made of a base (most frequently bicarbonate of soda), an acid and a stabiliser. It comes as a powder and is used to leaven breads and pastries. To act, baking powder requires both heat and humidity: after being kneaded in, the powder comes into contact with water, and once it is placed in the oven, the acid and base react to make carbon dioxide (CO_2), whose release 'proofs' the dough and makes it rise. This is what gives an aerated texture to culinary creations. To obtain an even rise and best results, the baking powder must be mixed and sifted with the flour. Take care to follow the amount listed in the recipe, as adding too much baking powder will make it rise strangely and add an unpleasant flavour.

CORNFLOUR

Cornflour is a very fine white powder extracted from corn starch. It is often confused with cornmeal, but their compositions differ: in cornmeal, the entire grain is ground, but cornflour contains only starch. Its texture is therefore finer. It is used in cooking and pastry making for its thickening and setting properties. If used to replace part of the wheat flour, cornflour can make cakes lighter and more airy.

POTATO STARCH

Potato starch is a fine white powder made from potatoes that have been dried and milled into a powder. In cooking, it is primarily used for its thickening properties. In pastry making, it is used to lighten desserts and give them a moist texture. It is also one of the ingredients used in pastry cream, and provides the cream's smoothness. As it has no gluten, it is perfect for the gluten-sensitive, but it cannot be used alone, as it does not rise: essentially, potato starch cannot be used to make bread.

FRESH COMPRESSED YEAST

Fresh compressed yeast is made from one or several species of Saccharomyces cerevisiae, a microscopic living fungi. Unlike baking powder, it acts through the fermentation carried out by living organisms. It is widely used to make bread, Danish pastries and brioches during the rising process (the 'proofing' of the dough). Sold fresh (pressed into a cube, as a powder or as a liquid) or dry (active or instant), yeast eats the sugars (glucose) in flour and causes a chemical reaction. Yeast does not need heat to act; you need only leave the dough standing at room temperature, (however, a certain amount of time is required, between two and three hours.) Take care not to mix it directly with salt, as the salt will 'kill' the living organisms in the yeast and the dough will not rise.

GROUND ALMONDS

Ground almonds are, as their name suggests, a powder made by grinding whole almonds. Their uses in pastry making are well-known and diverse: doughs, tarts, financiers, macarons, almond paste, etc. It is a key ingredient in macarons, frangipane and financiers, where ground almonds are one of the main ingredients. It can also be used more subtly to flavour cakes, creams and blancmanges. In tarts and tartlets, ground almonds can be very useful, as they absorb any excess fruit juice, leaving your tart cases crisp.

GROUND HAZELNUTS

Made by toasting and grinding hazelnuts, ground hazelnuts are used in a number of sweet creations, primarily to flavour desserts: macarons, cookies, ganaches, tart cases, etc. When ground for longer, they are used to make hazelnut paste, the key ingredient of the famous hazelnut spread loved by young and old alike. Take care not to mistake ground hazelnuts for hazelnut flour; to make hazelnut flour, the oil has been extracted, and the powder left behind. They do not have the same properties.

UNSWEETENED COCOA POWDER

Unsweetened cocoa powder is made from the nib of the cocoa bean. The nib must be treated to remove its bitterness: it is fermented, then sorted and toasted.

It is then cooled, crushed and milled. This produces cocoa mass (liquor), which contains fat: cocoa butter. After extracting this fat, a presscake is left behind; ground and sifted, this becomes unsweetened cocoa powder. Widely used in pastry making, unsweetened cocoa powder gives a chocolatey flavour to your sweet preparations. When mixed with milk, it is used to prepare the well-known drink called hot chocolate.

AGAR-AGAR

Agar-agar is a gelling agent that comes from red seaweed ground into powder. Calorie-free, odourless and flavourless, it is perfect for vegetarians who wish to use it as a substitute for gelatine (made from beef or pork). However, its gelling power is eight times stronger (meaning less should be used) and the way in which it is used is different. It should be mixed into a cold liquid and brought to the boil for 10-30 seconds before being added to a preparation. It will then set as it cools. Agar-agar gives preparations a very firm and almost brittle texture, which is something to take into consideration when using it. To make your agar-agar based desserts smoother, you may wish to consider adding crème fraîche, compote or fresh cheese.

PECTIN AND YELLOW PECTIN

Vegetable in origin, pectin is found mainly in apples, citrus fruits, quinces and redcurrants. It is used for its stabilising, gelling and thickening properties. There are many different kinds of pectin, with the two main types being NH pectin and yellow pectin. NH pectin works in an acidic and sugary environment, creating a firm, shiny texture. Glazes made with this pectin are reversible, meaning that they can set and be re-melted

many times while still retaining their properties. Yellow pectin is a slow-setting pectin that also works in very sugary, acidic environments; however, once set, it cannot be re-melted with heat. It is therefore perfect for fruit jellies, jams or gelled confections.

GLUCOSE

Glucose is a pure carbohydrate made from corn or potato starch. Used in many pastries, it rarely appears in recipes and is primarily used by professionals. Glucose is four times less sweet than table sugar, but has the same number of calories. Most often, it comes in the form of a colourless, thick, viscous syrup. In ice creams, it is used as a stabiliser and to improve texture. In pastry making, glucose syrup is used for its anti-crystallising and preservative properties. It stops sugar from crystallising, and has a similar effect on water during freezing, for example in ice creams. In addition, it plays a major role in extending the shelf life of your creations, making them softer and more tender. When used cold, it is diluted in a liquid before being added to the preparation; when used hot, it should be melted in order to combine it fully with the other ingredients.

GELATINE

Made through the hydrolysis of collagen-rich materials, like the skin and bones of pigs, cows or fish, gelatine is a product used as a gelling agent. Colourless, odourless and flavourless, it is used in a wide variety of food preparations, both savoury and sweet. It gives them a smooth, creamy texture. Gelatine most often comes as leaves. To use them, you must let the leaves soften in water for 10 minutes, squeeze them out and dissolve them in a hot liquid. However, this must not boil, or the gelatine will lose all its gelling power. To use gelatine in cold preparations, heat a small quantity of liquid to dissolve the gelatine leaves, then add this back in to the cold mixture. Take care, as certain fruits, such as the kiwi, pineapple and papaya, contain an enzyme that prevents gelatine from setting. To avoid this small problem, poach these fruits before using.

FOOD COLOURING

Food colourings are used to intensify the natural colours of a food or to liven them up by adding bright, eye-catching hues. There are two main categories of food colouring: hydrosoluble and liposoluble. Hydrosoluble colours are those that dissolve in water. These are recommended for colouring products such as macarons, creams, cakes, almond paste, etc. Liposoluble colours, in turn, dissolve in fat; they are recommended for colouring chocolate, butters and glazes. Food colourings (both hydrosoluble and liposoluble) come in different forms: liquid, gel or powder. Liquid colours should be avoided in eggbased preparations, as they can liquefy the mixture and cause it to fall. Gel colours are concentrated and therefore allow you to obtain very bright tones, as well as having the advantage of not affecting your preparations. Lastly, powdered colours should be used sparingly, and are often found in macaron recipes.

GOLD POWDER

Ideal for bringing flair and brilliance, edible gold powder provides a festive, professional finish to your creations. Once only used by specialists, it can now be found fairly easily online or in specialised shops. It is used on the surface of desserts; a damp brush is used to decorate them with a golden coat. It adds a final touch to perfect the aesthetics of a creation. It is not advisable to mix it into a dough, cream or any other pastry preparation, as the golden effect will be uneven and will not colour the whole mix. It can be used, according to your taste or the occasion, on macarons, chocolates, tarts, or yule log cakes, but also to decorate plated desserts.

NEUTRAL GLAZE

Very easy to make, neutral glaze is made of water, sugar, glucose and a gelling agent (usually pectin or gelatine). It brings brilliance and will serve to embellish your tarts, desserts and other sweet preparations. Neutral in colour and flavour, it is the perfect final touch for desserts, immediately giving them a professional, highly aesthetic look. Neutral glaze, once made, is applied to the surface with a brush.

FONDANT

Fondant for pastry making is a preparation made of sugar, water and glucose used to ice cakes, entremets and other sweet creations, such as mille-feuilles, choux puffs, religieuses and éclairs. The sugar syrup is heated to between 114 and 116°C before being cooled to 75°C and worked to make a homogeneous mass of syrup. The fondant then becomes an opaque white. It should then age (typically for 3 days in the refrigerator) before being used. It can also be coloured according to your preferences or the main flavour in your creations.

Cocoa butter

Cocoa butter is the fat extracted from cocoa mass (liquor) by squeezing it in a hydraulic press during the manufacture of unsweetened cocoa powder. It is solid at room temperature, but has a fairly low melting point (35- 37°C). However, it may be sold in different forms: as a powder, liquid or block. Cocoa butter has an almost neutral taste and a light aroma of cocoa. It is used in many different foods, pharmaceutical products and cosmetics. A very versatile ingredient, it can be found in chocolate, and can be used to cook as well as to blind bake tart cases: it seals the dough and prevents it from going soggy from fruits or fillings. Cocoa butter is very healthy, never goes rancid and keeps very well (around 2 years) if not exposed to air.

Inverted sugar (Trimoline®)

Inverted sugar, or Trimoline®, is a sweetener about 25% sweeter than table sugar. Inverted sugar is produced by hydrolysing sucrose: this produces a half-and-half mix of glucose and fructose. Used only by professionals and very expert amateur cooks, Trimoline® is valued for its anti-drying properties. It prevents sugar crystallisation, improves fermentation and colour and boosts flavours. Notably, it allows moister preparations to be made, cooking times to be reduced and ice creams and sorbets to be stabilised. Sold as a liquid or paste, it can only be found in specialised shops or online.

PASTRY CREAM

PREPARATION TIME: 30 MINUTES
CHILLING TIME: 30 MINUTES

MAKES ABOUT **500** G PASTRY CREAM
370 ml milk, 25 g unsalted butter, 3 egg yolks
(70 g), 80 g sugar, 20 g plain flour,
25 g cornflour

Adjust the quantity of ingredients to your chosen recipe.

Traditionally, pastry cream is made from milk,
which may be vanilla-infused. However, the
milk is sometimes replaced or enhanced with
fruit purée, coconut milk, fruit juice, etc., to
give it different flavours. A plain pastry cream
can also be flavoured after cooking by adding
chocolate, coffee or praline, for example.
It is made in a similar manner to crème anglaise
in that it requires particular care and slow
cooking. The main difference lies in that pastry
cream is thickened with flour and/or starch
and must be boiled. This is what gives pastry
cream its consistency. Widely used in pastry
making, pastry cream is used to make desserts
(either plain or with added butter or whipped
cream), frangipane, filled choux pastries (éclairs,
religieuses) and as a soufflé base.

CHEF'S TIP

To keep the cornflour or flour from
forming lumps, the cream must
be stirred throughout the cooking
process. As pastry cream burns
easily, it is advisable to make it in
a fairly deep saucepan and to stir it
continuously, making sure to reach
the full extent of the bottom and
sides of the pan while stirring.

1 In a saucepan, bring the
milk and butter to the boil, then
remove from heat.

2 In a bowl, whisk together
the egg yolks and sugar until the
mixture becomes pale and thick.

3 Add the flour and cornflour,
then mix with a whisk.

4 Tip in a third of the hot milk,
whisking well.

5 Tip the whole mixture back
into the saucepan with the rest
of the liquid and cook over a low
heat, whisking continuously,
until the cream thickens. Boil for
1 minute, stirring continuously,
then remove from heat
immediately.

6 Tip the pastry cream into a
bowl with the help of a silicone
spatula.

CRÈME ANGLAISE

PREPARATION TIME: 15 MINUTES

MAKES ABOUT **500** ML CRÈME ANGLAISE
350 ml milk, ⅓ vanilla pod,
4 egg yolks (80 g), 85 g sugar

Adjust the quantity of ingredients to your chosen recipe.

Like pastry cream, crème anglaise is made of milk, egg yolks and sugar, but contains neither flour nor starch.

It should be made with care: during cooking, it must be stirred constantly with a wooden spoon to avoid cooking the egg yolks, and cooked until it reaches 'coating' texture (the crème anglaise coats the spoon).

Classic crème anglaise is flavoured with vanilla, which is generally infused into the milk from the beginning. Crème anglaise can also be flavoured after cooking with chocolate, coffee, praline, pistachio, etc.

1 Split the vanilla pod lengthwise and scrape the inside with a knife to obtain the seeds.

2 In a bowl, whisk together the egg yolks and sugar until the mixture becomes pale and thick.

3 In a saucepan, bring the milk to the boil with the seeds and the vanilla pod.

4 Pour a third of the hot vanilla-infused milk into the egg yolk-sugar mixture, whisking vigorously.

5 Tip the whole mixture back into the saucepan and cook over a low heat, stirring with a spoon, until the cream thickens and covers the back of the utensil: dip out a little cream on the spoon, angle it and draw a horizontal line through the cream on the spoon with your finger. The edges of the line should remain very neat.

6 Place the crème anglaise in a bowl and leave to cool in the refrigerator.

CHANTILLY CREAM

PREPARATION TIME: 10 MINUTES

MAKES **500** G CHANTILLY CREAM

500 ml cream, 50 g icing sugar, 1 vanilla pod

Adjust the quantity of ingredients to your chosen recipe.

Chantilly cream, a favourite of food lovers everywhere, is very easy to make and is the perfect accompaniment to many desserts.

The key to success: a very cold bowl and very cold cream, kept ahead of time in the refrigerator.

Using cream with a fat content of at least 35% is absolutely essential; if the cream has less fat, it will not whip up.

Classic Chantilly cream is flavoured with vanilla, but many different versions exist today: chocolate, coffee, pistachio, etc.

1. In a bowl, whip the cream until it thickens.

2. Add the icing sugar and the seeds from the vanilla pod (previously split in half). Continue to whisk vigorously until the cream is firm and clings to the tip of the whisk.

CHEF'S TIP

If you do not have any vanilla pods, you can also use vanilla powder or liquid vanilla extract to good effect. As vanilla extract is fairly concentrated, take care to add it sparingly.

CHOUX PASTRY

PREPARATION TIME: 15 MINUTES

MAKES 500 G CHOUX PASTRY

170 ml milk, 70 g unsalted butter, 7 g sugar,
½ tsp fine salt, 100 g plain flour,
3 eggs (150 g)

Adjust the quantity of ingredients to your chosen recipe.

Choux pastry, a French pastry classic, is the base
for many traditional preparations, including
éclairs, chouquettes, religieuses, choux puffs,
and even the Saint-Honoré and Paris-Brest.
Follow this method, step-by-step, to obtain
a consistent, even-textured pastry that will
provide best results once baked.

1 In a saucepan, heat the milk,
butter, sugar and salt until the
butter melts completely. Bring to
the boil. Remove from heat, then
tip in all the flour at once.

2 Mix with a wooden spoon to
make a smooth, uniform paste
that wraps around the spoon.

3 Place the dough back on
the hob to dry, stirring until the
dough comes away from the sides
of the pan.

4 Transfer the dough to a bowl
and leave to cool for 5 minutes.

5 Mix in the beaten eggs little
by little by beating them in with
a spoon, reserving a little egg to
test the dough.

6 Next, test the dough to see if
it is ready to use: take up a little
with the spoon, then let it drop.
If it makes a 'V' as it falls from
the spoon, it is ready. If not, add a
little more beaten egg and repeat
the test.

GÉNOISE SPONGE

PREPARATION TIME: 30 MINUTES

MAKES **500** G GÉNOISE SPONGE MIXTURE

3½ eggs (175 g), 130 g sugar, 25 g unsalted butter, melted, 135 g plain flour, 30 g ground almonds

Adjust the quantity of ingredients to your chosen recipe.

Génoise sponge is a light preparation used as a base for many entremets, including Fraisier and Black Forest gateau.

It is often cut into two or three discs; these are generally imbibed with syrup and filled with cream or mousse, then stacked on top of one another during the assembly of the entremets. It is a good idea to whisk up a génoise sponge with an electric whisk to ensure that it thickens well and reaches the 'ribbon stage'. This stage is the key to success with a génoise; without it, the sponge will not rise when baked, and it will be dense and difficult to cut.

1 In a bowl, whisk together the eggs and sugar with an electric whisk.

2 Place the bowl over a bain-marie and continue to whisk until the mixture becomes pale and thick. It should be a little hot to the touch.

3 Remove the bowl from the bain-marie and continue to whisk until the mixture is completely cool and achieves 'ribbon' consistency: when the whisk is lifted, the mixture should fall off in an unbroken stream, forming a ribbon.

4 Mix a little génoise mixture with the melted butter in another bowl, then recombine with the main mixture.

5 Sift the flour and mix it into the mixture along with the ground almonds.

6 Fold with a silicone spatula until just smooth.

JOCONDE "BISCUIT" SPONGE

PREPARATION TIME: 15 MINUTES

MAKES A **30** x **38** CM TRAY OF CAKE

4 eggs (200 g), 140 g ground almonds,
125 g icing sugar, 45 g plain flour, 25 g unsalted
butter, melted (optional), 4 egg whites (120 g),
35 g sugar

Adjust the quantity of ingredients to your chosen recipe.

Joconde "biscuit" sponge is a particularly soft
cake and does not need to be imbibed with
syrup, as is often the case with basic "biscuits"
or génoise sponges.

It differs from a basic "biscuit" or génoise in the
way in which it is made: the flour is mixed with
the eggs at the beginning, while in the others,
the flour is added last.

In general, Joconde "biscuit" sponges are spread
onto a baking tray before being baked; they are
not baked in a tin, as Génoise sponges are.

CHEF'S TIP

For your egg whites to whip up well,
they must be at room temperature;
your cooking utensils should also be
very clean to avoid introducing any
fat that could prevent the whites
from frothing.

1. Whisk together the eggs, ground almonds, icing sugar and flour. Add the warm melted butter (optional).

2. Whisk the egg whites until they cling to the tip of the whisk.

3. Add half the sugar and whisk together, then add the rest of the sugar to form stiff peaks.

4. Use a spatula to gently fold the flour mixture into the egg whites.

MERINGUE

Meringue is a classic French pastry preparation made from beaten egg whites and sugar.

There are three types of meringue: French meringue, Italian meringue and Swiss meringue. Each is used for different purposes, including to make petit fours, parfaits, frozen soufflés, dacquoises, toppings for tarts or entremets or simply to decorate desserts.

FRENCH MERINGUE is the most traditional and, above all, the easiest to use. It is made by whisking egg whites and adding nearly double their weight in sugar. Traditionally, two types of sugar are added in more or less equal proportions: sugar and icing sugar.

ITALIAN MERINGUE, highly valued by pastry chefs, is made by pouring cooked sugar over beaten or whisked egg whites. It is generally used to lighten creams, as well as to mask and decorate tarts and desserts.

SWISS MERINGUE is made by whisking egg whites with double their weight in sugar over a bain-marie.

FRENCH MERINGUE

PREPARATION TIME:
10 MINUTES

MAKES 300 G FRENCH MERINGUE
100 g egg whites,
100 g sugar,
100 g icing sugar
Adjust the quantity of ingredients
to your chosen recipe.

1. In a bowl, whisk the egg whites until thick and foamy.

2. Continuing to whisk, gradually add the sugar until the whites are smooth, glossy and hold stiff peaks.

3. Fold in the icing sugar using a wooden spatula.

ITALIAN MERINGUE

PREPARATION TIME:
15 MINUTES

MAKES 350 G ITALIAN MERINGUE
100 g egg whites,
200 g sugar,
80 ml water

Adjust the quantity of ingredients
to your chosen recipe.

① Make a syrup by heating the sugar and water in a saucepan until the temperature reads 119°C on a cooking thermometer. Meanwhile, whisk the egg whites until soft peaks form.

② Once the temperature of the syrup reaches 119°C, tip immediately over the whites, whisking continuously.

③ Whisk vigorously until the meringue is completely cool. It should be firm and hold stiff peaks.

SWISS MERINGUE

PREPARATION TIME:
15 MINUTES

MAKES 300 G SWISS MERINGUE
100 g egg whites,
200 g sugar

Adjust the quantity of ingredients
to your chosen recipe.

① Whisk the egg whites and sugar in a bowl over a bain-marie until the temperature reads 45°C on a cooking thermometer.

② Once the temperature reaches 45°C, remove from the bain-marie and whisk vigorously until the meringue is completely cool. It should be firm and hold stiff peaks.

PASTRY DOUGHS FOR TARTS

Pastry dough is an essential element in pastry making; with good technique, you can create delicious, completely homemade tarts.

Sweet pastry, shortbread and sweet shortcrust pastry doughs are easy to make, and take only about 15 minutes to prepare. Puff pastry, on the other hand, requires considerably more time, and its preparation is also a more delicate process.

In this book, the Chefs have sometimes chosen to lightly flavour the pastry with ground almonds, but this ingredient can be left out or replaced with hazelnuts, vanilla or cocoa powder to give the pastry different flavours.

SWEET PASTRY DOUGH AND SHORTBREAD PASTRY

SWEET PASTRY DOUGH is particularly rich, but is a good fit for many tart recipes with a relatively heavy filling, such as an almond cream or chocolate ganache.
SHORTBREAD PASTRY has a sandy, crumbly consistency and is fragile when rolled out, but its texture is delightful when eaten.

Shortbread and sweet pastry doughs can be made using two methods: 'creaming' or 'rubbing in'.
The creaming method involves working room-temperature butter with icing sugar (creaming) to give it a light, creamy consistency, then adding eggs. The rest of the ingredients are then added.
The rubbing-in method involves mixing the butter directly with the dry ingredients by using your hands to rub the ingredients together with your fingertips (rubbing-in/*sabler*) before smearing it along the work surface to mix *(fraser)*. The main advantage of the rubbing-in method is that it requires less chilling time than the creaming method.

MAKES **250** G SWEET PASTRY DOUGH
105 g plain flour,
50 g unsalted butter,
50 g icing sugar,
1 tablespoon ground almonds,
½ egg (25 g)
Adjust the quantity of ingredients to your chosen recipe.

MAKES **250** G SHORTBREAD PASTRY
110 g plain flour,
65 g unsalted butter,
45 g icing sugar,
Pinch of salt,
1 tbsp ground almonds,
20 g egg
Adjust the quantity of ingredients to your chosen recipe.

THE CREAMING METHOD

PREPARATION TIME: 15 MINUTES – CHILLING TIME: 1 HOUR

THE RUBBING-IN METHOD

PREPARATION TIME: 15 MINUTES – CHILLING TIME: 30 MINUTES

 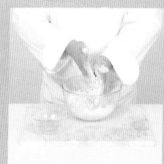

① In a bowl, whisk the butter until light and creamy.

② Add the icing sugar and whisk until homogeneous and smooth.

① Place the flour, butter, icing sugar, salt and ground almonds in a bowl.

② Work the dough by mixing it and rubbing it between your fingertips (rubbing-in/*sabler*).

③ Add the ground almonds.

④ Add the egg and mix well.

③ Add the egg and mix using a wooden spatula.

④ Turn the mixture out onto your work surface and smear until a smooth dough comes together.

⑤ Lastly, add the flour and mix until the dough is smooth.

⑥ Form the dough into a ball, flatten slightly and refrigerate for 1 hour.

⑤ Form the dough into a ball and flatten slightly.

⑥ Wrap in cling film and refrigerate for 30 minutes.

SWEET SHORTCRUST PASTRY

PREPARATION TIME: 15 MINUTES
CHILLING TIME: 30 MINUTES

Makes 250 g sweet shortcrust pastry
125 g plain flour, 75 g unsalted butter,
pinch of salt, 2 tsp icing sugar, ½ egg (30 g),
1 tsp water

Adjust the quantity of ingredients to your chosen recipe.

Rubbing-in method only

Shortcrust pastry, which is less fragile, contains
less butter and sugar and is an ideal base for
liquid fillings such as those found in fruit tarts.

1 Place the flour, butter, icing sugar, and salt in a bowl.

2 Work the dough by mixing it and rubbing it between your fingertips (rubbing-in/*sabler*).

3 Add the egg and water; mix using a wooden spatula.

4 Turn the mixture out onto your work surface and smear *(fraser)* until a smooth dough comes together.

5 Form the dough into a ball and flatten slightly.

6 Wrap in cling film and refrigerate for 30 minutes.

PUFF PASTRY

PREPARATION TIME: 1 HOUR
CHILLING TIME: 1 HOUR 40 MINUTES

Makes 500 g puff pastry
Détrempe: 105 ml water, 1 tsp salt, 45 g hot melted butter, 190 g plain flour
155 g 'dry butter' (84% fat)

Puff pastry is entirely different from the other three pastries in both texture and the way in which it is made. The process is much longer and more delicate, creating the flaky, crunchy result characteristic of this pastry.

It is prepared in two stages: the creation of a détrempe made from flour, water, butter and salt, then the addition of the dry butter in a series of 'turns', which involve folding the dough over on itself. Classic puff pastry is given 6 turns. Its production also requires a significant amount of chilling time.

There is also a kind of pastry called inverse puff pastry in which the détrempe is wrapped in the butter. This is used to make the famous mille-feuilles, but also certain fine tarts and small pastries.

1 Tip the cold water and salt into a large bowl, then mix in the hot melted butter.

2 Add the flour and mix the dough with a plastic dough scraper. This dough is called 'détrempe'.

3 Place the détrempe on a lightly floured work surface. Slap it down several times on the work surface, then knead gently to make a smooth dough.

4 Flatten the dough slightly with a rolling pin. Wrap in cling film and refrigerate for 30 minutes.

5 Soften the butter by tapping it repeatedly with a rolling pin.

6 Cut into a square, place the trimmings on top of the butter block and flatten slightly.

7 Lightly flour your work surface and quickly roll out the détrempe.

8 Place the butter square on top and fold the dough over it.

9 Lightly tap over the top to ensure the butter is securely wrapped in dough.

10 Roll out the entire assembly to seal the butter inside the détrempe and make a rectangle. Flour lightly if necessary.

11 Take the bottom third of the dough and fold over the middle third.

12 Then fold the top third over the middle third (1st turn).

13 Rotate the dough 90 degrees on your work surface.

14 Roll out the dough into a rectangle again.

15 Fold over the bottom third of the dough, then the top third, as above (2nd turn). Gently flatten the dough.

16 Mark the dough with your fingers to remind you how many turns you have completed (2). Wrap the dough in cling film, then refrigerate for 20 minutes.

17 Take the dough out of the refrigerator, remove the cling film and set the dough in front of you. Repeat the above steps (the 2 turns) 2 times, completing 6 turns in total, refrigerating for 20 minutes after each 2 turns.

18 Shape the dough into a rectangle again. Wrap in cling film and refrigerate for 30 minutes.

LINING A TART, TARTLET RING OR TIN

PREPARATION TIME: 10 MINUTES

Make a shortbread, shortcrust or sweet pastry dough, as suits your chosen tart recipe.

Lining a tart ring or tin with homemade pastry is a simple technique that is nevertheless essential to avoid damaging the pastry which, at this stage, is generally fragile.
Shaping the edges once you have lined the tin will let you dress up your tart's presentation.

1 Cut out a 3-mm-thick round of pastry approximately 5 cm larger in diameter than your ring/tin, setting the tin on top of the pastry as a guide.

2 Roll the pastry up on a rolling pin, then unroll it over the buttered ring/tin, letting it hang over the edges.

3 Line the ring/tin with the pastry by pressing it down, making sure the pastry goes all the way to the bottom corners.

4 Push the pastry gently into the sides so a little folds over the top of the ring/tin.

5 Roll the rolling pin over the top of the ring/tin, pressing down firmly to cut off any excess pastry.

6 Use two fingers to pinch the excess dough around the top, making it stick up a little above the top of the ring/tin. If you are going to blind bake your tart case, refrigerate for 10 minutes.

BLIND BAKING A TART CASE

BAKING TIME: 10 MINUTES

Prepare the pastry of your choice and use to line a tart/tartlet ring or tin (see recipe on page 493), then refrigerate for 10 minutes.

Blind baking allows you to partially bake a tart case before adding the filling (cream, fruit) and continuing to bake.

This type of baking is used for fruits that cannot take a long baking time, fillings that would soak into raw pastry and even when the filling needs to be cooked for less time than the pastry.

TEMPERING BY SEEDING

PREPARATION TIME: 30 MINUTES

Adjust the quantity of ingredients to your chosen recipe.

Milk chocolate is melted and heated to 45°C, then cooled to 28-30°C.

White chocolate is melted and heated to 40°C, then cooled to 28-30°C.

1 Preheat the oven to 180°C (gas mark 4). Take the case out of the refrigerator. Lay a sheet of heatproof cling film over the tart case, then pour a layer of baking beans on top.

2 Wrap the cling film back over the baking beans, taking care not to touch the dough too much.

3 Bake for approximately 10 minutes (the pastry should not be allowed to brown). Take out of the oven and remove the cling film with the baking beans.

1 Heat the dark chocolate until its temperature reads 45-50°C on a cooking thermometer.

2 Remove from the bain-marie and add a third of the chopped chocolate.

3 Mix until the added chocolate melts and cools the entire batch to between 30 and 32°C.
Test to see if the chocolate is well tempered and ready to use.

TEMPERING CHOCOLATE OVER A BAIN-MARIE

PREPARATION TIME: 30 MINUTES

Adjust the quantity of ingredients to your chosen recipe.

Milk chocolate is melted and heated to 45°C, cooled to 26°C, then reheated to 29°C.

White chocolate is melted and heated to 40°C, cooled to 25°C, then reheated to 28°C.

1. Chop the dark chocolate (preferably couverture chocolate). Prepare a large bowl filled with cold water. Melt the chocolate over a bain-marie. The water should simmer without boiling; avoid allowing it to come in contact with the chocolate, as this may cause it to become dull and lose its fluidity.

2. Once its temperature reaches 45°C, remove the chocolate from the bain-marie and place in a bowl of cold water, stirring continuously with a silicone spatula to cool it to precisely 27°C.

3. Remove the chocolate from the bowl of cold water. Reheat over the bain-marie, stirring gently and frequently to prevent the bowl from warming too quickly and raising the temperature of the chocolate too rapidly. Once the temperature of the chocolate reaches 30°C, remove immediately from the bain-marie. It should be smooth, glossy and therefore ready to use (chocolate can be used between 30 and 32°C).
Test to see if the chocolate is well tempered and ready to use.

TESTING THE CHOCOLATE

1. Pour a little tempered chocolate onto a piece of aluminium foil. Let the chocolate harden for 7 minutes in the refrigerator, then peel off the foil.

2. If the resulting piece of chocolate is smooth, glossy and snaps easily, the tempered chocolate is ready to use.

GLOSSARY

AGAR-AGAR
Plant-based gelling agent used as a substitute for gelatine. In fact, the gelling power of agar-agar is eight times stronger than gelatine's, and it is used in a different way.

APRICOT GLAZE
A liquid jelly with a neutral colour and flavour made from jam (apricot or raspberry) that has been melted to cover pastries or fruit tarts in order to give them a glossy, appetising appearance.

BAIN-MARIE
A method of cooking or re-heating that involves placing the vessel holding the preparation over a saucepan of simmering water. Used when a preparation should not be boiled directly (e.g. sabayon), to keep preparations warm (e.g. sauces) or even to gently melt certain ingredients (e.g. chocolate).

BAKING POWDER
An odourless powder, baking powder is made of bicarbonate of soda and cream of tartar. It is often sold in 11 g sachets. To act, baking powder requires heat and humidity: the baking powder comes into contact with liquids during mixing.

BISCUIT CUTTER
A metal or plastic kitchen utensil that comes in a variety of shapes (round, oval, semicircle, etc.) and is used to cut out regular shapes from a sheet of dough.

"BISCUIT" SPONGE
A light preparation made of egg yolks, sugar, flour and whisked egg whites.

BLANCH
1. To whisk together egg yolks and sugar until the mixture becomes pale and thick.
2. To drop a food (e.g. citrus) into boiling water to pre-cook, soften or remove excessive bitterness.

BROWN SUGAR
Refined beet or cane sugar with a brown colour and soft consistency. Both dark and light brown sugar can be bought in shops.

BUTTER
1. To coat a container with melted or room-temperature butter using a brush to prevent preparations from sticking to the container.
2. To work butter into a preparation.

CANDIED
A description of a food that has been preserved by saturating it with sugar.

CARAMELISE
1. To cook sugar until it takes on a darkened colour. This can then be used to glaze a preparation or make a caramel sauce.
2. To coat a mould with caramel.
3. To use the oven grill to brown a dessert (e.g. crème brûlée).
4. To add caramel to a preparation to flavour it.
5. To cover choux buns in caramel.

CHANTILLY CREAM
Whipped cream with added sugar and vanilla.

CHINOIS
A fine cone-shaped metal sieve with a handle.

CHOCOLATE COMPOUND COATING (PÂTE À GLACER)
A preparation made of cocoa powder, sugar and dairy products, finely ground and mixed with a vegetable fat. It is used to coat entremets and other pastry products to create a glossy, crisp finish.

CHOP/MINCE
To cut candied fruits, chocolate, hazelnuts, almonds, etc. into small pieces using a knife or mincer.

CHURN
To set a mixture in an ice-cream maker until it solidifies into an ice cream or sorbet.

CLARIFIED BUTTER
Butter whose milk solids have been removed by heating it over very low heat. It burns less easily and goes rancid more slowly than normal butter.

COAT
1. To cover a dessert with glaze to perfect its appearance.
2. To pour a coulis or cream over a dessert.
3. To cook crème anglaise until it reaches a consistency that covers the spoon evenly.

COATING
To entirely cover one food with another ingredient (e.g. chocolate, cocoa powder, sugar, etc.).

COCOA BUTTER
A fat with an almost entirely neutral flavour and light cocoa aroma; extracted from ground cocoa beans during the production of cocoa powder. It is used in the making of chocolate.

COCOA MASS (LIQUOR)
A paste made by grinding cocoa beans. It is the raw material for all chocolate and cocoa-based products. It can be found at specialised grocers.

COCOA NIBS
Crushed pieces of toasted cocoa beans. They can be found at specialised grocers.

COMPOTE
Cook a preparation very slowly until the ingredients break down into a compote.

COOKING THERMOMETER
A kitchen utensil that allows you to find the exact temperature of a food or preparation while it is cooking. Often equipped with a probe.

CORE
To cut out or remove the insides of a food (e.g. an apple).

CORNFLOUR
A very fine white powder extracted from corn starch. Finer than cornmeal, it is used in cooking and pastry making for its thickening and gelling properties, allowing cakes to be made lighter and airier.

COULIS
A very fine liquid fruit purée made by mixing fresh or cooked fruit, either with or without sugar, then filtering them through a sieve.

COUVERTURE CHOCOLATE
High-quality chocolate that contains at least 32% cocoa butter. Because of its properties, couverture chocolate is the chocolate used for tempering.

CREAM
1. To beat butter and sugar together until they make a creamy, pale mixture.
2. To add cream to a preparation.

CRÈME ANGLAISE
A smooth vanilla-flavoured cream made from milk, egg yolks and sugar. Served with many desserts, it is also the base preparation for making ice cream. The vanilla in a crème anglaise can also be replaced with another flavour (e.g. chocolate, pistachio, etc.).

CRUSHED GAVOTTES® CRÊPES
Fragments of wafer biscuit (in France, *crêpes dentelles*).

CUT OUT
To cut out shapes from a rolled-out sheet of dough using a biscuit cutter or knife.

DEEP-FRY
To cook foods by plunging them into a hot oil bath.

DÉTREMPE
A mixture of flour, water and salt; the first step in making puff pastry.

DILUTE
To thin out with a liquid.

DOCK
To make small holes in the base of a pastry case with a fork to ensure it does not inflate when baking.

DRY OUT
To remove any excess water from a preparation by stirring it constantly over heat with a wooden spoon until it comes away from the sides of the pan and curls around the spoon (e.g. choux pastry, fruit jellies, etc.).

DUST WITH FLOUR
To cover a work surface, preparation, mould or even a baking tray with a thin layer of flour.

EGG WASH
Beaten egg or egg yolk, sometimes with water added, brushed over doughs before baking.

EXTRACT
Highly concentrated extract of an ingredient (e.g. coffee) used to flavour a preparation.

FONDANT
A preparation made of sugar, water and glucose used to ice cakes, small desserts and other sweet creations, such as mille-feuilles, choux buns, religieuses and éclairs.

FONDANT ICING
A preparation made of icing sugar, egg whites, liquid glucose and food colouring. Highly mouldable, fondant icing is used to make pastry decorations.

FRESH COMPRESSED YEAST
A fungi used to make bread and yeast-based pastries. In floury, damp, warm environments, it causes fermentation that

releases carbon dioxide: it is this gas that proofs the dough as it tries to escape.

GANACHE
A mix of cream and chopped chocolate used to fill small desserts, cakes and sweets, among other things.

GELATINE
A colourless, odourless and flavourless gelling product most often sold as leaves. To use the leaves, they should be allowed to soften in cold water, then squeezed out and dissolved in a hot - but not boiling - liquid.

GÉNOISE SPONGE
A light preparation made by mixing sugar and eggs over a bain-marie, then whisking them until they cool and the addition of flour sprinkled in. Génoise sponge is the base for many cakes and can be flavoured with various ingredients (e.g. almonds, hazelnuts, chocolate, etc.).

GLAZE
1. To brush a pastry with beaten egg or egg yolk to give it a glossy, golden crust when baked.
2. To cover the surface of a dessert with glaze or icing sugar to perfect its appearance and make it look more appetising.

GLUCOSE
A colourless syrup with a thick, viscous texture used in pastry making and confectionery for its anti-crystallisation and preservative properties. It also makes preparations softer.

IMBIBE
To soak a preparation (e.g. baba, génoise, etc.) with syrup or alcohol to moisten and flavour it.

INCORPORATE
To gradually add one element to another while mixing gently.

INFUSE
To leave aromatic items (mint, tea, etc) steep in a boiling liquid so that it acquires their flavours.

INVERTED SUGAR (TRIMOLINE®)
A sweetener about 25% sweeter than table sugar.

KNEAD
To mix, blend and work the ingredients of a preparation to make a dough.

LINE
1. To top the surface of a mould or tin with a preparation, dough or baking parchment.
2. To use a rolled-out sheet of dough to cover the sides and bottoms of a mould or container.

MACERATE
To steep fresh or candied fruit or nuts in a liquid (e.g. alcohol, syrup, tea) to infuse them with the liquid's flavour.

MARBLED
A word used to describe a dessert made of two preparations whose composition is identical, but that have contrasting colours and flavours (marbled cake, marbled ice cream, etc.).

MELON BALLER
Small, deep round cutter used to make small fruit or vegetable balls.

MELT
To make a solid element into a liquid (e.g. butter, chocolate, etc.) by heating it.

MERINGUE
A mixture of whisked egg whites and sugar. There are three types of meringue:
1. French meringue, where the whites are whisked and into which sugar is whisked progressively until stiff peaks form.
2. Italian meringue, where cooked sugar is folded into egg whites whisked to stiff peaks.
3. Swiss meringue, where the egg whites and sugar are whisked together over a bain-marie.

NOZZLE
A hollow conical tool made of metal or plastic used with a piping bag to pipe preparations onto a baking tray or to decorate desserts. Nozzles can be either plain or star.

NUT BROWN BUTTER
Butter that has been heated until it begins to brown and the milk solids stick to the bottom of the saucepan.

OIL
To coat a tray or mould with a fine layer of oil to prevent sticking.

PASTRY CREAM
A thick cream made from milk, egg yolks, sugar and flour, traditionally flavoured with vanilla, that is used to fill a variety of pastries. The flour can also be replaced with starch or custard powder.

PASTRY RING
A metal ring that can come in a variety of diameters (6 to 34 cm) and depths; used to assemble desserts (e.g. entremets, mousses, etc.). Pastry chefs prefer these to moulds for making tarts and flans.

PÀTON
The French term used to describe puff pastry whose turns have been completed, but which has not been baked.

PECTIN
Made from plants, pectin is used for its stabilising, gelling and thickening properties. There are many different kinds of pectin, with the two main types being NH pectin and yellow pectin.

PINCH
A small amount of an ingredient (e.g. salt, sugar, etc.) picked up between the thumb and forefinger.

PIPE
Evenly distribute portions of a preparation such as choux pastry over a baking tray using a piping bag fitted with a plain or star nozzle.

POACH
To cook foods in a lightly simmering liquid, particularly fruits in a sugar syrup.

POTATO STARCH
A fine white powder made from potatoes dried and milled into a flour. In cooking, it is primarily used for its thickening properties. In pastry making, it is used to lighten desserts and give them a soft texture.

PRALINE
Stage of coating almonds or hazelnuts with cooked sugar.

PRALINE POWDER
Preparation made from almonds and/or hazelnuts, caramelised and finely ground. Praline sold in sachets can be found in shops.

PROOF
A dough whose volume increases due to the fermentation process of fresh compressed yeast.

QUENELLE
An ice cream or mousse preparation moulded into an egg shape with two identical spoons.

REDUCE
Bring a liquid to the boil and keep it there so that it evaporates and loses volume. The preparation will become thicker and the flavours more concentrated.

Rhodoïd®
Relatively thick plastic (acetate) bands or sheets used to line entremets rings for the preparation of mousses or creams.

Ribbon
Used to describe a preparation that, once adequately whisked, is smooth, uniform and falls from the whisk in an unbroken stream, making a ribbon.

Roast
To evenly toast nuts (walnuts, almonds, pistachios, etc.) on a baking tray in a hot oven.

Roughly chop
Chop an ingredient with a knife or crush it coarsely with a mortar and a pestle.

Rub-in (sabler)
To mix flour with a fat to distribute it evenly. Stop when the mixture becomes crumbly.

Score
Decorate a dough that has been brushed with an egg glaze and is ready to bake using the point of a knife, like for a Three kings' cake, apple turnover, etc.

Set aside
To remove an element (which may be either chilled or kept warm) from the main work area in preparation for later use.

Shape
To give a particular shape to a preparation.

Sift
To run an ingredient (e.g. cocoa powder, icing sugar, baking powder, etc..) through a fine drum sieve or fine sieve to remove any lumps.

Simmer
To heat a liquid to the point just below the boil; bubbles should be just barely visible.

Skin or blanch
To remove the skin or peel from nuts or fruit (e.g. almonds, peaches, pistachios) after plunging into boiling water.

Sliced
To cut nuts (such as almonds) lengthwise into fine slices, either by hand or using a machine.

Smear (fraser)
To squash a dough by pushing it away from you with the palm of your hand, homogenising it without overworking it.

Smooth
To whisk a set or stiff mixture vigorously to make it supple.

Softened butter
Room temperature butter worked with a spatula or beaten until it has a creamy consistency: soft and pale.

Stop cooking
To lower the temperature of a preparation (e.g. caramel, sugar syrup) by gradually adding the required amount of cold liquid, giving it a soft consistency.

Strain
To filter a liquid or semi-liquid preparation through a sieve to remove any solid particles.

Stuff
To fill the inside of a sweet or savoury item with a preparation (e.g. choux buns, stuffed sweets, etc.).

Temper
To run chocolate through three distinct temperature stages to improve its gloss and snap. Once tempered, chocolate may be used to make moulds or decorations or to coat chocolate bonbons.

Thinly slice
To cut a product, for example a fruit, into fine, regular pieces.

Turn
To fold and re-fold a dough (puff pastry, croissant dough, etc.) around butter to incorporate it.

Well
Flour made into a ring or crater into which the other ingredients needed to make a dough are placed.

Whipped cream
Whipping cream whisked until it holds firm peaks.

Whisk (whip)
1. To beat an ingredient (e.g. egg whites, cream) with a whisk to increase its volume.
2. To beat a preparation with a whisk to cream, lighten or soften it.

Zest
To cut off the outer peel of a citrus fruit (e.g. orange, lemon, etc.) with a zester or vegetable peeler. Zest can be added to a preparation to flavour it.

INDEX OF RECIPES
in alphabetical order

INDEX OF RECIPES
by ingredient

ACKNOWLEDGEMENTS

The publication of this book would never have been possible without the professionalism, constant attention and enthusiasm of the coordination teams, led by Émilie Burgat and the Chefs Jean-François Deguignet and Olivier Mahut, or without the photographer Olivier Ploton. We must also thank the administrative team: Catherine Baschet, Kaye Baudinette, Isaure Cointreau, Marie Hagège, Charlotte Madec, Leanne Mallard and Sandra Messier.

In particular, we would like to thank Isabelle Jeuge-Maynard (President - Managing Director) and Ghislaine Stora (Joint Managing Director) from Larousse, as well as their whole team: Agnès Busière, Émilie Franc and Coralie Benoit.

For this edition in English Le Cordon Bleu wishes to thank Grub Street Publishing directed by Anne Dolamore.

Le Cordon Bleu and Larousse would like to thank the Le Cordon Bleu Chef teams around the world, located in nearly 20 countries at more than 35 institutes, who have allowed this book to be written thanks to their creativity and skill.

We would like to express our heartfelt gratitude to **Le Cordon Bleu Paris** and Chefs Éric Briffard MOF, Philippe Groult MOF, Patrick Caals, Williams Caussimon, Olivier Guyon, René Kerdranvat, Franck Poupard, Christian Moine, Guillaume Siegler, Marc-Aurèle Vaca, Fabrice Danniel, Laurent Bichon, Jean-François Deguignet, Oliver Mahut, Soyeon Park, Vincent Valton, Éric Verger, Olivier Boudot, Frédéric Hoël, Vincent Somoza & Gaultier Denis

Le Cordon Bleu London and Chefs Emil Minev, Loïc Malfait, Eric Bediat, Anthony Boyd, David Duverger, Reginald Ioos, Colin Westal, Colin Barnet, Ian Waghorn, Julie Walsh, Graeme Bartholomew, Matthew Hodgett, Nicolas Houchet, Dominique Moudart, Olivier Mourelon, Jerome Pendaries, Nicholas Patterson & Stéphane Gliniewicz

Le Cordon Bleu Tokyo and Chefs Gilles Company, Katsutoshi Yokoyama, Philippe Wavrin, Grant Kells, Yuji Toyonaga, Hiroyuki Honda, Jean-Francois Favy, Philippe Dégé, Dominique Gros, Manuel Robert & Kiyoaki Deki

Le Cordon Bleu Kobe and Chefs Philippe Koehl & Vincent Koperski.

Le Cordon Bleu Ottawa and Chefs Hervé Chabert, Aurelien Legué, Stéphane Frelon, Ilan Dagan, Yannick Anton & Serge Martin

Le Cordon Bleu Korea and Chefs Georges Ringeisen, Roland Hinni, Javier Mercado, Pierre Legendre, Fabrice Cardelec & Régis Doré

Le Cordon Bleu Peru and Chefs Jacques Decrock, Torsten Enders, Eric Germananges, Franco Alva, Cecilia Aragaki, Facundo Serra, Marc Le Dantec, Javier Ampuero, Bruno Arias, Gregor Funke, Fabian Beelen, Annamaria Dominguez, Andres Ortega, Daniel Punchin, Jean Georges Spunck, Jean Marc Mathes, Olivier Roseau, Andrea Winkelried, Christophe Leroy, Patricia Colona, Samuel Moreau, Juan Carlos Gormez, Gabriela Zoia & Joao Castello

Le Cordon Bleu Mexico and Chefs Arnaud Guerpillon, Aldo Omar Morales, Denis Delaval, Carlos Santos, Carlos Barrera, Edmundo Martinez, Cédric Carême, Richard Lecoq & Roni Kirkova

Le Cordon Bleu Thailand and Chefs Pierre Rimoneau, Dan Yvan Stella, Maxim Baile, Marc Champire, Willy Daurade, Frederic Legras, Marc Razurel, Supapit Opatvisan & Wilairat Kornnoppaklao

Le Cordon Bleu Australia directed by Chef Tom Milligan

Le Cordon Bleu Shanghai and Chefs Philippe Clergue, Régis Février, Jérôme Rohard, Olivier Paredes. Yannick Begel, Kristof Deschuymere, Yannick Tribois, Philippe Martel & Sebastien Gregory Crouzat

Le Cordon Bleu Taiwan and Chefs Jose Cau, Nicolas Belorgey & Sebastien Graslan

Le Cordon Bleu Istanbul and Chefs Erich Ruppen, Arnaud Declercq, Frédéric Amirat, Alican Saygı, Christophe Bidault & Richard Vacher

Le Cordon Bleu Madrid and Chefs Erwan Poudoulec, Franck Plana, Yann Barraud, David Millet, Carlos Collado, Diego Muñoz, Enrique Gonzalez, Amandine Finger & Martin Ducout

Le Cordon Bleu New Zealand and Chefs Sébastien Lambert, Francis Motta, Vincent Boudet, Michel Rocton & Thomas Holleaux

Le Cordon Bleu Malaysia and Chefs Rodolphe Onno, Sylvain Dubreau, Florian Guillemenot, Stéphane Alexandre, Thierry Lerallu & David Williams Morris.

Le Cordon Bleu Burj on Bay Lebanon and Chef Roberto Zanuso & Guillaume Sinden

Le Cordon Bleu São Paulo and Chefs Patrick Martin, Jean Yves Poirey, Renata Braune & Amanda Lopes

Le Cordon Bleu Rio de Janeiro and Chefs João Paulo Frankenfeld & Philippe Brye

This English language edition published in 2018 by
Grub Street
4 Rainham Close
London
SW11 6SS

Reprinted 2018

Email: food@grubstreet.co.uk
Web: www.grubstreet.co.uk
Twitter: @grub_street
Facebook: Grub Street Publishing

A CIP catalogue record for this book is available from the British Library.

ISBN 978-1-911621-20-1

Printed and bound in Slovenia